Th

ADVEN

o

OWEN HATHERLEY

in the

POST-SOVIET SPACE

The ADVENTURES *of* OWEN HATHERLEY *in the* POST-SOVIET SPACE

by

OWEN HATHERLEY

Repeater

Published by Repeater Books
An imprint of Watkins Media Ltd

19-21 Cecil Court
London
WC2N 4EZ
UK
www.repeaterbooks.com
A Repeater Books paperback original 2018
1

Distributed in the United States by Random House, Inc., New York.

Cover design: Johnny Bull
Typography and typesetting: Josse Pickard
Typefaces: DIN Next / Garamond

ISBN: 9781912248261
Ebook ISBN: 9781912248278

Printed and bound in Great Britain by TJ International Ltd, Padstow, Cornwall

CONTENTS

"The everyday routes go past houses which have been bombed in different ways. There are sections of houses which keep reminding you of Meyerhold's theatre sets. There are sections of small multi-coloured rooms with the little round stove still intact, painted the same colour as the wall, or an intact door, sometimes ajar. Grim stage-set doors, carefully made and leading nowhere. The house sections illustrate the storeys, the thin layers of floor and ceiling. You begin to realise with astonishment that as you sit at home in your room you are suspended in space, with other people similarly suspended above your head and below your feet. You know about this of course, you've heard furniture being moved about upstairs, even wood being chopped. But all that is abstract, unpicturable, like the way we are borne along through space on a sphere rotating about its axis. Everybody feels as if their floor rests on some kind of soil, covered over with planking. Now the truth had been revealed in a dizzyingly graphic fashion. There were skeletal houses with preserved façades, shot through with darkness and depth. And the sky can be seen through the empty window sockets of the upper storeys. There were houses, especially small ones, whose beams and flooring had collapsed under their crumbling roofs. They hung at an angle and looked as if they were still sliding down, perpetually falling, like a waterfall.

A new attitude to houses developed. People began to talk about houses, think about houses. The accepted unit of the city became the apartment house, just as previously it had been the street, with its merged undifferentiated façades. Unobservant people suddenly saw what constituted their city. It was made up of discrete areas of incomparable Leningrad beauty, out of astonishing complexes of stone and sky, water and foliage, and for the rest, apartment houses of the second half of the nineteenth century, with a certain trace of pre-revolutionary modern and boxes dating from the first years of the revolution. The wretched architecture of the second half of the last century, with its fear of line and plane, the flat surface and the unfilled space, which prompted it to cram every unoccupied space with some sort of stucco nonsense. Now we saw those houses, shabby and bare, standing in damp and rusty streams of poor-quality paint. In grim autumn days it seemed that the rusty dankness was oozing out from inside them. They presaged nothing good."

– Lydia Ginzburg, *Notes of a Blockade Person* [1]

A SHORT INTRODUCTION

The book you are reading is a guide to cities in what was once the Union of Soviet Socialist Republics. It is intended to be useful both to visitors, for whom this will tell them things they do not know, and to curious citizens, who will find an interpretation of what they do already know, which they may or may not agree with. There are many books on Soviet architecture today, bridging a gap between academic history and Instagram, and they tend to be heavy on images, low on description and context. This one, as a guide, has somewhat different ambitions, in that I hope for it not to sit on a coffee table, but to actually be placed in people's pockets as they walk around. Accordingly, my model for these is not photobooks or historical monographs but the series of foreign language Soviet city guides published in the 1970s and 1980s by Progress Publishers. You can often find these in second-hand bookshops, in both East and West. They are unusual objects, insofar as they are not particularly useful as conventional guidebooks.

There are driving and travel tips, which say nothing about the guards and checkpoints you might meet on the way. An abundance of goods fill the pages – local wines, fruits, sweetmeats, along with the buildings and the folk costumes. Maps are beautifully illustrated with schematic drawings of the important buildings and monuments, but are not to scale, so that you can't really use them to get around anywhere, even before so many of the street names were changed after 1989. Looking at these books – I've accumulated a minor collection – you get some sense of the extreme geographic scope of the Soviet Union, the "last Empire", as the Ukrainian historian Serhii Plokhy calls it (the USA might have something to say about that – but certainly the last *contiguous* land Empire). Like all empires it had a centre – Moscow, of course – and a periphery, although the ways in which the two related to each other bears little resemblance to the way the European transcontinental empires worked. Money and investment most often flowed from the centre out to the periphery, whereas high culture (and, crucially for this book, architectural ideas) often flowed from periphery to centre. The guides to this empire encompass a geographical territory far larger than Europe, but whether you're in Lake Baikal near Mongolia, in Vladivostok a day's sea voyage from Japan, in Central Asia on the borders of Afghanistan, in the Caucasus wedged between Turkey and Iran, or in Estonia, a short ferry ride from Helsinki, the story is always basically the same. First, there is a section on the historical development and monuments of the city in question, and this is relatively impartial. Then you hear about how the city was incorporated into Russia – something that is usually considered a "progressive" move, despite the "reactionary" nature of Tsarism. You are then told about how it participated in the 1905 Revolution, then in the 1917 one. You are regaled with stories of the years of socialist construction (or of bourgeois degeneration, in the Baltics), then of the heroic efforts of the local populace in the Great Patriotic War. We end with a present in which your city has a prominent place in the socialist family of nations, and is building up the productive forces for the eventual transition to Communism.

This linear progression from great ancient history to the bad days to the optimistic present of "transition" resembles that found in the guidebooks you can find in any airport bookshop. The historical part is much the same, and the participation in revolution is shifted into the age-old struggle for national independence, which stretches usually from sometime in the Middle Ages (earlier, in the Caucasus) to its final achievement in the 1990s,[1] and the eventual transition to capitalism (never quite satisfactorily achieved, it seems, but always *getting there*). There is more description of landscape, and in some places, there is the suggestion that what you're doing might be slightly naughty – *stalking the forbidden zones of the Soviet Empire*. These, in summary, are all the things this book tries to avoid. Naturally, the Soviet narrative is absurd in many respects – in its pandering to Russian nationalism, its hilariously paradoxical attempt to pretend that the societies being described are totally open to travellers, in its frequent outright rewriting of history, especially when concerning those countries caught between the Molotov-Ribbentrop pact. But the Lonely Planet version just replaces the goal of Communism with that of becoming a "normal country", and refuses to concede the slightest legitimacy to the revolution of October 1917 and the country it created, while encouraging you to enjoy the cheapest of thrills within its ruins. Because of this, the emphasis of the book you are reading remains on the results of the revolution and its aftermath in these countries, largely because that revolution and its results are still a historical puzzle, one towards which total dismissal or apologism are equally suspicious.

The book includes eleven countries, out of the fifteen that once made up the USSR (joined at the time of writing by no less than six mostly unrecognised republics, five of them the direct creations of Russian military intervention). These eleven are, in rough order of size: Russia, Kazakhstan, Ukraine, Belarus, Georgia, Kyrgyzstan, Lithuania, Latvia, Estonia, Moldova and Armenia. We can also include the relatively devolved Republic of Tatarstan within the Russian Federation as a "country" of sorts. There is a bias towards those countries that it is easier and cheaper to get to – cost, distance, and the expense and hassle of complicated visas, has meant that there is nothing either on the architecturally hugely important modern city of Baku in Azerbaijan, or on the historic cities of Tashkent, Samarkand or Bukhara in Uzbekistan – these are major absences which I have not had the budget to rectify. I've divided what I do have into four parts, because of those immense geographical differences. It should be noted that the inclusion of a country in here as "Post-Soviet" is not intended as some sort of statement that they were and are eternally affected by their incorporation into the USSR, nor is it intended to imply that that incorporation was voluntary: in the case, for instance, of the Baltic states and Georgia, it very clearly was not.

Some of these nation states are in the European Union; some are in the post-Soviet umbrella Commonwealth of Independent States; some are in the Eurasian Union recently set up under the auspices of the Russian government. However, I've found a geopolitical approach to definition less than useful. Strongly "pro-Europe" and democratic Ukraine is in terms of its approach to architecture and town planning a messier correspondent to "pro-Russian" and dictatorial Belarus. There is more in the way of "planning" in the aggressively anti-Communist Baltic states than in anywhere else in the former USSR, and they've generally cared for the Soviet legacy in mass housing much better than countries where hammer and sickles and Stalin portraits are still normal. Some countries are strongly influenced by other geopolitical "poles" altogether – for instance, Kazakhstan looks both towards Turkey and China as models, the Baltics and Georgia to Central Europe, with varying degrees of plausibility. Above all, the Baltic and the Caucasus feel "different" to the rest, due to an architectural, topographical and cultural specificity that would have been equally obvious before, during and after the USSR.

What all of these places have in common is a certain much mythologised, usually regretted "betweenness", in a space which is not wholly Europe *or* Asia in the way in which it is conventionally defined, and in which a usually deeply rapacious and crass capitalism is forced to develop, or more often affix itself parasitically to, an infrastructure built up by an enormous, unfinished and abandoned attempt to build an ideal Communist society. The division I've made, then, is not "civilisational", between the democratic Europeans and dictatorial Eurasians, but between different regions that may include different aspects of these in the same place. Everywhere has its stereotypes, but the former Soviet Union is still overwhelmingly defined by them nearly thirty years after its collapse. As an alternative, the book contains a relaxed intelligentsia city on the Chinese border in Kazakhstan and a despotic oil state a boat away from Sweden in western Latvia; the capital of a miniature Islamic Republic in the heart of Russia, an industrial city riven by socialist nostalgia in Ukraine; a historic city redesigned by fashionable Italian and Dutch architects in Georgia; and we begin with a portrait of a town where the dying Union tries to represent itself. The cities include current capitals, two former capitals, several formerly "closed cities", some small towns, a resort, new towns and historic cities. It's the product of several years travelling in these countries.[2]

Some of the chapters are based on repeated visits over many years – to Kyiv, Moscow, Petersburg – others are based on more or less extended visits to particular places (Ukraine outside Kyiv in autumn 2015, the Baltic in summer 2016, Belarus in spring 2017, Armenia and Kazakhstan in summer and autumn 2017, Kyrgyzstan in spring 2018), something reflected in their differing lengths and approaches. The information related is partial and largely monolingual; it's an incomplete portrait, one which, given the vast size and punitive visas of much of the territory in question, will probably remain so. It draws heavily on an enormous amount of English-language research made in the last decade by scholars, researchers and activists in these countries, to whom I am immensely indebted. However all judgements, unless otherwise credited, are my own responsibility, not theirs. This is a subjective book, the things that were found interesting by an effete Western Marxist on foot, with a camera, and absolutely crucially with the benefit of many much more informed (if by no means remotely typical) interlocutors. The photographs are my own, and are intended, to quote John Berger, as "simple memoranda", rather than as artworks.

MICROCOSMOS
SLAVUTYCH

In the main secondary school of Slavutych, a town of 25,000 people founded in 1986 in the north of Ukraine, is a full-length mural that tells a strange tale about technology, revolution and human progress. A Neanderthal plays with a Rubik's Cube. Byzantine monks bring Christianity to ancient Rus. Red Guards storm the Winter Palace. A beaming Yuri Gagarin, in spacesuit, rises from his parachute like Botticelli's *Venus*.

The Perestroika vision of history

And in the centre of it all, a blonde girl in shorts runs from an exploding nuclear power station, as figures in protective suits fight to put out the conflagration.

This is the foundation myth of the last city built in the Soviet Union. Its purpose was to rehouse those who lost their homes with the evacuation of Pripyat, the new town that served the Chernobyl Nuclear Power Station. It was built as an extraordinary act of Soviet internationalism, not with standard plans laid down in Moscow, but with distinct, separately conceived districts, each designed by the architects – and built by the builders – of eight different Soviet republics: Estonia, Latvia, Lithuania, Russia, Azerbaijan, Armenia, Georgia and Ukraine. It is "the last ideal city", according to Ukrainian architectural historian Ievgeniia Gubkina, whose just published *Slavutych Architectural Guide* is the first work on the subject in English. A "humanist utopia", opposed to the "technocratic utopia" of the nuclear power station and of Pripyat, an answer to a loss of faith in progress, technology and socialism that was the consequence of the nuclear disaster. The place itself, however, is ideal to begin a study of the Soviet city. Not only was it a showcase of planning, it was also a conscious showcase of one of the least understood aspects of the Soviet Union: its attempt to create what a post-Soviet scholar called an "affirmative action empire"[1], where expressions of "national" culture – whether musical, sartorial, architectural, literary or linguistic – were officially encouraged (albeit frequently interrupted by counter-waves of Russification), just so long as they didn't coalesce into movements for national independence. A variety of enduring slogans enshrined this move; Socialist Realist architecture, for instance, was described as "national in form, socialist in content", while the "Friendship of Nations" was taken as the self-description of what was in reality a unitary state where Moscow's word was always final. By the time Slavutych was built, national independence was exactly what the "nations" did demand, especially in Ukraine, the Baltic and the Caucasus. In the small space of Slavutych, the Soviet experiment in delimited nationalism is pushed into close proximity with a confrontation with the failure of another cliché, the "Scientific-Technological Revolution", encouraged from Khrushchev onwards. Accordingly, this place is the USSR in microcosm.

The loss of faith in the "Scientific-Technological Revolution" came as a catastrophe to many of the Soviet citizens who were affected by, or took part in the relief effort to alleviate, the disaster. In her recently republished *Voices from Chernobyl*, Svetlana Alexeivich quotes one worker on how even the robots that were sent to repair the reactor after it was considered unsafe for even protected human beings succumbed: "our robots, designed by Academic Lukachev for the exploration of Mars".[2] But according to the local Party boss at the plant, later the long-serving Mayor of Slavutych, "I had dozens of letters on my desk by people asking to be sent to Chernobyl. Volunteers. No matter what they say now, there was such a thing as a Soviet person, with a Soviet character."[3] As first dozens, then hundreds of relief workers became sick and died from radiation sickness, that enthusiasm began to seem incomprehensible. A Belarusian nuclear engineer who took part in the clean-up told Alexeivich:

> I don't remember that any of our colleagues refused to go work in the Zone. Not because they were afraid of losing their Party membership, but because they had faith. They had faith that we lived well and fairly, that for us man was the highest thing, the measure of all things. The collapse of this faith in a lot of people eventually led to heart attacks and suicides. A bullet to the heart.[4]

Slavutych was a town that attempted to alleviate that trauma, a city that would renew the Communist faith in a new way – an environmentalist, humanist, internationalist socialism, rather than the technocratic, polluted, standardised form represented by Pripyat

Pripyat has long been a cult destination, a modernist ghost town much frequented by "urban explorers" – despite not having been lived in since 1986, it is probably more visited by Westerners than Slavutych. However, the replacement town provides a striking contrast to Pripyat's image of post-nuclear modernist ruins. Gubkina writes that "one of the tasks confronting the planners was to emotionally and psychologically rehabilitate people who were moving here from Pripyat", in order to "avoid exposing them to negative memories arising from the tragedy", with deliberate avoidance of propagandistic or nuclear imagery. "The antagonistic dialogue with a dead town exists in a town which is itself alive".[5]

I visited Slavutych in July 2016, to take part in a summer school on The Idea of the City, organised by Gubkina with the Kharkiv-based Urban Forms Centre.[6] The first thing that strikes a visitor is the combination of classic Soviet spaciousness with "green city" gestures. Past a derelict, never-completed hotel is a forested park, containing a memorial for the first group of relief workers, all of whom died of radiation sickness within days of the explosion;

The oversized centre of Slavutych

then you reach a gigantic, empty square, with (what was) the Party headquarters, department stores, an art gallery, a House of Culture, all the essentials for a Soviet new town. This centre was designed by architects from Ukraine, aside from the Minsk department store – the only contribution from Belarus, the republic most affected by the disaster. Forested pedestrian streets and cycle paths lead from here to the districts designed by each republic. Uniquely for Ukraine, you see more bicycles than cars.

The tone was set in the "Tallinn Quarter", designed and built by Estonians. The architect Mart Port insisted on retaining the tall pines in "their" suburb, and most others then followed suit. As well as the density of trees, each republic's district was notable for having a school, a sports hall, a restaurant or a cultural centre. The greater innovation was the inclusion of large single-family houses with gardens in each quarter, among the taller blocks of flats that dominate the view. They're not bunched away in an affluent suburb, but placed

The trees of "Tallinn"

within the mid-rise, flat-roofed, prefabricated modernist flats, so as not to accentuate class differences. By the 1980s, Soviet housing had a waiting list system, with rents at around 5% of income; these houses were originally granted to "heroes of labour" at the power plant, though since all housing here was privatised in 1992, they sell on the open market, naturally for more than the flats. These are also impressive, though, cleverly arranged to create courtyards, views and ensembles. The other Baltic republics took a similar approach – the houses (terraces and semis in "Riga", detached in "Vilnius"), and the maisonette flats could easily be in affluent Sweden or Finland rather than Ukraine. The only giveaway that you're in a post-Soviet country is the high fences built by some house dwellers. In what will become a familiar paradox of East-West geographical nomenclature, the renovations that make the houses look less Scandinavian are dubbed "Euroremont", Euro-renovations.

A single family house in "Vilnius"

The placid elegance of "Tallinn", "Riga" and "Vilnius" was part of a "humanism in Soviet architecture" that had developed since the Fifties, especially in the peripheral republics; Gubkina tells me that "these values were well-known by ordinary people and architects and were frequently used in theory of the Stagnation Period in the USSR, but timidly applied in practice. For 1986 it was really new and interesting that the individual, the human experience and even attention to people's trauma started to be considered. Environmentalist topics became a strong component. There was also a strong and consistent work with communities. Although, as you can understand, there is also a contradiction: a new, planned city in a forest is not so environmentally friendly." Indeed it isn't. As she points out, people aren't cycling in Slavutych because the city is so well-planned for it, though it is – it's because they can't afford cars.

The idea to have each district designed by a different republic was an improvisation, intended to take pressure off Ukraine; Gubkina quotes Fedir Borovyk, one of the Ukrainian architects, that "the town was largely created over the phone", collectively and democratically, as an example of Perestroika in action.[7] The only decision the Ukraine co-ordinators made without consultation was the tower blocks that fringe the square, which help give some vigour to the vast empty space at the heart of the town. "According to the architects", says Gubkina, "everything was directed to a comfortable, healthy and democratic life as they understood it." The unifying idea of an "eco-city", meanwhile, fit into certain already existing Soviet traditions: environmental ideas "were quite clear and easy to understand for Soviet architects and people, because they fit into a concept of struggle, the condemnation of exploitation, healthy lifestyle and the legacy of interwar modernism." In that, it forms links across the different eras of the USSR, connecting the aspirations of the 1920s to the realities of the 1980s. The city pivots between egalitarianism and individualism.

A telling factor is that the "centre", "Moscow" itself, clearly couldn't be bothered with the project, and its contribution – aside from the

The drained canals of "Leningrad"

Thanks, comrades – "Moscow"

cash – is by far the least interesting aspect of the entire project. Of the two Russian quarters, "Moscow" is a standardised grid identical to anything built in Russia in the Seventies or Eighties. "Leningrad" is a little more imaginative, with a rhythm of open loggias and (never completed) water features, intended to evoke the canals of old St Petersburg.

Aside from the Baltic quarters and the Leningrad district, the most popular has always been the Armenian "Yerevan Quarter". Barbecues were built into each balcony and into the public square between the flats, faced with Armenian pink tufa and entered through grand archways, surrounding caravanserai-style houses.

These are similar to houses in "Tbilisi", along which cypress trees were planted in reference to the Georgian capital. The least favoured is Azerbaijan's "Baku Quarter", largely because of flaws in the prefabrication system used, although this did not affect the private houses – in one of which, we found a nuclear engineer from Yorkshire (the still-ongoing Chernobyl clean-up and protection effort is an

A barbecue in "Yerevan"

international operation in its own right). At the heart of "Baku" is a school for orphans, its grounds full, like each of the quarters, of delightful, surrealist sculptures designed in abstracted versions of local folk art. Here, unlike in all the other quarters, the artworks have been smashed up, and the buildings left half-derelict. That aside, the town is in strikingly good condition, especially by Ukrainian standards. Mostly, Slavutych's residents are caring for its unique features, and "Decommunisation" has affected it little, but for a mooted change of name from the "Leningrad Quarter" to the "Neva Quarter". Based on the interviews she made for her book, Gubkina tells me that "residents show a keen interest in the architecture and urban design of their city", and my own part of the summer school was surprisingly well-attended, for a talk on post-war British new towns. That said, residents remain disgruntled with the poor transport connections (one daily train to Kyiv) and with the future of the power plant itself, which is being wound down as the final touches are put to the "sarcophagus" that

Sculpture in "Baku"

encases the toxic structure. Slavutych workers recently protested in Kyiv, knowing that there is no plan as to what happens to the town when those jobs go.

Given the Russian-backed conflict in Eastern Ukraine, this built expression of the Friendship of Nations is all the more remarkable. So too in the context in which it was built, when nationalism was already spiralling out of its control by "socialist content" – here are Armenia and Azerbaijan, peacefully side-by-side, on the eve of the two countries collapsing into inter-ethnic warfare. Within a couple of years co-operation between the Baltic republics would hasten their independence from the USSR, but this close, democratic and humane co-operation between the Baltics, the Caucasus, Russia and Ukraine still seems remarkably utopian on the eve of the end of the Soviet Union's demise. Rather than seeing it as a proof that the USSR could be reformed, Gubkina sees it as the fulfilment of Gorbachev's policies of Perestroika, a "reconstruction" of Soviet socialism from the ground up which never got the chance to be widely implemented.

This "humanist utopia" didn't arrive any more than did the "technocratic utopia" promised by Pripyat. None of the ideas in the town about pedestrianisation, cycling, environmentalism, urban democracy or public space were influential in the former USSR, aside perhaps from the Baltic states and scattered civic activists elsewhere. Instead, architects, now commissioned largely by private business, fell into "a primitive fulfilment of their clients' wishes and needs", resulting in what Gubkina calls a "complete loss of professional and aesthetic skills, and of the moral and ethical concerns of an architect". The results in a city like Kyiv, with its chaos of overpowering advertising, towering nouveau riche penthouses and underground shopping malls, piled onto creaking, unrenovated Soviet infrastructure, are dispiriting. The paradox is that, even given their rejection of all things Soviet, these Perestroika ideas are, she argues, much more connected to the demands of contemporary Ukrainian protest movements than Ukrainian capitalism as it is currently practiced. The demand that

Ukraine become more "European" also means advocating "things like cycling, democracy in the city, human rights in architecture and urban design, the promotion of a healthy lifestyle and public spaces that are basically very similar to those emerged in the period of Perestroika. Almost any of the principles applied in Slavutych have their counterpart in modern urban planning." She admits, though, that she couldn't live here.

I thought about this wandering around Slavutych's largest building – the hospital, a rich and complex design at the edge of the city, placed just where it meets the forest. It began, of course, largely catering for the needs of those facing radiation poisoning, and other injuries and conditions caused by the clean-up operation, but it has long since settled down into a normal provincial hospital. Graffiti on the pavements consists of declarations of love, and congratulations from husbands to wives on the birth of children, chalked with hearts onto the asphalt, presumably visible from the maternity ward of this multi-storey building. It's charming, and ordinary.

There are many aspects of Slavutych that suggest there was life in the system still. A swerve could be made from standardisation, car-centred and pedestrian-hostile streets, domineering scale and alienation towards something that is, to use the current term, "sustainable", warm, friendly, pastoral and attractive. And the Soviet command economy's ability to direct resources and enforce planning meant that it was all achieved incredibly rapidly, with great completeness. The comparison with really existing Ukrainian capitalism is not flattering, as it has left the town almost completely alone, incapable of finishing off any of what the Soviets left unfinished – the fountains and ponds, and the large derelict hotel opposite the railway station, sit permanently in limbo in a place built from scratch in little over two years. Anything new comes from civic action – maps by the Urban Forms Centre, sculptures in the parks from local lobbying – in a context of governmental indifference. Other aspects of the project show how incredibly limited and inflexible the Soviet

Mosaic at Slavutych hospital

system was, even at its most open-minded and humane. This is still a single-industry town, devoted to doing one thing – in this case, aptly enough, dealing with the aftermath of a man-made disaster – with no plan as to what happens next. You are miles from anywhere – the nearest city, Chernihiv, is a long way away, and it would, as Slavutych's architect Fedir Borovyk later pointed out, have made a lot more sense just to build a new suburb for that city rather than put another tabula rasa in the forest, yet another showcase, another experiment, this time one that shows off how good and reformed the system could be. After twenty-five minutes walking, you always come to the forest, an absolute limit. You're kept continually in a capsule, a delimited field for trying out ideas, without any organic connection to any other place, a humane urban machine but a machine nonetheless.

And all of this emerged not as the result of peaceful changes in Soviet thinking and planning, but as a rushed result of an appalling catastrophe. As one relief worker tells Svetlana Alexeivich:

> "Don't call these the 'wonders of Soviet heroism' when you write about it. Those wonders really did exist. But first there had to be incompetence, negligence, and only after those did you get wonders: covering the embrasure, throwing yourself in front of a machine gun. But those orders should never have been given, there shouldn't have been any need".[8]

It took the most horrendous nuclear disaster in history for Soviet architects and planners to make their last attempt at the ideal city.

Part One:

THE WESTERN PERIPHERY

Kaunas synagogue

Orthodox in form, Catholic in content

FORGOTTEN CAPITAL

KAUNAS, Kowno, Kovno

"Multiculturalism is European genocide", read the torn, partly ripped-off sticker on the mirror of the bathroom in the Romuva Cinema in Kaunas. It's standard far-right rhetoric across the continent now, but seeing it in Kaunas felt especially strange. When I visited the place in December 2016, its historic architecture was very obviously that of a deeply multicultural city. Just at the edge of an old town of one-storey houses and Baroque churches, you can find a large late-nineteenth-century Synagogue. In the dead centre, streets radiate from the bulbous domes of a sprawling, Byzantine Orthodox church (long since reconsecrated to Catholicism, but you'd only know that from walking inside). Most surprisingly of all, there's a Mosque built in 1933, its art deco design one part Hollywood and one part Samarkand, pretty and diminutive, but prominent – it was designed by the Lithuanian architects Vaclovas Michnevicius and Adolfas Netkyska for the Lipka Tatars who have lived in Lithuania for centuries. All of these in close proximity are rare in larger cities to the West, let alone on the Baltic

This conflicts with Kaunas's reputation, garnered from its status as de facto capital of the Lithuanian Republic of 1918-1940, as the most "truly" Lithuanian city in Lithuania. If it isn't multicultural anymore, then it's *because* of a genocide that took place here between 1941 and 1944. The sticker is baffling as much as offensive, but then the modern city built here during the interwar years – just granted UNESCO World Heritage Site "tentative listing" – is pervaded by similar lacunae.

Kaunas became Temporary Capital of Lithuania in 1920, two years after Lithuania became independent with the collapse of the Russian Empire. Vilnius, a mostly Polish and Yiddish speaking city, which had nonetheless been the acknowledged capital of Lithuania since the Middle Ages, was the de jure capital, but de facto, it was a provincial city in the north-east of Poland, after a military operation to seize it. Accordingly, says heritage researcher and journalist Agnė Sadauskaitė, Kaunas, a small garrison town near the Prussian border, "lacked almost everything that other European capitals had, infrastructure, accommodation, representational buildings and inhabitants". Necessity – the loss of Vilnius – made them create a new capital in Kaunas. Development was especially intensive after a brief democratic

Kaunas mosque in its park

period was extinguished by nationalist leader Antanas Smetona's coup of 1926. One of his first acts was to execute the leadership of Lithuania's small Communist Party. By the 1930s – when most of the major buildings of the temporary capital were built – Lithuania was a one-party state, adopting the slogan "Lithuania for Lithuanians" (Jews made up over a quarter of the population of Kaunas in the 1937 census).[1] Kaunas grew fast, but Lithuania's economy remained overwhelmingly rural, and it was by far the poorest of the three Baltic republics that had a brief independence between 1918 and 1940.

The Kaunas Republic, as nobody calls it, was milder than regimes to its east and west (not a high bar after 1933), and was not a fascist country, as such – more than one coup attempt from the far-right was thwarted, and it was hostile to Nazi Germany, who had irredentist ambitions for the port of Klaipeda – but its political character is seldom considered when the architecture and ambition of the interwar capital are discussed. Unlike "the spider's web of unsolved questions about Soviet architecture, the interwar period rises as an idyllic picture of the independent Lithuanian creators of the First Republic", says Sadauskaitė. Yet its architecture is dominated by the sort of architecture the Nazis regarded as "Jewish" – flat roofs, smooth surfaces, economy and modernity. It doesn't *look* like the architecture of a parochial rural dictatorship.

Partly this is because the state encouraged foreign study for Lithuanian architects. "Vytautas Landsbergis-Žemkalnis and Stasys Kudokas studied in Rome, Arnas Funkas in Berlin", notes Sadauskaitė, and aspects of both the classicised modernism of Mussolini's Rome (Smetona was an admirer of Mussolini) and Weimar German flamboyance can be found in the temporary capital. Asked how this connects with the government's aggressive nationalism, she points to how "traditions were intercrossed with international trends" – buildings that look from a distance like those of Weimar Berlin, like the Central Post Office, the Headquarters of the Pienocentras Milk Processing Company or the Pazanga Publishing Company, with their swooping corners and plate glass, have subtle ornamental reliefs and decorative interiors deriving from Lithuanian folk art.[2] More noticeably, the town planning is totally traditional, a dense grid. Much of the construction is brick with render, not concrete and steel.

The centrepiece of all this rises above the city, on a hill where a bourgeois villa district was planned: Christ's Resurrection Church, designed by Karolis Raisonas after a competition intended, in Sadauskaitė's words, to express "nationalism, patriotism and establish a symbol of a free nation" – Lithuania had also been "resurrected" as a state in 1918. Building a giant Catholic church was not especially modern a gesture, but architecturally, it is the temporary capital's most enduring and indelible monument, its light rectangular tower dominating the skyline. It was only recently finished as a church; it

The Pazanga Publishing Company

was left uncompleted when Lithuania was occupied by the USSR in 1940, and was then turned into a radio factory. The combination of modern motifs and a traditional street plan makes Kaunas a pleasure to walk in, every corner full of delights for fans of steamboat balconies and streamlined curves; aside from the church, the major buildings are the expressionistic rotunda of the Ciurlionis Art Museum and the stripped classical Vytautas the Great War Museum, with its Mussolini-moderne campanile.

Kaunas ceased to be even a temporary capital when the Molotov-Ribbentrop pact saw the Soviets move into the Baltics. As a sweetener, Vilnius was taken from Poland and given to the newly Sovietised Lithuania, which was soon after annexed to the USSR after a spurious election; mass deportations to Siberia ensued. Kaunas was again a

Pienocentras Milk Processing Company

provincial town, and it was made particularly so by the massacre of the city's Jews, which meant that the city became "truly" Lithuanian in a way even the Smetona government never imagined. Soon after the start of Operation Barbarossa, Lithuanian nationalists and the German Einsatzgruppen organised the Kaunas pogrom, the most violent in history up to that point; and then ghettoised the survivors. Most were killed at the Ninth Fort on the city's outskirts.[3]

In the look of the city, Soviet re-occupation in 1944 led first to a straightforwardly "colonial" era of Socialist Realist architecture usually designed by Russian architects – there are a few obvious examples of this, typically Stalinist structures like the Railway Station and the Knigos bookshop. But after 1956, Lithuanian architects came into their own, and the city became first an area of modernist experiment, and then a pioneer of the peculiar genre of Soviet Postmodernism. On foot, you'll find Kaunas's pretty old town is suddenly severed by a dual carriageway leading out of the city. On the way out, you can see peculiar late-Soviet architecture like the Sorrow Palace of Ritual Services, an example of organic Brutalism left rotting unassumingly by the roadside like a derelict petrol station. The road leads to two emblematic Soviet projects – the forest of towers of the Šilainiai mass housing district, and the monumental concrete memorial at the Ninth Fort. They look out at each other at either side of a multi-level motorway, one flat and square, and the other exploding outwards in wild angles.

Architect Matas Šiupšinskas grew up in Šilainiai in the 1980s. "Most people around were young families, young professionals who got an apartment from their workplace. There were a lot of factory workers, but also some artists, academics." The story of the district's construction is one of decline; the first parts were "green, with lots of nature, views from the hill towards the city and the river bank", inspired, as with much Baltic Soviet architecture, by the example of Finland, but with curved balconies perhaps recalling the streamlined architecture of the temporary capital. The first part was "built more

The Resurrection Church, seen from below

or less as planned", but in subsequent parts, numbers took over, and "schools, kindergartens, playgrounds, landscaping were finished only partly". The buildings have had none of the Styrofoam and render renovation you'd find in Poland or the Czech Republic, but were more imaginative than the norm in Russia or Ukraine, with fortress-like details in their concrete panels. Pixellated digital numerals and names were painted on the blocks, an Eighties futuristic gesture that neglect has preserved.

Opposite is the Fort. The low but extensive buildings where the massacres took place were turned into a museum showcasing fascist atrocity already in the Sixties, but the museum and memorial date from 1984. Šiupšinskas indicates the lack of any Soviet symbolism, something suggestive of the confidence of the architects, and the sculptor Alfonsas Ambraziunas, "using as universal a language as possible" and avoiding overt propaganda. The main memorial is a pure

The Ninth Fort Memorial

image of agony, stretched bodies in extremis etched into shuttered concrete. The museum itself anticipates much "Deconstructivist" memorial architecture in its savagely distorted angular forms, shoved rudely into the Fort's grounds, but is more subtle than today's gestural memorial museums, set low into the landscape, with public walkways across. The complex resembles Soviet memorial spaces like Kyiv's roughly contemporary Museum of the Great Patriotic War with all the heroism stripped out, with no chiselled Red Army men rushing to the rescue. In the 1980s, Šiupšinskas remembers, "kids were brought there during school excursions in order to educate them about the war crimes of fascist Germany", but "even if it was close to Šilainiai we were not going there often". It has become more popular in recent years, as a "cool strange monolith structure". A debate about whether or not it was appropriate to take selfies here was, he says, "caught by the pro-Russian media", always eager to find stories of Baltic fascists.

The last Soviet architecture in Kaunas, though, is much less a matter of twentieth-century complexities, and more about finding solace in the past. Unlike other old towns in the region, Kaunas's medieval streets, Baroque churches and Hanseatic Gothic warehouses had been unaffected by war. "Kaunas was happy enough to escape major war bombings", critic and architect Martynas Mankus tells me, and "the old-town reconstruction plan of 1961 and regeneration plan of 1977 were important benchmarks" in preservation. Much 1980s infill in the old town is gently Postmodernist, with steep roofs and gables recalling Gothic and Baroque, but without ornament. "Quite obviously", Mankas notes, "we had (Soviet) Postmodernist architecture without Postmodernist discourse", and "the vocabulary of postmodern historicism in the 1980s seemed to be a perfect language" for the historic city. Some examples, like the Žilinskas Art Gallery, are visibly inspired by the work of the Italian architect Aldo Rossi, with decontextualised, abstracted cubes, pediments and columns. Kaunas Postmodernism was not an escape from politicisation, but quite the reverse, "synchronized with sociocultural turning points in society". In the second half of the 1980s, the "Lithuanian independence movement was focussed on three things: economic self-dependence, ecological awareness, and attention to the historical environment". Warning me he may be being a little speculative, Mankas suggests that "historic sensitivity was considered to be a form of resistance".

Agne Sadauskaite, similarly, points out that "Kaunas became the symbol when regaining independence in Lithuania", and is "now a historical moment of affiliation". She hopes that when UNESCO permanently list the temporary capital, as they're expected to, Kaunas will become a stop on an emerging map of modernist tourism, along with cities like Berlin, Le Havre or Tel Aviv. This image of modernity is seductive, but it can easily give the sense that everything that happened to the city outside of an interwar golden age was illegitimate or uninteresting. At the same time, the city's story reminds that nationalism and identity are constructions, something

The renovated Kaunas Old Town

that has to be "built", and how shaky the identification of modernism with social progress can be. In the 1930s, Kaunas architects found a small medieval town and built a modernist capital around it, and the results are attractive, intriguing and worthy of preservation and care. Enthusiasts for Soviet architecture in Lithuania know to separate their aesthetic and political tastes. If that's possible, then the temporary capital's architecture could also be extricated, from the dubious project of Lithuania for Lithuanians.

A GUIDEBOOK OF REVOLUTIONARY RELICS

KULDĪGA, Goldingen

Kuldīga is a small Hanseatic town in the Courland (*Kurzeme*, in Latvian) area of Latvia, and I spent a summer there on a "writers residency programme", those wheezes that give you a quiet place to write in, on the proviso you write about them. Quiet is the most conspicuous thing about it; although in simple terms of distance, it isn't far from a major European metropolis (Riga, by far the biggest city in the three Baltic republics), the fact that it has no rail connection, and is linked only by a bumpy country road, means that you can almost forget, when here, that you're in the European Union in the early twenty-first century, with all the tensions, contradictions and possibilities that entails. That's why they have a writer in residence programme: because this is considered to be an appealing idea for writers. What this says about us may not be complimentary. Naturally, if you explore just a little, you find all the paraphernalia of contemporary Europe, the free Wi-Fi, the out-of-town retail parks and the Western-owned chain stores – in fact, one of the most picturesque aspects of Kuldīga, its cobbled roads, are a recent intervention, an EU-funded infrastructure upgrade deliberately calibrated to recall the historical texture of the town. On the weekend of the annual

Kuldīga Fair, you can also get a sense of a place that has marketed itself with moderate success as a tourist destination, with German, English and Russian all audible. But, walk down, say, Ventspils Iela on a weekday afternoon, and the only thing that really tells you that anything much has happened since the eighteenth century are the cars parked outside the attractively faded wooden houses. The scarlet and white Latvian flags flying from outside many houses date the town, too, given that these could hardly have been displayed before 1918 or between 1940 and 1990. Part of the town's appeal, nevertheless, is that this is a place where nothing much appears to have happened. Duke Jacob of Courland is the main, or only historical figure worth honouring, part of an almost impossible history where a small Baltic Duchy managed to colonise parts of West Africa and the Caribbean

Kuldiga Forever

(this they did – the Dutch and British soon muscled in and took Courland's colonies over, however). As for twentieth-century history, Kuldīga appears on the face of it to have been blissfully absent, its fabric barely touched. This sits oddly with an overwhelming fact about contemporary Latvia. This small country, dominated to an extreme degree by its capital city, underwent very recently the sort of economic contraction usually seen in the aftermath of total war or environmental disaster. After a real estate boom in the 2000s – at one point, property prices in Jurmala, for instance, "matched those in Monte Carlo"[1] – in 2009, the Latvian economy contracted by 18%, the largest single crash among the EU countries affected by the financial crisis – larger even than Greece. Whereas Ireland, Greece, Spain, Slovenia, Portugal, Italy and eventually even Britain responded to the crisis with a surge in strikes, activism, and the formation and electoral success of new left-wing protest parties, Latvia, and similarly, if not as severely stricken Lithuania and Estonia, were remarkably peaceful. Aside from one 2009 protest that ended in a spontaneous riot in Riga, this crash on a historic scale coincided with complete social peace. Within a few years, impressive economic growth had resumed, helped to a degree by mass emigration (in 2013, Latvia's population was 7.7% lower than it had been in 2008) and by what economists call "internal devaluation", that is, the driving down of wages and working conditions.

This shouldn't be overstated. As Paul Krugman pointed out,

> Latvia suffered a huge, Depression-level economic contraction after 2007, followed eventually by a fast but as yet incomplete bounce-back – which the latest data suggest may be slowing – that has left unemployment much higher than it was pre-crisis. Actually, Latvia's numbers from 2007 to 2013 look fairly similar to those for the United States from 1929 to 1935. Today, everyone considers America in 1935 to have been still in the depths of the Great Depression, so if one

looks at Latvia through the same lens the country doesn't look very good – better than Greece, perhaps, but not good.[2]

But the fact remains that, in comparison with, say, the continuing drama of Greece, even a huge economic collapse passed peacefully in twenty-first-century Latvia. Aside from the depopulation brought on by emigration, and a lack of maintenance of many houses that actually enhances the place's picturesqueness, this crisis is totally invisible in Kuldīga – to a degree that not only contrasts with southern Europe, but also, for instance, with the streets of central Riga, with their empty flats, casinos and charity shops. There are some possible explanations for this phlegmatic response. One, for instance, is the fact that in living memory, Latvians experienced an economic contraction on an even larger scale, in the immediate aftermath of the collapse of the Soviet Union, with a recession of -10.4% in 1991, an unbelievable -34.9% in 1992, and -14.9% in 1993.[3] The eventual pay-off for that, after a decade or so of misery, was EU membership, well-stocked supermarkets, EU-funded infrastructure improvements and the safety valve of emigration. Latvians have become well trained at coping with crises that would have led to insurrection pretty much anywhere else.

In that case, Kuldīga is a place where you can almost pretend there is no crisis; the pace of life is slow, the signs of modernity are subtle to non-existent, the houses, right down to their carved doorways, have stood for centuries, their paint peeling off elegantly, and could do so for another few centuries more until they're finally eaten away as the wood degrades. The churches are timeless – Lutheran, Catholic and Orthodox, rustic and emblematic, forming an elegant skyline. So far, so sleepy. Spend a little more time there, however, and you may notice something unexpected.

Here, on the Kuldīga Law Courts, is a plaque that tells you the site of the Revolutionary War Committee in 1919. Here is another plaque, commemorating where a Red Army leader taught in a school. Here is another, on Baznīcas Iela, telling you that on this site, revolutionaries

The Catholic church

The Orthodox church

were massacred. And in the main park, you'll find a monument where two rugged men carrying a flag surmount a plinth with the year "1905". You'll also find another, newer plaque, telling you that in the lovely Biedermeier building you're looking at, the NKVD tortured and humiliated its victims, in the 1940s and early Fifties, and another, which you could almost miss entirely, on the site where the town's Jews were taken away to be slaughtered. These signs of social unrest, revolution, revolt, counter-revolution and ethnic genocide are placed almost imperceptibly onto the wooden houses and plastered classical public buildings; a couple are translated into Russian, another couple into English, and most, into neither.

Explore a little more and you'll find legacies of the USSR, in a town which could otherwise fairly advertise itself as one of the least visibly Soviet towns in the Baltic states.[4] There's a large housing estate, stretching along both sides of Piltenes Iela, and another, smaller, off Mucenieku Iela; there's the remnants of large factory complexes; there's

Red Base – the old Law Courts

a peculiar personal museum; and there's the sculpture park of a local artist, whose work will be instantly identifiable for anyone who knows the public art of the late-Soviet era. All of these are not only evidence of the ways in which Kuldīga has been deeply shaped by the events of the last 110 years, beginning with the sudden explosion of 1905, but they may also help explain exactly why the town is now so quiet, in the face of events that have elsewhere led to countries experiencing their own "1905"s. There is a carefully conserved absence at this town's heart, and this essay will be an attempt to fill it – something which is not so hard, so long as you pay attention to its inscriptions.

The Relics of 1905

During the Kuldīga Fair in July 2016, there were events in the 1905 park; folk singing and dance contests were held in a marquee built onto the plinth of a monument; the two figures on that monument stared impassively as Kuldīgans and tourists loitered and enjoyed themselves. A few days later, the paraphernalia was removed, and the monument stood alone in the park again. Anyone who has the slightest familiarity with the Stalin-era artistic school known as "Socialist Realism" will straightaway know what they're dealing with here. Hewn from grey granite, the statue depicts two full male figures; one, younger, very handsome, with a quiff, high cheekbones and dramatic eyebrows, and a shorter, older moustachioed figure. Between them they carry a banner, which you can be quite sure was coloured deepest scarlet when the events the statue refers to were taking place. Both wear crude, ill-fitting clothes, the garb of the early-twentieth-century factory labourer and peasant; their gaze is aimed firmly forward; behind them is the signature of the sculptor, Livija Rezevska, and the year, 1955. Beneath them is the year "1905", with no further explanation; and that's what the park and the street are named after too. What is this, and what is it (still) doing here?

Whereas monuments to the revolutionary events of 1917-1920 can be rare in those EU countries which were once, entirely or not, part

The year 1905

of the Russian Empire (Finland, the Baltics, Poland), monuments to the 1905 Revolution appear with remarkable regularity. In a sense, this is strange. In Marxist historiography – whether official Soviet, dissident libertarian or Trotskyist – 1905 was the "dress rehearsal" for 1917. Beginning with strike waves in St Petersburg and Poland, it was a pan-imperial working-class uprising, culminating near the end of the year in a failed Bolshevik insurrection in Moscow. Unlike 1917, it was successfully suppressed, in a combination of carrot (the Tsar's "October Manifesto" promised various liberal freedoms, mostly honoured in the breach) and stick (thousands of protesters were killed in 1905, and on into 1906 and 1907). Some of the revolutionary leaders in 1905 would later become central to the nation-building projects of the interwar years, such as Jozef Piłsudski in Poland, or Kārlis Ulmanis in Latvia; and the anti-imperial aspect of this explosion means that it can be seen in a sense as a nationalist uprising, although at the time it was largely interpreted in socialist terms. But, surely, pretty little Kuldīga could not have been much of a part in the rising? At this point, it is worth referring to another plaque, this one on the

Town Hall Square, showing the EU Cobbles

front of Kuldīga's mid-nineteenth-century neo-Gothic Town Hall. It reads: "In this building in Autumn 1905 was based the Kuldīga Revolutionary Committee".

Kurzeme, Kurland Gubernia was one of the most turbulent provinces in the entire Russian Empire during the 1905 Revolution, and within that, the dominant political trend was not agrarian populism, as it was in much of Russia itself, and there was no Father Gapon figure promising to intercede with the Good Tsar. On the contrary, 1905 was dominated by the Latvian Social Democrats, the local wing of the Russian Social-Democratic Labour Party, then only vaguely divided into Bolshevik and Menshevik factions. In Anatol Lieven's account, the centrality of this avowedly revolutionary Marxist party to the events owed something to Latvia's proximity, both economically and physically, to Germany. More industrially and agriculturally developed than most of the Russian Empire, Latvia had – Kuldīga, or then, usually, Goldingen, included – a large factory proletariat, who had been further radicalised with the Marxist literature brought back from Germany by Social Democrats such as the poet couple Rainis and Aszpazija. "Based on the large Latvian (and Russian) working class in Riga and Liepāja, the Latvian Social Democratic movement in 1905 is said to have been bigger than the Russian Menshevik and Bolshevik organisations combined".[5] An active working class, organised in large factories, with ideas being circulated by radical, peripatetic intellectuals – it's a fairly classic revolutionary scenario. You can also get a sense of why it occurred when you look at the larger houses in turn-of-the-century Kuldīga, such as the sprawling, redbrick Dutch Baroque residence on Mālu Iela, with the fateful year "1905" inscribed onto its gable.

The impression of Social Democratic dominance is also stressed in the work of Andrew Ezergailis, who describes the 1905 Revolution as "perhaps the most important event of the twentieth century to Latvians" (in the early 1970s – opinions may have changed since). He argues that "among Latvian historians of 1905 and in the memoir histories of the participants, the general conclusion is that Latvia showed more enthusiasm, violence and revolutionary maturity in 1905 than any other area of the Russian Empire".[6] Widespread strikes of farm-hands were organised across Kurzeme by the Latvian Social Democrats, and events soon escalated even out of their control – the province was hit by a series of "church demonstrations", where priests were dragged out of their churches and made to carry red flags or flogged. In August 1905, Martial Law was declared in Kurzeme, and the revolutionary committee which occupied the Town Hall was the response to that.

The extent of the events is an enduring contrast with the smallness of the canvas – an armed rising in Tukums is obviously less celebrated than one in Moscow, but both took place. As everywhere else, the revolution was violently suppressed, but it left long-lasting legacies. According to the Latvian Social Democratic leader, and brother-in-law of Rainis, Pēteris Stučka, naturally not an unbiased observer, 1905 may have appeared at the time like a national uprising, with Latvian liberals and populists joining in a struggle against Tsarist administrators and Baltic German landowners, but whereas they compromised afterwards, accepting some paring back of Tsarist restrictions on Latvian language and culture, the socialist demands carried by the Latvian workers naturally could not be fulfilled.[7] The immediate effect was emigration – Latvian exiles from the later Chekist Jēkabs Peterss, born just outside Kuldīga, to the mythical "Peter the Painter" found themselves crammed into the slums of London's East End or New York's Lower East Side.[8] Around twelve years later, however, many would return.

The continuity between the two revolutions can be read, too, in the inscriptions on Kuldīga's Soviet-era plaques; at the corner of Liepājas Iela and Baznīcas Iela, you find that "in this house in 1905 lived Janis Septe (Žanis Millers), chairman of the revolutionary committee and President of the Soviet in 1918". The second revolutionary sequence, from 1917 to 1919, is not a part of Latvian historiography today in the way that 1905 is; the legitimate government, it is assumed, was that set up by the Latvian Declaration of Independence in late 1918, signed by members of 1905's populist and liberal parties, and the Menshevik wing of the Social Democrats; the subsequent Latvian Soviet Republic, merely a facet of a "Latvian-Soviet War". Of course, for the USSR, after 1940, this brief Republic was the legitimate government and the liberal government a foreign plant; something which has very probably discredited it in the eyes of post-Soviet observers. Even so, Kuldīga has not removed the many 1919 plaques and monuments around the city, and from them, you can piece together aspects of the much more murky revolutionary events that took place in the aftermath of the First World War.

The Relics of 1919

Livija Rezevska's monument representing "1905" and her later sculptural ensemble on "1919" are strikingly different, linked only

The women of 1919

by the events described, and by the fact that neither work has any added commentary, just a simple year appended to the figures and the plinths. It is placed in a courtyard just in the corner of, but contiguous with, 1905 Park. This courtyard is entered through the very early, timber-framed house at the junction of Liepājas Iela and Baznīcas Iela, where you can find another of Kuldīga's revolutionary plaques. This one, unlike most, is bilingual in Russian and Latvian, on a stark black plaque with angular sans serif letters, in a style much more immediately recognisable as "Soviet". It reads: "in the courtyard of this house in 1919 the Landeswehr killed more than 100 revolutionaries". It is this act which Rezevska's sculpture draws attention to, rather than the (briefly) victorious seizure of power in the town by Bolshevik revolutionary committees; rather than triumphalist, like the two men of 1905, this is instead an image of suffering and defeat; perhaps it is the fact we're dealing with an image of victimhood that has enabled this monument to survive, given that the events it deals with are enduringly controversial, in a way that 1905 is not.

As you can find in the progression of Rezevska's works in her Sculpture Garden at the heart of the town – which we will come to later – the 1919 monument marks a major shift in style. The 1905 monument is traditional Soviet Socialist Realism down to its chiselled cheekbones, musclemen with their eyes set with total focus towards the future; they are realistically rendered, with their clothes and hairstyles modelled with historical veracity. By the mid-1970s, when she created the 1919 monument, Rezevska shifted towards a more stylised kind of figurative sculpture, with some ancestry in early-twentieth-century modernism, of the sort that was proscribed in the USSR from the mid-Thirties to the mid-Fifties – Gaudier-Brzeska, Brancusi, Lipschitz, are all possible influences, as well as a continued remnant from more approved sculptors like Maillol. The body remains recognisable in work like this – it is not abstract sculpture, which remained extremely controversial in the USSR from the Thirties right up until the very end in the late Eighties, but it is abstracted, so that the recognisable bodies are reduced to sharp lines, their faces sketched in rather than realistically rendered, and organised as formal, pattern-like groups. In painting, this shift, visible as early as the mid-Fifties under Khrushchev, was called the "severe style", and this describes well what happens to Rezevska's work. You can also see this in monuments from the entire Soviet space, so it isn't unique to her, by any means. But the 1919 monument is an intelligent, subtle example of the severe style, particularly in the way it integrates with architecture.

This is paralleled by the materials Rezevska used for this ambitious work. Approached from the 1905 Park, all you find is a stark, crumbling wall – this monument to a hundred revolutionaries killed by German military adventurers immediately recalls Mies van der Rohe's monument to Rosa Luxemburg and Karl Liebknecht, two rather more famous revolutionaries murdered by Freikorps in 1919. The rugged brick wall of Mies's monument was selected to evoke the wall against which the two were shot; it seems likely Rezevska's use of poor-quality bricks was for similar reasons. Walk within this, towards the building that bears the plaque, and the wall is revealed to be a two-part composition, made up of two hard, black beaten metal panels. In one, six naked male figures stretch and writhe, their bodies reduced to the lines of chests, their faces just noses and jaws; they are pulled into a formal composition, with the tallest figure embracing his comrades in agony. In the adjacent panel are the mourners, a group of head-scarved women looking in sorrow over one of these murdered naked men. Aesthetically, this is all considerably more radical and ambitious than what the younger Rezevska had produced to commemorate the earlier failed revolution, but the iconography here is conservative, with struggling men and women left as mourning mothers. The headscarves of these women became something of a motif in Rezevska's work, an item of clothing that abstracts and depersonalises the wearers to much the same effect as the diagrammatic features of the men. Flowers had been laid in front of the memorial.

This is maybe surprising, as official Latvian history quite

unsurprisingly ignores or downplays the revolutions that took place here in 1917 and 1919.[9] As in, say, Poland or Czechoslovakia, the important thing is the declaration of independence that immediately followed the collapse of the German Army at the end of the First World War. The subsequent two years of chaos were simply a War of Independence, where the new state bravely established itself against Bolshevik invaders, German Freikorps and White Russian nationalists. This not wholly untrue, but it neglects one obvious fact – the events can also be considered, in Anatol Lieven's description, as a Civil War, caused in large part by the huge popularity of socialist revolution in Latvia,[10] and particularly, the overwhelming popularity of the Latvian Social Democrats, who were by mid-1917 the local branch of Lenin's Bolshevik Party. In the work of Andrew Ezergailis on 1917 in Latvia, it is clear that this was actually one of the most solidly Communist parts of the Russian Empire, comparable in that respect with the factories of Petrograd or the mining areas of Donbass, rather than with more conservative provinces nearby such as Lithuania or eastern Poland; given how much the Bolsheviks' organisation rested on the Baltic Fleet, it would be strange were it otherwise. Latvia, with its ethnically diverse, tightly organised and literate working class and its modernised agriculture, was natural territory for early-twentieth-century socialism. However, in 1917, Kurzeme was occupied by the German Empire, who had plans for a puppet state of Courland on the territory; many Courlanders were in exile, or fighting in the famous Riflemen's Division. It was later, in 1919, that it was itself affected by revolution.

Nonetheless, it's necessary to understand what happened in the unoccupied Vidzeme, Latgale and Zemgale in 1917 to understand what happened in Kurzeme two years later. 1917 was peaceful in Riga, with power falling into the hands of the local Soviet with ease. Latvian exiles in Britain or the US made their way home, no longer in fear of arrest or torture by the Okhrana. One gave an account of a depopulated capital:

> Was it really Riga, the busy, industrial city? The silence that reigned in the streets made me doubt it. The factories which we passed did not work. The slender factory smokestacks had not belched for some time. It seemed like a metamorphosis had changed the entire city into an old, paralytic invalid.[11]

The Latvian Social Democrats had hitherto occupied a "Unionist" position, advocating co-operation between the Bolsheviks and Mensheviks; the course of events, with the Bolshevik emphasis on immediate transfer of power to the workers and soldiers' councils, and on immediate abolition of capitalism, had more appeal than the Mensheviks' support of a coalition with liberals and populists. This is perhaps strange, as the Latvian Riflemen, so many of them Courlanders, could have been expected to be sceptical, given the Bolshevik insistence on immediate peace – something which one Latvian Bolshevik worried "would place Kurland outside the blessings of the revolution"[12] – but the desire for revolution seems to have overrun nationalism or patriotism, something which Ezergailis is keen to stress. The Latvian Social Democrats of 1917 wanted a "free Latvia in a free Russia", nothing more. It is worth pausing over the reasons why, as Ezergailis argues, it was the apocalyptic, visionary aspect of Bolshevik rhetoric – rather than the more prosaic promise of national autonomy – that really convinced the population.

A mid-1917 article in the paper *Social Democrat*, for example, justified the union with the Bolsheviks as follows: "We will merge our work with our mighty proletariat. Our petty fanciful 'I' will disappear, and brightly and forcefully will ascend the demolition of the past and the builder of our beautiful future – we."[13] A hostile liberal observer, in the paper Lidums, examined this in greater detail:

> The Social Democrats loom large not only because they know how to appeal to the psychology of the Mob, but mostly because they are inspired by an eschatological sense of the world. Each and every

> Social Democrat believes that the doomsday of the old world has arrived and a new everlasting life has begun. And it depends on every individual member, on his unceasing activity, whether the new life will arrive or not.[14]

This is especially crucial because, as Ezergailis puts it, "in Latvia there was no right wing to speak of; there were only competing views of progress, change and social transformation... Moreover, Latvia in 1917 was a socialist country, which, considering the circumstances, meant that it was a Marxist country".[15] If this was the case, the party that offered the most complete vision of transformation, the most unadulterated socialism, and the most convincing promise of its swift achievement, was unsurprisingly the most popular. To give some measure of how popular, the Social Democrats won elections to Latvian Soviets from early 1917 onwards, and in the unoccupied part of the country, won the Constituent Assembly elections with a landslide 72%[16] – compared with just over 25% in the Russian Empire as a whole. All this of course meant little when the whole of Latvia fell to the Germans over the next year, with the Treaty of Brest-Litovsk envisioning it as a German satellite. The collapse, as the German army mutinied and Soviets sprang up along Germany's Baltic Coast, enabled the Declaration of Independence in November 1918, but it also meant that the Latvian divisions of the Red Army could cross over and retake what they considered to be rightfully theirs. After all, the Red Army's first commander in chief, Jukums Vācietis, was a Courlander. You can still find a plaque honouring him in Kuldīga, along the sleepy, dusty, wooden curve of Ventspils Iela.

The mood of the Latvian Communists in January 1919 was, it would seem from most accounts, unforgiving. They had to fight for the country with the same German Freikorps that were then violently suppressing Communist revolution in Germany itself, in the Spartacist uprising in Berlin and the Bavarian Soviet Republic, and they also had to fight against the centre-left government established with the

Declaration of Independence, backed by British gunboats. The year appears to have been one of apocalyptic carnage, the "doomsday of the old world" truly made apparent. But it will not do to make this a local event. What happened in Kuldīga that year is comparable with what happened in Kiel, in Helsinki, in Munich, in Budapest, in Glasgow, in Turin, as Europe convulsed into a flurry of failed revolutions and equally, if not more, violent counter-revolutions. David Mitchell's lurid history of that year, *1919 – Red Mirage*, gives Latvia a particularly central role. Relying on hostile, mostly German accounts, he sees the Red Army's entry into the country in terms which evoke the account of late medieval chaos in Norman Cohn's *The Pursuit of the Millennium*:

> On January 3rd, 1919, the Red Army appeared in the streets, terrifying in its very dirtiness and raggedness (rifle slings made of pieces of string, greasy red banners with unintelligible inscriptions, a military band whose instruments, musicians and music produced an impression of almost incredible dilapidation and cacophony). The sight of a detachment of women soldiers, rumours of whose more-than-male ruthlessness had flown ahead of them, struck a special chill into bourgeois hearts. Were not these Bolshevik gunwomen said to be recruited from the ranks of strumpets and ungrateful female domestic servants?[17]

Aside from giving a very different picture of revolutionary gender roles to that depicted in the sculptures of Livija Rezevska – women as an active and angry revolutionary vanguard rather than as mourning, head-scarved ghosts – this helps elucidate what a strange place Kuldīga must have been in 1919, as its attractive little streets, evaporating within a couple of miles to pasture, forests and (crucially) Baltic German manor houses became the setting for a ferociously fought revolution and counter-revolution, and as the Kuldīga Courts, a beautiful, idiosyncratic classical building set on the canal, became the headquarters of a committee of revolutionary war – something still immortalised on a plaque, and by the small memorial to the revolutionary fallen in the town cemetery. The strange combination of horror and anticipation that Kurzeme must have been undergoing is particularly well captured in a 1919 poem, published in the Social Democratic paper the *Red Flag*, which gives a sense of a world turned upside down:

> We are the Vandals of Justice,
> We are the barbarians of Right,
> We carry freedom on our shields
> The freedom of the human race!
> There is a trembling and a groaning,
> Through the empty spaces of a worn-out civilisation,
> There is thunder and lightning where we step,
> And fertility rises like vapour from our tracks.
> We are the modern Vandals,
> Wandering with heavy tread,
> In iron-spiked sandals,
> Along the highway of the future![18]

In Kurzeme itself, this fervent, eschatological air, this sense of the final righting of some historic wrongs – the oppression over hundreds of years of the poor by the rich – was expressed in some drastic actions. The tombs of the Dukes of Courland – including Duke Jacob, now Kuldīga's candidate for a figure for a useable past – were opened in Jelgava by the Red Guards in early 1919. Locals threw objects at them or shot at them, as if in doing so they could finally achieve a redress of their ancient grievances.[19]

The Relics of 1940

What happened after this is probably better known. With major assistance from first the Germans, and then from the British, the Communist threat was seen off (something which was hardly helped by

Bolshevik land policy, which saw the Communists essentially starved out, as the country was wracked by famine). A liberal democratic republic – whose most popular party, for as long as democracy lasted, was the Latvian Social Democratic Labour Party, i,e, the Latvian Mensheviks – was set up instead. One of its first acts was to nationalise the Baltic Germans' estates, something which immediately fulfilled one of the main demands of 1905, and was, incidentally denounced by Washington and London as a Communistic measure.[20] Given the convulsions the new state to the east would undergo in the 1930s, Latvians were lucky to stay out of the USSR, something reinforced by the fact that so many of the thousands of Latvian exiles who had opted for Soviet power were massacred in 1937 – Latvians were among the nationalities specifically targeted during the Great Purge. The Latvian Communists we've encountered here – like the Courlanders Vācietis and Peterss – were killed. Today, no serious historian would argue that the annexation of Latvia to the USSR, when it eventually came, had much to do with actual Latvian events or Latvian enthusiasm for socialism or visionary utopias, or for the Soviet state. Because of this, it's fair to say that 1905 and 1919 had more in common than 1919 and 1940.

The official line, as expounded in a small propaganda guide on the Latvian Soviet Socialist Republic, was as follows:

> In the second half of June 1940, a tide of demonstrations swept the country, calling for a Soviet Latvia and its Union with the USSR. The fact is that a revolutionary situation had developed in 1940 [...] Of course, the very existence of the Soviet Union and its historic achievements, which were of world significance, exerted a revolutionary influence on other peoples, including the Latvian people.[21]

Although there was widespread discontent with the right-wing dictatorship of Kārlis Ulmanis, there's no evidence whatsoever for this narrative – not that there was either any genuine call for union with the USSR, nor that there was any sort of popular revolution. In 1919, the Red Army – commanded, after all, by a Latvian – sent its Latvian divisions into the country, as if to stress the point that this was not a colonial occupation or a return of the Russian Empire. Latvians had been targeted so heavily in 1937 that there were few respected leaders left who could have served to head the new puppet Republic; at first, its driving force was the Pole Andrey Vyshinsky, the notorious prosecutor at the Moscow Trials – who was, it is worth noting, a Menshevik in 1917. According to Anatol Lieven, even the Latvian Communists who organised the "spontaneous" demonstrations[22] to welcome the Red Army were shocked when they realised the country was simply going to be annexed, and tried unsuccessfully to convince Moscow to give it the "autonomy" enjoyed at that point by Mongolia.

And whereas actual opposition to Stalin existed by 1940, if at all, in the concentration camps, in Latvia, as in the other areas annexed under the Molotov-Ribbentrop Pact, there were thousands of potential (more than actual) counter-revolutionaries, who were deported en masse in 1941. On their arrival in Kurzeme, the Nazis would expose locals to the bodies of prisoners killed as they approached, and, in the usual fashion, make an entirely spurious association between Jews and Communists,[23] something which may at least have contributed to the passivity of most of the local population as the Latvian Auxiliary Police and the Einsatzgruppen between them killed nearly all the Jews of Latvia, by far the single greatest atrocity to have happened in the country's history.

This is remembered in Kuldīga – where, Ezergailis notes, Jews were exterminated by the local police – only by a small, and recent plaque on the Synagogue, an elegant and well-restored building that now serves as the municipal library. Unusually, though, in a country which today is assiduous in sustaining the memory of the deportations, occasionally and offensively conflated with the Holocaust as a "double genocide", there are also very few memorials in Kuldīga to the atrocities which came with the first phase of Stalinism. In the Catholic Church, there is a panel on one martyr who was killed by the Soviets during the deportations in 1941, but that aside, there is only one major example. That is, a recent plaque – like that on the Synagogue, translated into English – on the building where the NKVD had its cells, from 1945 until 1956. The text is unusually elaborate and affecting: "here people were humiliated and tortured. They were deprived of home and family, freedom and life"; next to it are verses about freedom. This emotional tenor contrasts with that on the Synagogue, which simply tells you that there were Jews here, and then that they were killed. The town is so minuscule that it's impossible to imagine that anyone in the city could have been ignorant of what happened to the Jews, and equally impossible to imagine anyone passing the NKVD building without being fully aware of what happened inside.

The main monumental legacy of this "revolution", the atrocities it perpetrated and the (often equally atrocious) resistance to it, is two graves at either ends of St Anna's Cemetery. At the main entrance is a 1970s memorial to the fallen of the Red Army. Presiding over a great

The monument to the Red Army

grass circle of Soviet dead – nearly as many people as in the entire rest of the cemetery put together – are two more of Livija Rezevska's head-scarved, and here practically hooded, figures. Here is maybe one case in which Rezevska had been allowed to dissent just a little from the accepted monumental norm, insofar as there is no image here of heroism, of the eventual victory over the Third Reich, but another image of women – here, one older woman, and a little girl – left in mourning after their menfolk have been sacrificed. They're made up of hulking great polygons of granite, their bodies indistinguishable from their headscarves, and their faces could be considered to be contorted in mourning, or equally plausibly, be making little inscrutable Attic smiles. Since the late 1990s, they've faced off against a much smaller – both in terms of amount killed and space taken up in the cemetery – grave of anti-Communist partisans. In some ways, the response to the Soviet advance in 1944-5 resembles some of the tactics used by the Latvian Social Democrats in 1905 – guerrilla warfare in the forests, and escapes into exile through Ventspils and Liepāja. That shouldn't imply any similarity in their politics, but it does mean that some aspects of Latvia's revolutionary history were still remembered, even or especially by those who refused to accept the rule of the (however grossly degenerated) heirs of 1905. The graves are laconic, around a single gaunt cross. Some of the names are first names, with patronymics unknown. Some, in fact, just read "unknown". Outside here though, you can walk throughout the town from end to end without being aware of the fact these events ever happened. That's not the case with the later aspects of the Latvian Soviet Socialist Republic.

Relics of 1968

In terms of architecture and new space, the interwar Republic of Latvia left very little in Kuldīga. A Neoclassical bank just off Liepājas Iela with the year 1934 on its pediment (which could quite easily have been constructed a century earlier), and the milestone at the edge of the city marking the construction of the Kuldīga–Skrunda highway – and that's about it. That isn't a comment in itself on an era that was, in economic measures, mildly successful, whatever its democratic deficit in later years, but it is a conspicuous absence. On the other hand, the USSR saw quite widespread construction in Kuldīga, although it can take a little while to discover it. Most of it dates from the years after 1956, as the Khrushchev "Thaw" started to ease the grip of Stalinism on the USSR, although its application to Latvia outside of aesthetics was fairly limited – terror ended, but a quasi-colonial migration of Russian-speakers continued, as did repression of any attempts at "national Communism" in the Soviet Republic – something that led to an official "Letter of 17 Latvian Communists" in protest, forwarded to the Western Communist parties. Accordingly, the results of the "Thaw", broadly conceived to be the period from 1956 to 1968, can be quite ambiguous.

The transformation of the wooden Baltic German Villa Bangert on the edge of the municipal park into the Kuldīga District Museum in 1940 was the earliest act of the occupation authorities in the new Latvian SSR; the construction in the late 1970s of the Livija Rezevska sculpture garden around it provides a more ambiguous Soviet space. But there are also some much less pleasant Soviet interventions into the town. There's the radio tower behind the post office that disfigures an otherwise lovely skyline, its spindly metal outline rising way above the spires of the Lutheran, Catholic and Orthodox churches; and there is the department store on the oversized town square, and although that incongruously vast parade ground-cum-car park was actually laid out in the 1930s, the over-restored modernist department store that dominates it is a Soviet construction of the early Sixties. There was also a Lenin statue here once – not, unlike nearly every other major piece of public sculpture in the city, designed by Livija Rezevska. It was removed in 1990.

The sculpture park, however, is an excellent way to track Rezevska's journey, and its parallel with Soviet art of that era in general. Like more celebrated sculptors such as Ernst Neizvestny or Lev Kerbel, she embraced the possibilities offered by the "Thaw" to shift away from monumental pomposity into a more subtle kind of figurative work. The earliest work in the sculpture garden, the "Violin Player" of 1951, has the extreme, almost cartoonish veracity that can be seen in much of the public sculpture of late Stalinism, comparable to the work of heroic sculptors like Matvey Manizer or the Latvian-born Vera Mukhina. This strong-featured young woman involved in strenuous creative labour could be imagined as the centrepiece of pretty much any Stalinist Palace of Culture. Within less than a decade, in the 1960 piece "Contemplation", the figure has gone from a specific, verifiable, dressed female figure with the prop of her work, to a tightly composed, abstracted, almost faceless feminine body, with thought implied by posture, not by the furrowing of the figure's brow. One could usefully compare these with later work like the 1986 "Path of Sorrow", with its clustered, angular bodies bunched into one hulking mass of granite, or the 1980 "Suitu Folk Singers", with another mass of head-scarved, depersonalised women, and you can see what has changed in Soviet aesthetics as much as in Rezevska's own work. However, in the sculpture garden, the propaganda aspect of Rezevska's work is absent, unlike in the monuments left elsewhere in the city for the heroic deeds and great sufferings of 1905, 1919 and 1941-45. A text in her small studio, preserved for the last fifteen years, describes the sculpture garden as "22 sculptures characterising the Latvian nation, its unity, musical talent and love".[24] This is pretty much how it could have been described in the Soviet era, although perhaps then it might have been described as the "Latvian SSR". What is more notable in them, perhaps, is a talented sculptor with an unfortunate bent to sentimentality trying to experiment within very tight limits.

Another important monument to the "Thaw" era can be found in the small housing estate that begins along Piltenes Iela. The first phase of it can be dated quite easily to the very end of the Thaw, from the dates that are placed on the gable ends – 1967, 1968, outlined in a red brick that deliberately contrasts with the grey-beige of the rest of the

The Villa Bangert and the Rezevska Sculpture Park

Moomin singers

buildings. These are "*Khrushchevki*", the standardised housing that was built en masse in order to solve the housing crisis created by Stalinist industrialisation and wartime destruction. Though there would soon be experiments, inspired by the French example, with prefabrication and mass production, at first these were built at extremely rapid speed out of standard bricks, without lifts. The bricks and the doorways varied from area to area, but that's about it – here, we have the white bricks and pitched roofs that were common to Krushchevki in the Baltic states – in north-eastern Estonia, for instance, there are almost entire towns made up just of these. The innovation, in so far as there is one here, is in layout. In Kuldīga, this is actually quite a sharp break. Kuldīga's housing is characterised by single-family houses, usually, of course, of wood, though the more cramped, working-class housing that can still be found along Mucenieku Iela is often in red brick. The

Manicured Khrushchevki

houses often have large gardens, in which you can grow produce, as many people still do – the "green space" is there to be used, as a kind of production for food and sale, but in the 1967-68 housing estates in Kuldīga, it is there to be contemplated passively – trees and open space to bring birdsong and light into your cramped fourth-floor walk-up flat. Standardised and identikit as it is, it's also a totally different typology to anything else in the city up to that point.

So what's it doing here? Kuldīga, already with some industry in the early twentieth century, expanded as a small industrial town in the Soviet era – there was even a concrete panel factory, the results of which we will soon see. One paradox is that these construction projects, as was often the case in towns that hadn't been substantially damaged during the war, left the old towns neglected, but largely intact. New construction – largely aimed at skilled workers and intelligentsia – was begun on virgin sites just outside towns, while the town centres and inner suburbs were usually left alone, and remained as a dilapidated concentration of private ownership and commerce, with most housing still privately owned, as opposed to the state ownership of the new *Mikrorayon*.[25] So on that level, one of the reasons why the old town of Kuldīga is so well preserved – more so, than a similar town in, say, the UK, might be – is precisely because the Soviet preference for showcase construction on untouched sites meant that it could avoid the results of the property speculation that usually goes along with economic growth. That is – the reason why Kuldīga appears as such a time-capsule, is because the growth in population and industry that happened here between the Fifties and the Eighties was accommodated elsewhere.

Relics of 1989

The sheer fact that a concrete panel factory was built at all on the outskirts of Kuldīga reveals the sheer reach of the Soviet mass housing programme, penetrating even into this small town of wood and, more seldom, brick. Aside from the obvious fire safety question, there is no rational reason why Kuldīga could not have continued to build in much the same way as it always had, expanding a little further out into the countryside, on an Anglo-Saxon suburban model; it would make more sense than using a heavy-industrial technology to build high-density housing on the town's edge, but this is exactly what happened.[26] However, as the *Mikrorayon* at Piltenes Iela expanded, the approach to architecture in the new district became ever more determinedly local, veering away from the interchangeable designs of the first, 1960s phase, towards more elaborated, more sophisticated architecture – while remaining prefabricated in its components. Eventually this would end on the literal eve of the USSR's collapse and Latvia's regained independence, with a shift towards Postmodernism. Arguably, this could be paralleled with the political history of the town during the same time. In the Kuldīga District Museum is a short film showing a demonstration marching through the town in 1990 demanding independence – there are enough people there that you could imagine at least half of the town was on that demonstration, which would make it the largest political manifestation in the town since 1919. The turn to Postmodernism and localism in architecture could be presented as a deliberate move from Soviet universalism and a Russified "internationalism" towards more local values; or, equally plausibly, it could be seen as proof that there was a little more mileage in the system's approach to architecture and planning than it was given credit for.

As Philipp Meuser and Dimitrij Zadorin write in their dry, obsessive catalogue of prefabricated housing in the post-Stalin USSR, the layouts and approaches of the different eras of the micro-district can be compared to kinds of games – the straightforward "chessboards" of the first *Khrushchevki*, laid out in banal grids, the more spaced out "Ville Radieuse" of the Sixties and Seventies as "dominoes", and the last, more complex, articulated structures as "Tetris".[27] Of these, the Kuldīga *Mikrorayon* is mostly dominoes, with a bit of Tetris creeping in. But probably more significant is something else, which Meuser and Zadorin point out – the development of different regional variants of the large panel housing estate. Here, the Baltic states were by some way more advanced than the bulk of the USSR, with a local enthusiasm for the new towns and new suburbs of nearby Sweden and Finland (both of which also made extremely extensive use of concrete panel systems) spilling over into both the layout and the aesthetic of their new estates, something that became obvious mainly in the 1970s and 1980s, which was, paradoxically, a period of particularly acute Russification in Latvia and Estonia. So, to the street, facing Piletenes Iela itself, is a row of five-storey blocks using a series developed in the Lithuanian SSR, with abstract patterns in the concrete relief; some of these have been painted and insulated. These look only slightly more differentiated, but it's inside the estate that you really notice a difference. One thing that has been added to most of the blocks is individually designed entrances, where brick and concrete steps, often with built-in benches, lead to patterned screens as a perhaps vain attempt to introduce variety in the standardised buildings.

Would prefer to be in Finland

Then, you'll notice that things have changed in the buildings themselves. Many of them use wood as a decorative device, something very widespread in Scandinavian modernism, either to create rhythms in the façades or to create balconies and loggias; like the tall pines which run between the buildings, these are ornamental, not "useful" like the wooden houses and the fruit trees of the old streets a few yards away. Other blocks boast redbrick stair-towers emphasised against the yellowing concrete panels, creating a slightly medieval rhythm. At the far edge of the estate, where it meets a stream, a series of garages and the end of the town altogether, the stair towers have been emphasised further with fluted brickwork, reminiscent of German Expressionism and brick Gothic. A Hanseatic kind of Gothic is of course a vernacular architecture in much of Latvia, and especially in Riga, but bar the early-twentieth-century Lutheran church, there is actually very little of it in Kuldīga. The real architectural vernacular here is a slightly folksy version of Neoclassicism. So while the building committees of the Latvian SSR were able by the early 1980s, when these blocks were built, to have a kind of system-building that displays an engagement and continuity with the traditions of Latvia, it couldn't do the same with individual towns, preferring a general "Latvian" look that didn't necessarily suit everywhere.

Or, at least, not until the end of the 1980s. Cross the road from the large estate and past an empty space which was very probably going to be more housing before 1991, and you'll find two more redbrick Soviet tenement blocks, one of them insulated and painted an unsympathetic pastel green. Beyond these are two terraces of single-family houses. This is a type which might be normal in, say, Britain or the Low Countries (or as "row houses" in nineteenth-century America), but is rare anywhere in continental Europe – including in Kuldīga, where the pre-twentieth-century type is detached houses, however small some of them may be. Some of the design gestures are similar to those on the *Mikrorayon*, especially the stepped entrances, but the articulated solid-and-void rhythm of the houses themselves is something else,

Prefab Gothic

indebted perhaps to De Stijl, Dutch rather than Finnish modern; though where the wooden towers that crown some of the houses come from is anybody's guess – most likely the private invention of the architect. The year is outlined on the gable: 1989. At the centrepiece is an office block for the local Forestry Commission, which is even more elaborate, to the point where it is obviously a work of Postmodernism, a "complex and contradictory" (as Robert Venturi put it) montage of historic forms – a bulging, modernist corner, a traditionalist gable, all tilted at conflicting angles. And then it all stops, there and then, in the year that the Soviet Empire fell in Central-Eastern Europe, two years before it would leave Latvia. What has happened since turns to a more ingratiating wood-cladding commercial architecture, or something more banal in the new retail parks; but there's no more housing, bar the odd single house. The expansion of Kuldīga

1989

stops here, the end of its history. And certainly, given the amount of empty houses in the town, a housing shortage is the least of the contemporary town's problems.

Relics of an Alternative Present

There are a few places which offer a good explanation of why history ending might have appeared rather seductive. One of them is the extraordinary homemade museum on Baznīcas Iela, Cits Laiks, or "Other Time", as it translates itself. This one-man collection of Soviet memorabilia is all of the things that the town is otherwise keen to forget or regard as a terrible mistake breaking out all over the place, a chaos of giant busts of leaders (Marx, Lenin, "the Georgian, Stalin"), flags laid on top of each other, a mini-library of Latvian Communism and a repository of forgotten or repressed iconography.

The Forestry Commission

Marx, Lenin, and 1990s rationbooks

In one room, an impressive photograph mural of Lenin, taken from the Party headquarters in Jēkabpils, takes up one wall, and a series of hagiographic panels on the Latvian Riflemen takes up another. Some of it has personal meaning – the museum's owner/founder/collector points to a map of the "Russian" Civil War, and points out that three million were killed, including his great-grandfather – I didn't ask what side he was fighting on, but given his fixations and the allegiances of most Latvians in 1917, it wouldn't be hard to guess. The map, which was mounted on the classroom of a Kuldīga school in the 1970s, shows the international interventions that aimed to suppress the Bolsheviks – armies coming from Britain in the north, France up the Black Sea, the US and Japan in the east, Poland in the west. It's entirely in Russian.

These were "very hard times", he tells me at the start, with a well-practiced patter; "Christmas was criminal, only New Year", as he points to a selection of rather pretty New Year's Cards on a table, under glass. It's hard to concentrate, though, with this historical pile-up of pomposity, optimism and kitsch. A painting of the young Lenin walking through a forest, paintings of landscapes with smoking chimneys, a Latvian-language primer in Dialectical Materialism, portraits of Gorbachev, Gagarin and Brezhnev, a mock-up "Party leader's table with vodka glass and telephone", the flag of the Kuldīga District Communist Party.

A lot of this would just be rubbish in any other context, and the small selection of Soviet ephemera in the Kuldīga District Museum gives a strong impression of why this society might have felt so oppressive, even after the terror from 1945 to 1953 ended. That effect is created through the sheer concentrated weight of cultism – more Lenins than you could ever want to see. Yet, when the museum's director points to the "hardest times", he reaches through the piles and piles of tat to several printed strips of ration cards from 1992; here as elsewhere, the collapse was economically disastrous; the fact that this didn't lead to much of a neo-socialist reaction is proof of just how discredited the system was by that point. It's also a useful reminder that what happened here in 2009 had very recent precedents. Either way, if anti-capitalism means what is on display as an example of the "Other Times", it's little wonder it has so little appeal. It's not all hideous – some of the posters and pamphlets show an optimism and modernity that contrasts with the morbidity of the rest – but the most radical response it could elicit is "hmm, well, those were the days".

In the same room as all the many and varied busts of Lenin, is a set of matchbox lids, with different designs on them, mostly on Soviet themes, with odd little surprises, like a set on the architecture of Sverdlovsk/Yekaterinburg (see Part Three of this book). These have particular significance, because the Vulkans match factory was the town's main employer, before, during and after the Soviet era. Some of the EU funding mainly intended for re-cobbling the streets went into a commemorative vitrine on Liepājas Iela, where you can learn about matches, Spartakiadas and the Komsomol, all as things which happened to be done by employees of the factory. Much of the factory itself still exists, but you might find it entirely by accident, as I did. The Vulkans factory's remains are down a back street, off Skrundas Iela. The monumental redbrick chimneys still stand, but the buildings around them – Soviet and pre-Soviet – are either in ruins, destroyed or part-destroyed. That particular kind of social change, that which happened in 1905 – workers in large factories and landless peasants taking action against a repressive state, agitated and organised by a leadership of factory agitators and intellectuals – is obviously never going to happen here ever again, and wasn't open as an option to protesting about what happened here in 2009.

One possible way out of this is to look at the history of this place more critically, and to think about some of the things that didn't happen. Outside the Synagogue/library at the time of writing is a giant wooden cat. Inside the adjacent building, the Art House, is "the Grand-land's Museum", and an accompanying text promises the following:

The chimneys of Vulkans

> The "Grand-land's Museum" working group has received a fragmented information from the Universe about a mysterious story that has silently been developing in parallel to our "reality". That other "reality" that we are dealing with, in general tells the same story as the one we live in. Except, something surprising happened there during the first decade of the 20th century. After the World War I, the fathers of the idea of an independent Latvia joined forces with the founders of the Soviet Union and together changed the course of history in an ideologically more innovative direction than the history we are familiar with. Grand-land was founded. Thus, the entire global landscape of the geopolitical history that followed in this parallel reality, looks completely different compared to the history which is familiar to us. We can only speculate on how the representatives of these seemingly different, even opposite ideologies, found a common language and it is our task to find it out. One thing is clear – Latvian virtues of hard work in combination with Russian comradeship has produced a unique chemistry and led to the establishment of a civilised state never previously known in the history of civilisation – the Grand-land. The famous Latvian poet Aspazija was unanimously chosen as the ruler of the Grand-land. Considering the fact that Aspazija was one of the first Latvian feminists, Grand-land was created on the basis of matriarchy, which has considerably reduced the number of unnatural deaths in society, replaced competition with cooperation as one of the main values of the society and elegantly combined industrial progress with deep and true love of nature.[28]

So how is this vision of a transnational socialist-feminist-environmentalist state that never actually existed translated into actual exhibits, like that giant cat? It's "the Grand-lander Cat, and is a multifunctional object that has served also as a tribune for Aspazija to address the nation. It was also a boudoir for the ruler on her annual journey across the borderless country, while currently it serves as a shrine, since the legendary stateswoman left her physical state of being more than half a century ago, and has joined the eternity. Mysteriously allured, the famous Latvian sculptor Aigars Bikše undertook the restoration of the Cat following the instructions from the parallel reality." To approach history like this is quite different both from how the official history of the town and the country proceeds – that is, to ignore the revolutionary history of the area completely – and also, from how this essay has progressed, in which we've tried to find real traces left by those events. The reason for this has been to make clear that in Latvia – even, or especially, in a town as "deep Latvian" as Kuldīga, with a nearly non-existent Russian population and comparatively little industry – there is actually an abundant revolutionary history, an apocalyptic, utopian heritage which is only inadequately represented by the Soviet state that the country first narrowly escaped becoming part of, and then was annexed by. But these objects left around – the housing estates, the sculptures and the

The Grand-land Museum outside the Synagogue-Library

plaques – are quite easily read, as easily understood as they are easily ignored. The Grand-land project is considerably more cryptic. Its authors suggest that the relics genuinely left by a different civilisation from ours might be totally incomprehensible. However, as time goes on, the relics left by the revolutionary movement's very ambiguous heirs may become equally baffling. All it would take is a repainting of the housing estates, a removal of ten or so plaques, the removal of three statues and practically the entire twentieth-century history of Kuldīga would be impossible to read in its built landscape. And that's not an implausible prospect; one day, all there will be here is a waterfall, pretty houses, Duke Jacob and supermarkets.

An Aivars Lembergs mug

A TOUR WITH THE CITY ARCHITECT

VENTSPILS, Windau, Vindava

Ventspils is widely considered to be the best managed city in Latvia. In Latvia, outside the capital, which does have its concentration of big businesses and tourist draws, this means a lot. What if there was a future other than managed decline and emigration? Frequently, in discussions with people about the depopulation and decline of their town, and what they can do about it, they will point to Ventspils as an example of what could be done. Simultaneously with being considered the best managed city, it is considered to be the most corrupt city in Latvia, with its long serving Mayor and former head of the local Communist Party, Aivars Lembergs, seemingly perpetually under investigation for dubious deals and kickbacks, although it has never resulted in him actually being prosecuted – or losing an election. Although Ventspils has a relatively small Russian minority, Lembergs has been unexpectedly sympathetic towards the erstwhile imperial overlord, claiming NATO to be a bigger threat to Latvian independence than the USSR ever was, and recently jetting over to Russia for talks with Dmitry Medvedev – especially curious given that "de-Sovietisation" of the city's aesthetic has been part of his programme as Mayor. I had the unexpected pleasure of a tour of the city from its city architect in summer 2016, a surreal experience of a city managed as a combination of industrial company town, theme park and children's playground. If being more like Ventspils is a possible solution to the rather sad, worn look of many Baltic towns outside the three capitals, it is worth finding out exactly what this alternative is – and how they managed to fund it. Ventspils' history can be read in the glossy guidebook published by the city council, a contemporary equivalent of the Progress Publishers Guides that would tell you about the achievements of the Soviet republican capitals. The current edition, *Ventspils – 700+25*, begins with a valedictory foreword from Lembergs: "We have built ourselves a city, a city where we and others feel good [...] We carefully consider all new things and choose only what is best for our well-being, convenience, comfort, urban aesthetic and growth".[1] The history told therein is the usual attempt to create a monoethnic narrative out of Kurzeme, once the multicultural imperial province of Courland, shifting between the land of the ancient Livonians, to the Grand Duchy – a German governed autonomous part of the Polish-Lithuanian Commonwealth, whose fleet once claimed colonies in West Africa and the Caribbean – through the Russian Empire and independence. More controversial matters are avoided, from the 1905 Revolution, when Ventspils – Windau, Vindava – erupted, like all of Kurland, in a ferocious socialist uprising, before being brutally pacified by Tsarist troops – to the brief 1919 Latvian Soviet Republic. The silence extends to the Holocaust, when Kurzeme's large Jewish population was exterminated, largely by the Latvian Auxiliary Police. However, it does take time out to note the "genocide of the Livs", apparently caused when the Soviet army forced the Finno-Ugric speaking Liv population out of their fishing villages when they militarised the Baltic coast (undoubtedly a bad and cruel thing, but an odd one to consider more important than the murder of every single Jew in the city). History then leaps from 1944, and the flight of the liberal Latvian Central Council to Stockholm, to the 1980s environmental movement that would lead to independence. As a narrative, there's nothing in the story that Ventspils tells about itself that could possibly offend a Latvian nationalist. That mention of the

Classical Ventspils

environmental movement, however, is crucial for understanding what has made Ventspils the strange "success story" it is today. In the 1970s, an oil terminal was built here with the assistance of the American investor Armand Hammer and his company Occidental Petroleum, for the export of fossil fuels from the Soviet interior through the Baltic to northwestern Europe. The large Free Port of Ventspils is still based around this, and it has been a Special Economic Zone since 1997, during which it has become a highly profitable capitalist enterprise. It is the Oil Terminal that first makes it obvious quite what sort of a town you are in, on arrival from the bus station. Nearby, is a small square, built around the Lutheran Church, a diminutive piece of Petersburgian classicism, and an ensemble of little houses, wood and stucco, leading down to the historic market square. As you step down towards the market, you can't help but see the Terminal – a continuous metal conduit, stained red and black, suspended on tiny little metal

A view of the Oil Terminal

struts, connected by pipes and gantries to domed containers, leading further to rusty cranes, and in the middle of all of this, dwarfed, a couple of grimy, late-nineteenth-century dock buildings. The sudden shift from the Lilliputian scale of the houses and the church to this Constructivist monster is the most remarkable thing in the town, and a constant reminder of what exactly it revolves around. In front of it, dotted along the quayside promenade, and the passenger port that can take you to Sweden, north Germany, Denmark, is a series of fibreglass cows. They have been decorated in a variety of costumes. Suitcase cow, decorated with stamps and stickers from foreign destinations. Riot police cow, with shield and armour. There's also a little group of souvenir shops, where you can buy a mug with the face of Aivars Lembergs.

I'm not here to look at the port, rather, as one of a group of writers taking part in a residency in nearby Kuldīga, on a visit to the "Writers

Pig Cow

Latvian Hansa Aalto – the Samrode building

House", opposite the Lutheran Church; you can tell it is the writer's house, because there is a giant sculpture of a quill outside, another example of the public art that has been bestowed upon the city in the last ten years. Here we were met by Daiga Dzedone, the chief architect of Ventspils, who in that capacity has been responsible for much of the makeover the city has received. Very kindly, she offered us a tour of the city, so we could see how it had been transformed, as she described it, from a depopulating and extremely polluted industrial port, its very air poisoned by ammonia, with a town centre people would actively avoid due to the proximity of the dirty, filthy dangerous industry, to a local tourist draw, with a blue flag beach, a public art programme, and very unusually for Latvia, a growing population. She avoids taking us around the oil terminal, but it is clear this is where the money for it all has come from – that, and the European Union structural funds that have been ploughed into the country since accession, which are actually more conspicuous here than in the pot-holed, half-decrepit, financial crisis-stricken boulevards of Riga. Some of the new work

Bolshevik Municipal

has taken place in the town centre; next to the Writer's House is a neat little municipal library designed by Juris Poga, which bridges between a historic building and a new, mildly modernist new wing with wooden slats; nearby, is the Samrode building, a little office block by architects Krists Karklins and Arhitektūras Birojs, in a knobbly, Hanseatic brown brick. In front of these is a hilariously walrus-faced statue of a Red Army general, Janis Fabricuss, one of the very many Courlanders to throw in his lot with the Bolsheviks. Its survival is surprising. The strident working-class politics that the Riflemen stood for is harder to find.

Rather than lingering here, Dzedone whisks us off to the Juras Varti House of Culture, on the other side of the docks. It's an area dominated by tiny wooden houses, which, at the turn of the century, could be built here at a discount, as a means by the Tsarist government to attract residents to an area that, even then, was beset by pollution, with the prevailing winds blowing in precisely this direction. The result is a little fragment of the sort of villagey townscape you can find in somewhere like Kuldīga: winding streets, recently repaved with EU money, between modest, one-storey clapboard houses, painted yellow, red, blue, green. She doesn't linger on these, though – the point is the new building, which is in fact a remodelling and expansion of a typical Soviet House of Culture, with the same sort of multifunctional high culture you'd have got in one those – classical music, opera, theatre, maybe a bit of panto to bring in the receipts, and some very bad painting exhibited on the walls. The no doubt worn and creaking Soviet structure has been overlaid with shiny but cheap-looking materials, everything bright and wipe-clean; we get a rather too extensive tour, shown everything about it from the mechanism that lowers and raises the stage to the small and large dressing rooms (the latter for stars, the former for dancers and the like).

The "humanisation" of the Soviet legacy exemplified by the House of Culture is one of the main concerns of the town architect – several districts of *Khrushchevki* have been renovated, in the manner common in Poland or the Czech Republic, with pastel colours and garish patterns, which seldom happens in Latvia – "apartment buildings are transformed entirely, as traces of Soviet legacy in the architecture of Ventspils are wiped away by a more modern, better-looking design"[2], says *Ventspils – 700+25*, but the spacious, parkland layouts are untouched by new construction. The landscaping of the green strips between with fountains and lots and lots of flower arranging feels very Soviet, though – the place it most resembles in the region is the Baltic states' apparent antithesis, for its institutionalised Communist nostalgia – Belarus.[3] Affluent, clean, conformist, fully employed, and run by a popular big man.

There are un-humanised parts of the city, particularly one big housing estate of untouched panel slabs, which could be absolutely anywhere in the USSR – these, Dzedone tells us, are known as the "Belarus Station", housing as they originally did workers from the slightly more southerly Soviet republic. The streets have been repaved, but the seams between the panels here are visibly coming loose. On the other side of the Free Port is another large Soviet estate of the 1980s, and a much more interesting one – the standardised type, but the Latvian SSR standard rather than a generic Union one, and superior to it both functionally, and, with their expressive brick details, visually. Dzedone tells us this one is soon to get the Styrofoam and lime-green paint treatment, and here, if nowhere else in the town, it would be a shame.

Oddly, however, the underlying message from the city architect's version of the city is that buildings don't really matter. What she wants us to see are things like the campsites in the woods, which apparently have a several months-long waiting lists, and are indeed very attractively designed, in lightweight, crisp little chalets under pines. She wanted us to see the endlessly sprinkling fountains and incredibly literal sculptures – around ten giant anchors, on all the entrances to the beach, a big chair made up of chains by the car park. The several sports centres, and a seemingly interminable quantity of playgrounds:

cynical local opinion puts these latter down to Lembergs having recently sired. No child, apparently, ever has to queue for a slide or a swing in Ventspils. The huge amount of children's infrastructure – from a ski-jump to a genuinely rather delightful children's railway running between the beach and the woods, which doesn't quite compensate for the closure of the city's railway station – helps make the place feel a tad infantile, as if it were planned not to accommodate children, but *just* for children. For them, too, there is little space for surprise or discovery – everything is spelled out.

Architecturally, some of the new work in Ventspils is excellent, especially by post-Soviet standards. The City Council itself is housed in an eco-friendly HQ (in an oil town), with a subtly drizzly, greenscreen draped across it; it's placed in a very affluent looking villa district, with wooden terraces and the rangy Arts and Crafts houses of the disappeared Baltic German bourgeoisie. Today, the area is apparently popular with Russian emigres. Similarly interesting is the suburban Parventa Library, in a workaday area of renovated *Khrushchevki*,

The Seat of Ventspils

with murals on their gable ends. Two brittle curved steel and glass curves interlocking around a multi-storey atrium over benches with beanbags, to a competition-winning design by INDIA architects – this one even made its way into the English-language architectural digests.[4] The confidence of the design is somewhat contradicted by the awful paintings of nudes and landscapes on the wall, the sort of stuff a street-corner tourist painter might think twice about exhibiting; it all feels oversized, the readers made tiny by the space. With a big EU-funded concert hall slated to supplement the Juras Varti House of Culture, there's almost an over-provision of culture here, more than a town of 40,000 people could really need. There is a lot of cultural spending, but no sign of the "creative class" or anything remotely bohemian or "alternative". In this too, the town resembles a Baltic Belarus; Lukashenkaism without the need for the KGB.

It is hard to resent this city – the boom ended, as it always would, but at least they have something public that they can point to and say "this is what we did in that time". You can mock it easily. "A city that is also a brand!" say some excited people in *Ventspils – 700+25*. The head of MALMAR steel says, as well he might, "we liked Ventspils the most" of all towns in Latvia. "The industrial charm of the terminal is praised even by artists".[5] There is in the book, and the investment in industry in the town, an unlikely emphasis on factories and the people who work in them – no wonder that Ventspils won "European local government of the year 2012"! What has made this a "success" is the way in which just enough of the cash made here – it is no coincidence that Lembergs has become one of the richest men in the Baltics, significantly enriching also his family and greasing several palms, as the Panama Papers investigation uncovered – has been put into the town, and enough to make people grateful, perhaps because they know that in many other towns not very far away, they won't even get that trickle. "Thank you Ventspils," says one schoolgirl in the town's promotional book, "for making me so happy. Ventspils, always stay ahead of the curve!"[6]

NUCLEAR MODEL VILLAGE

SILLAMÄE, Sillamäggi, Narva 2, Leningrad 5

One unique factor of the independence movements of the 1980s in the Baltic states was the role environmentalism played in agitating for an end to empire. This happened across the board – against nuclear power stations in Lithuania, against destruction of historic cities in Latvia – but it was intense in Estonia. This small and pretty northern country was transformed in the Soviet period into a comprehensively mined and exploited landscape, usually using imported Russian labour, which had major effects on the country's demographics – even today, around one-third of inhabitants are Russophone (not necessarily "Russian"), a large proportion of them made non-citizens by the stringent citizenship system instituted after 1991. Many of the locations found and filmed by Andrey Tarkovsky in 1979's *Stalker* as emblems of post-industrial decay and warped nature were in Estonia, and many of these are now unrecognisable after being cleaned up by post-independence governments. Abroad, the country sells itself on the untouched medieval old town of Tallinn and an "E-Stonia" of ultra-fast Wi-Fi, with easy "e-citizenship" deals offered to foreign business (a strange concept in a country otherwise so specific about who can and can't be a citizen). There is a little more to the country's economy than that. At the Venice Architecture Biennale in 2016, a trans-Baltic team of curators tried to investigate the networks that ran through these three countries, so obviously crucial to places like Ventspils, while pointedly ignoring the still extremely heated national and post-colonial discourses in each. Then, you can find that through following geological deposits, train lines and pipelines, yesterday's coloniser easily becomes today's oppressed minority. Outside of the capital, Russian-Estonians are concentrated in Ida-Viru county, on the border of Russia's Leningrad Oblast. Slovakian architect Maros Krivy's contribution to the pavilion argued that the widespread 1980s opposition to phosphorite mining in eastern Estonia with its overwhelmingly Russophone population was couched in apparently ecological but actually "identitarian" reasoning: "I recently asked (the Soviet-Estonian geologist Anto) Raukas to explain how *exactly* phosphorite mining could cause environmental damage, he responded by making reference to 'the Russians'. It seems there is no clear boundary between ecological and ethnic pollution".[1] This was the start of a familiar political-economic process, one which was originally identified in the 1960s by Maoist geographers, who would be surprised to find their ideas fitting so well with an anti-Communist project. According to thinkers such as Samir Amin, in order to escape being re-colonised through trans-national capital, newly independent colonies should "de-link" themselves from the Western metropolis. In the early 1990s, this is more or less what happened in the Baltic states, with the technological, industrial and transport links between Riga, Vilnius and Tallinn with St Petersburg or Moscow forcibly ruptured. As with most projects of de-linking, whenever it has been tried (Soviet "War Communism", the Chinese Great Leap Forward), one immediate effect was mass immiseration; and as with the latter two examples, the noxious memory of the old regime, and the absence of desirable alternatives, meant that by and large people accepted their new poverty. However in the Baltic example, soon after old links to the metropolis were being cut, new links to a new and much more favoured metropolis were being established – that is, with the European Union, with one consequence being the fact that a large proportion of the independent Baltic's financial and mineral wealth is owned abroad, particularly in Sweden.

However much international links might change, minerals are minerals, and they remain valuable whatever networks are used to distribute them. So Ida-Viru county today is an area which independent Estonia is "mining the shit out of, using Russian labourers", in the words of curator Johan Tali.[2] The place where this project of relentless extraction began was Sillamäe, a tiny village right on the Baltic sea, not far from the industrial town of Narva. Shale mining began here before the war – owned, just like nowadays, by Swedish industry – but the discovery that uranium could be refined from shale here made Sillamäe crucial to the post-war nuclear weapons programme administered by Lavrentiy Beria. Some sense of the disparate territories' complex infrastructure can be imagined when

The Plant at Sillamäe

you realise scientists in Moscow and Kyiv were devising weapons using uranium mined and refined in Estonia to be tested in the steppe of Kazakhstan, a model of coerced transcontinental co-operation. The first Soviet citizens to mine these materials were Gulag prisoners, after the site of the town was destroyed in the last months of the war. Soon after, a civilian new town was constructed in Sillamäe for the atomic workers. The resulting townscape is now marketed locally as a minor tourist attraction, though it isn't competing with Tallinn old town just yet. Vacation rentals operate here; I stayed in the small 1980s flat of a Russian lawyer, who had the Constitution of the Russian Federation prominently displayed on the shelf opposite her sofa-bed.

In terms of the sort of "destination" it is, the town has the frisson of freely entering an area that was legally "closed", not appearing on maps for much of its existence – this was what was called in Sovietspeak a ZATO, a "Zakrytoe Administrativno-Territorialnoe Obrazovanie", a "Closed Administrative-Territorial Formation". For a time the town didn't have a name, and was referred to as "Narva 2", or "Leningrad 5". Unusually, it combines the kitschy thrill of entering somewhere that was once, and is no longer, dangerous to enter, with the quainter charms of the model village. As that, more or less, is what Sillamäe is. This is no ferroconcrete utopia/dystopia, not even quite a Stalinist showcase of monumental authoritarianism, as most of the buildings are in what today gets described as the "human scale", but what would under Stalinism be called "socialist humanism". Sillamäe is something else, something from the same family as Portmeirion and Disneyland, a little classical town of remarkable quaintness and disquiet, organised and assembled in an inorganic yet picturesque manner.

A grid of streets of diminutive flats and houses leads to a central axis around a Town Hall and a House of Culture (originally a cinema), all of it in a charming minimal classical style, with restrained floral details and pastel colours; a staircase leads down towards the Baltic Sea like a Lilliputian Odessa Steps. The pretty appearance is actually the product of a typically Soviet use of standardisation: these pedimented two-storey flats are duplicates of a system that can be found in other north-western republics of the USSR – there are whole districts of these in Minsk, for instance. But here there is nothing else, save for some perfunctory 1960s blocks on the outskirts and the 1980s blocks I stayed in, meaning that this is the closest thing you can find in the European Union to an ideal Stalinist town. In her MRes thesis "Small Voices, Big Narratives", Aleksandra Zavjalova describes her hometown as "atopian", a town that isn't just full of "displaced and dispossessed" people, but is also a place that is itself displaced, somewhere that could only have made sense in the Soviet Empire. It can only be a place of (frequently guilty, ambiguous) memory in a present in which it is permanently out of time.[3] In her interviews with early settlers, we find the village after the war as "a completely empty space [...] there was no residential housing at all. In front of us was a terrible grim picture: it was a site of battle during the WWII. There was barbed

Steps down to the Baltic

wire, scattered ammunition and tanks left behind after the battles."[4] The perfect tabula rasa.

Another of her sources remembers that immediately after the war, "all the workers at the mine were camp prisoners". A Gulag, she writes, "was established in August 1946 and was functioning until April 1953, having approximately 11,200 inmates', approximately the population of the town that would be built around it. 'People imprisoned for several years for various reasons (often for no particular reason) had to start the construction of the factory and the town, work in mines. Gulag prisoners also worked on the construction of town buildings and even public sculpture"[5], which was abundant in the town (some of which has been removed – a statue of Stalin in 1962, and heroic workers on the steps to the Baltic in the 1990s). Then came mass in-migration from the Union, with at least ten different nationalities moving to the tiny town, with Russian of course as their lingua franca. As with many of the more "remote" parts of the USSR – if you bear in mind its centre was Moscow – many of those working here had themselves been victims of Stalinism beforehand, and got jobs here because they were easier to get than in the developed heartland. One appealing consequence of this is that there is a Georgian restaurant here, whose staff were most surprised to find themselves serving Khinkali to an English visitor.

Finding traces of the things that Sillamäe is based upon – forced labour, mass migration, ethnic cleansing, nuclear weapons – is a game one can play after enjoying the charms of the town, which are what strike you first. The tree-lined streets of pastel houses are limpid and attractive, ironically in a style which owes something to the gracious proportion and subtle colour of Swedish classicism, although given that these were standard products, that is wholly accidental. The main square was originally named after Sergei Kirov and is currently called Kesk Square, Central Square, of course like all the other street signs solely now in Estonian, a language which is at best only a second language for most of the inhabitants. But unlike other north-east

Estonian cities, which have been extremely vigilant about renaming all Russian streets and standing firmly against Russian shop signs, there are many Russian language plaques to "famous" residents (engineers and directors of the plant, by and large), and streets named for Soviet generals and poets. On Kesk Square you have a standard House of Culture in a classical style, with an open pediment and a tall colonnade, made unusually commanding by its position at top of Sillamäe's "Odessa Steps". Alongside is what was once a "Board of Honour", which Zavjalova calls a "very typical socialist attribute", where local heroes of labour were celebrated, with their names and pictures on a board; whether as a consequence of ideological change or of mass unemployment there are no heroes of labour on there now.

Behind this is a park, and in front, the Town Hall, which is not a standard design at all, but a Leningrad-Classicist attempt to engage with Estonia's Lutheran "vernacular". The tiered tower with its black spire is obviously modelled on Protestant churches, and given that the

"Where am I" – "In the Village"

town didn't have one until the 1990s, it is a clear attempt to retain the symbolism of religious architecture without the actual use; Protestant in form, Stalinist in content. Certainly, it's an odd thing to put on top of a classical building. Opposite this you get one of the clues as to what sort of place you're in – a monumental statue of a giant metal man holding aloft an atom. The town might have been secret, but the uranium mining that took place here was celebrated, albeit for residents only, as a great human achievement; the splitting of the atom, the reconstruction of nature, the harnessing to the building of Communism of infinite power, in which the fact that slaves were the first people to bring the radioactive material out of the ground here is a mere irrelevance. The statue was built as late as 1987, by which time the ecological movement had already started up in Tallinn; it must have already seemed dated, and now it is a piquant reminder of the celebration of physical labour in a country which prefers to keep things immaterial – at least in theory, although the fact that extraction and refining still happens here can't be ignored, in Sillamäe. One of the axes that bisects the town leads not to the Baltic or to the Town Hall spire, but to the still-smoking chimneys of the refinery. Make it to the stony beach, down the "Odessa Steps", and you'll see it there too. As you go into the outskirts of the town to get the bus out – the only public transport connection – you'll see dereliction and flaking pastel plaster, and obviously empty houses. "More with less", as they call it in business.

For Zavjalova, in her thesis on the town, the very point of the place is its lack of place: "The propaganda culture of the 'USSR being one's homeland' rather than a sentimental bond of commitment to a particular place, town or region, would give birth to the impossibility of local resistance, since there would be very few 'locals'."[6] An after-effect whose dialectical import would surely have pleased Soviet thinkers is that what is now "local" to people in Sillamäe, what counts as "home", is this pure Stalinist product, this radioactive model village; they don't much want to be in "Russia" (wages are higher here, when

The Atomic Man

there are wages – and if there aren't, migration is easy and visa-free thanks to the EU), but they can't quite be in "Estonia" or be "Estonian" on anything other than geographical grounds. Eventually, after all the dust has settled, it may all seem as cute as any other industrial model village, as much as somewhere like Port Sunlight in Lancashire, where tourists will come to admire that familiar tension between the cute and the corporate, the homely and the sinister. But for now, the place still has a job to do.

In need of Structural Funds

THE CRADLE OF THREE REVOLUTIONS

ST PETERSBURG, Petrograd, Leningrad

Along with its three names, the city variously known as St Petersburg, Petrograd and Leningrad, used to be called "the Cradle of Three Revolutions". It was central to a succession of massive upheavals – the eventually failed empire-wide uprising of 1905, the February Revolution of 1917 that overthrew the Tsar, and the October Revolution that same year that began an experiment in total social transformation.[1] Nobody calls St Petersburg this anymore. Over the last decades, it has become something of a forgotten city, though it is the fourth largest metropolis in Europe, after Moscow, Istanbul and London. Its eighteenth century canal-side streets look to the untrained eye like a tougher Copenhagen, yet rather than being lined by bicycles, they're choked with traffic. A Petersburg "clan" dominates Russian politics, based around Gazprom and the secret services, but the city seems to have benefited little in terms of investment. Its piercing beauty coexists with a sharp carelessness. Aside from its revolutions, Petersburg is best known for a beauty that predates, and is irrelevant to, the revolution. At its heart is an ideal, diagrammatic plan, established in 1737, where the brittle classical edifice of the Admiralty, facing the river, marks the culmination of three grand boulevards, evenly departing from it – Ulitsa Gorokhovaya, Voznesensky Prospekt and Nevsky Prospekt, originally the Middle, Larger and Lesser Prospects.

Each of these leads to the delicate spike of the Admiralty's spire, although Nevsky also leads – if you turn right at its end – to the unforgettable dreamspace of Palace Square, best reached via the fictional route of the insurgent proletariat in Eisenstein's *October* – down Nevsky, through the arch of the General Staff building, into the square and towards the Winter Palace. These are the most famous of Petersburg's setpieces, but there are several. The central city, south of the Neva, is as uncanny as Venice, as calm as Amsterdam, with the streets overlooking the successive waterways of the Obvodnyy Canal, the Fontanka, the Griboyedov Canal, the Moika. There are the stark squares in front of the two Neoclassical cathedrals – Kazan Cathedral, a miniature Vatican, and Saint Isaac's, in its proportion Parisian, but completely distinct in the exotic chromaticism of its red granite columns, almost black stone walls and golden dome. North of the Neva is the equally geometric ensemble of the "spit" of Vasilyevsky

Cheap gas Copenhagen

Island, and the Peter and Paul Fortress, whose restrained Baroque spire mirrors that of the Admiralty – power there, punishment here. Each of these would, absolutely anywhere else in Europe, be absolutely choked with tourists snapping away at this unearthly beauty. Here, in summer, there's a few, mainly Chinese, but far less than outside far uglier buildings like Buckingham Palace or the Louvre. You can tell where tourism is happening, though, because someone will be yelling into a half-broken, feedback-emitting loudspeaker promising "excursions". The place that erupted three times in strikes, factory occupations and insurrections was not defined by this perfectly calculated Enlightenment classicism, but by nineteenth-century suburbs of tall, crowded tenements, wooden slums, redbrick mills and heavy metal engineering works. Petersburg's industry was monolithic, defined by a few enormous complexes employing thousands of people, staffed by workers whose grandparents were serfs. This made it an

Gorokhovaya to Admiralty

ideal city of what Bolshevik theorists called "Combined and Uneven Development". Yet Petersburg is extremely "even" in its planned structure. That centre like an ideal Renaissance town plan come to life is surrounded successively by equally homogeneous quarters of the nineteenth century, the avant-garde 1920s, the Stalinist 1930s to 1950s, the prefabricated 1960s to 1980s. It is these last where new development is concentrated, because of the most influential Soviet legacy – the historical preservation of the entire city centre, which is sometimes circumvented, but never quite defeated, by property developers and their friends in government. Instead, developers cram ultra-high-density complexes of Postmodernist "luxury" flats, quickly built by brutally treated Central Asian migrant workers, into tight plots in the former industrial districts. It's an unpleasant side-effect of conservation that the city government seem prepared to accept.

In memory of the Tsar, background, in memory of the workers, foreground

There are many traces of the revolution in the centre if you know where to find them. The cruiser *Aurora*, a volley from which was the signal for insurrection in October, still stands on the Neva, and was recently restored, although it currently downplays its revolutionary use. Plaques are sometimes to be found on the buildings occupied by the various revolutionary governments, like the Tauride Palace or the Smolny Institute. The most central monument is the exceptionally moving Field of Mars. It was commissioned from the young architect Lev Rudnev by the city's Soviets (here, in its original usage as "workers councils"). It was originally a Tsarist parade ground near the river Neva, overshadowed since the late nineteenth century by the Cathedral of the Savior on the Spilled Blood, a florid, polychrome design of asymmetric onion domes, built in honour of Tsar Alexander II, who had been assassinated by revolutionaries in 1881. Rudnev's design broke with these dominating surroundings completely, creating instead an anti-hierarchical space, a monument without monumentality – a processional route for revolutionary events, a burial ground for those killed in street fighting, and a place that could connect the victorious workers of Petrograd to the failed revolutionaries of the past. The texts on the monument's tufa stelae, written by the Commissar of Enlightenment Anatoly Lunacharsky, link Petrograd to Paris: "to the crowds of Communards are now joined the sons of Petersburg".[2]

The most interesting and enduring revolutionary legacy is more invisible – the *Kommunalka*. This hugely unequal and divided city's apartments were audited and divided during the bloody Civil War that followed the Bolshevik seizure of power, with one result being extreme subdivision – several families in one huge, high-ceilinged imperial flat. Few outside Russia realise that many of the opulent apartment blocks in the centre are actually still *Kommunalki*, with a tangle of doorbell switches to each door. This has two results today. The neglect of these lush tenements is obvious, but inner-city districts have mostly not been fully gentrified, as the complexity of who owns what often deters investors. Defying conservation laws, some developers find it easier to just knock down and build "sham replicas" instead, dispersing the residents and owners in one fell swoop rather than negotiating with them.

It's hardly utopian, but the persistence of the *Kommunalka* is nonetheless a definite revolutionary legacy in 2017, and remains popular with students and the young because of the fact you can live a stroll away from Palace Square for a decent rent, as long as you don't worry about privacy or mod cons. This extends to the easiest and cheapest way to stay here as a visitor. For a fairly paltry sum you can sleep in a tiny cubicle with a plastic door with a cupboard-sized shower, right in the centre, managed, or not, by a skeleton staff and inhabited by lost people who thought they'd only just be staying here for a little while. On one visit, I waited an hour for someone with responsibility to turn up and give me the key I'd paid for in one of these. Eventually arriving, he took a look at my passport and smirked "this is not like Britain". It's not, though it helps not to know Russian – if you know only the little I do, you soon realise that the names and phone numbers chalked and stencilled on the pavements round here are those of sex workers.

The Lunatic Asylum

With the admirable exception of Catriona Kelly's compendious and mindboggling 2014 book *Shadows of the Past,* St Petersburg after the end of the Second World War – during which the city was blockaded and starved nearly to death – is ignored in English-language histories. It was only really between the Sixties and the Eighties that the housing problem inherited in 1917 was seriously tackled, with the mass building of prefabricated housing – most of the results are nondescript, save the memorable Brutalist enfilades that line the canals in the north of Vasilyevsky Island. Perestroika Leningrad saw a late artistic flowering as a city of the post-punk avant-garde, via artists and musicians like Timur Novikov, Sergey Kuryokhin and Viktor Tsoi. It is also the hometown of Vladimir Putin, and his coterie of former secret

A sham replica in progress

servicemen. Its city government has been proudly reactionary – the recent law against "homosexual propaganda" was first tested out in Petersburg. The Northern Capital is among other things great evidence that start-ups, pop-ups and craft beer (at least one tap room in every city centre courtyard, it seems) do not a socially liberal city make.

And despite all of this, the centre endures probably the best preserved, least damaged Neoclassical metropolis on Earth, and the central paradox of the revolution is that it left the place where it happened so completely intact. So for instance there is only one Constructivist building in the centre of Leningrad, in a city that was a centre for the avant-garde for decades. And it's not accidental that the building in question is the Bolshoy Dom, the Big House, housing consecutively the NKVD, the GPU, the OGPU, the KGB, and currently the FSB, which means it's in better condition than any building of its era, here or in Moscow. It was designed by Noi Trotsky and

The Big House

Aleksandr Gegello, and it is an unusual example of Constructivist architects – very talented ones – applying modernist principles directly to the instruments of dictatorship, with all the minimalism, plate glass and Americanist/Bauhaus references pulled into a hierarchical composition that is pure Lubyanka. Apart from the Metro stations, there's very little Stalinist architecture here either. There's a smattering of post-1991 buildings, and perhaps one reason why so few is that those that do exist are so appalling that they're enormous evidence that the twenty-first century can do nothing of worth here – as in the "Regent Hall", a daring assemblage of columns, mirrorglass and supergraphics.

The neglect of the city centre also extends to the surprising quantity of industry that still exists inside it, long since expelled from Moscow. Obviously it doesn't make it a healthier country or a more pleasant one to live in, but my north-west European eye is immediately pleased by the closeness of industry and urbanity here: you can take a leisurely

Submarine, St Isaac's

stroll from submarines to Neoclassical institutes. You can find this a pretty short distance from the centre, as in the district around the typically delicate Neoclassicism of the Bobrinsky Palace, now the Faculty of Liberal Arts of the Smolny College (literally at the other end of the city from the famous Smolny Institute, formerly a girl's school, that was the centre of 1917). The area is dominated by Petersburg's main lunatic asylum, to the point where apparently this is shorthand for the area in general, though by now this refers to the backwater effect caused by the lack of a Metro station.[3]

You can find a glass box with a rusty chimney emitting a strong smell of polish opposite a fine block of art nouveau (or as they called it here, Style Moderne) tenements for shipyard clerks from 1908, looking untouched for decades, coated in a thin layer of grime and dust, as is almost everything in St Petersburg, from the buildings to the cars. For all its grandeur and order, this is not a fastidious city, or, at least to the untrained eye, a rich one; you sense it's a very, very long time since this was the Russian capital. The proximity of these different registers coincides with a seeming carelessness about which parts of it get restored and which don't. Nearby is New Holland, a planned island enclave of warehouses, which has spent years rotting away quietly despite dozens of competing plans, some of them involving major architects such as David Chipperfield and Norman Foster, to transform it into a multifunctional hipster playground. In terms of the failure of any of these consecutive ideas to actually take form in reality, it could be compared to London's Battersea Power Station saga, except that this is not a Thirties power station, but a UNESCO-listed ensemble of eighteenth-century classical buildings.

The NEP City: Narvskaya Zastava

In this showcase of planning, the first place to be specifically created by the Soviet planned economy is eclectic in style, straggling in form. South of the city centre is the Narva District – Narvskaya Zastava – a working-class district of wooden houses and tenements from before

Spires of Petersburg

Bobrinsky Palace

Illustrating Revolution

the revolution, clustering around the Putilov heavy engineering works, which provided the bulk of Bolshevik support in the revolution and Civil War (and at the end of it, moved towards opposing it, one of the reasons for the shift towards the mixed New Economic Policy, and the relative freedoms of the 1920s). From 1924 onwards, this district was rebuilt as a showpiece.[4] The only structure here that gets mentioned in Petersburg's many guidebooks is the Narva Gate, a green-painted triumphal arch, built both to celebrate victory over Napoleon and to provide a gateway to the city. After the area was replanned, it stood as the focal point for a huge and vague square, Ploshchad Stachek, Strikes Square. Almost everything around it is from the 1920s and early 1930s, the golden years of Soviet modernist architecture, the "Lost Vanguard", as the photographer Richard Pare called them. There is nothing else, save for a Stalinist Metro station and the horrific 1812 Shopping Centre, which with its mirror-glass, fibreglass columns and clumsy imperial symbolism is all of the worst things about Nineties architecture in the city summed up. It faces the Gorky Palace of Culture, designed in 1925 by two of the most prolific Leningrad Constructivists, Alexander Gegello and Dimitri Krichevsky, on a fairly conventional stripped classical plan, slightly resembling the Berlin Volksbühne, only with much more glass, and a lack of any explicit historical references, opting instead for the expression of pure volume and mass. Next to it is a furniture store designed in 1930 by the same architects, which was when built a Technical College. It has a peculiar decorative fenestration, with the lower two sets of windows stepping downwards, in a clumsy bit of cubo-futurism. In the original drawings, these were ribbon windows, slashing dramatically downward. Evidently, the builders took one look at this and swiftly revised it to the interesting botch-job you can see now, where the limitations of a largely peasant building industry meet the vaulting ambitions of the architects, and cancel each other out.[5] The rhetorical side of Strikes Square – the need to display revolutionary fervour while carrying out the post-revolutionary programme mural

– comes in an exciting mural of 1965, by the painter and illustrator Rifkat Bagautdinov, depicting the revolutionary deeds of 1905 and 1917. It is in the "severe style" of the "Thaw", so rather than being – as are the sculptural reliefs of the same events in the Metro station adjacent – an image of oppressive solidity and hierarchy, its figures are lively, energetic, with dramatically sketched factories and plotting revolutionaries, as if from a Khrushchev-era children's book. Visiting the square once with the Polish writer Agata Pyzik, she insisted on a photograph in front of it, as a rare place where you can feel the presence of real revolutionary energies, a feeling that here is where it all happened, which you never quite get in the city centre. This is no doubt also what lies behind the moving short film by the St Petersburg neo-avant-garde group Chto Delat, *Angry Sandwich People*, where a group of people carry sandwich boards reading out a Brecht poem about the dying of revolutionary hope, appropriate for a celebratory proletarian space declining into a deindustrialised "ghetto".[6] It hinges on the central problem of this place – somewhere created out of revolutionary optimism and creative fervour that has fallen into a depopulated depression, unable to imagine any way out of its own predicament. It's not really a square, Ploshchad Stachek, it's more a large traffic space attached to Stachek Prospekt, another long, wide street, which may once have felt public when the traffic was minimal, but now – perhaps as intended – feels far more of an artery than a public utility. The buildings don't feel as unified as they might, as to cross the road to get to them involves a certain amount of bravery; conceived as a unified ensemble, they don't coalesce together like a square should. So over the road from the Gorky Palace of Culture is the relatively well-kept School for the 10th Anniversary of the Revolution, designed by Alexander Nikolsky, a pupil of Kazimir Malevich. It's planned, arbitrarily but prettily, as a hammer-and-sickle, with a planetarium in the "hammer". Over the entrance is the same symbol, in travertine, only with a tennis racket added to the objects. On the same side of the square is a building in far worse condition than any of the others – the Kirovsky Fabrika Kuchina, or Sergei Kirov District Factory Kitchen – after his 1934 assassination, the entire Narva District was renamed after the former boss of Leningrad. This is an incredibly ambitious building, the most brilliant and fearless of three designed by the "psycho-technical" ASNOVA School of architects. On each side are huge plate-glass windows, in the middle is one extremely long, Corbusian ribbon window, and beneath it are the high vitrines of a department store; perhaps this didn't go down well in the Petersburg climate, but the actual fabric of the building seems fairly untouched, with additions being ad hoc and cheap rather than comprehensive, which at least doesn't affect the actual fabric. The originality and confidence of the design is still astonishing, but logos have been bolted onto every available surface, and the concrete is clearly in dire need of repair. The roof terrace is now a green-pitched roof. Follow Stachek Prospekt further down, and you find some more ordinary housing of the avant-garde era, five storey buildings in "Zeilenbau" (line-building) arrangements, a prefiguring of *Khrushchevki* in scale and

The Factory Kitchen

linearity. Cross here and you find the most surprising and all-round wonderful thing on Stachek Prospekt: the Traktornaya Ulitsa housing scheme, by Gegello, Krichevsky and Nikolsky, of 1926. It is Petersburg classicism gone cubistic, opened up, chopped up only seemingly at random, without the divide between the imposing front and the sordid backside that, as we will see, defines actual Petersburg classicism. While other compromises between Constructivism and classicism are just that – compromised, caught between two styles, leading to intriguing confusions – this scheme has total confidence about itself. It does many of the things that Seventies/Eighties Postmodernist housing would try and do – a teasing morphing of a familiar local "vernacular" into something palpably new, only, for reasons both political (i.e. an unsurprising lack of nostalgia for Tsarism in early Bolshevik Petrograd) and aesthetic (Petersburg's historic architecture is already abstract and dreamlike) it actually works. It's as neglected as everywhere else, but wears the knocks well.

Terminating the square to the south is the largest of the Ploshchad Stachek buildings – when it was built in 1932, perhaps the largest of modernist buildings anywhere, here or elsewhere – is the local town hall, or again, post-assassination, Kirov District Soviet, designed by Noi Trotsky, near-namesake of the more straightforwardly assassinated former leader of the Petrograd Soviet. In front is the first of many statues of Kirov, this one with the extraordinary quote on its plinth:

> Comrades, many centuries ago a great mathematician dreamed of finding a point of support, which if leaned upon, could turn the globe. Centuries have passed, and this support is not only found, it is created by our hands. It will not be many years until we, basing ourselves on the achievements of socialism in our Soviet land, turn both hemispheres on the path to Communism.

It is heady rhetoric for a public square to support. The Soviet itself is a very long block in concrete and granite, with strip windows leading to a curved cruise-ship corner on one side, and a thrillingly pure Constructivist tower on the other, with an illuminated hammer and sickle. Note that viewed from the square, the chimney of the Putilov Works is symmetrically aligned with the Soviet. Round the back of the tower is a slightly later extension, including the disused Progress Kino, where the lack of ornament and modern materials (somewhat dour, in this case) is replaced with granite mouldings for no perceptible architectural reason, other than a certain Stalinist horror vacui. Walking around this neglected space is uncomfortable. Opposite the closed cinema is the draft board – when I first walked round here in 2010 the loophole for university students that exempted them from conscription (and the horrendous hazing rituals that usually go with it) had just been closed, and there were stories of the militia dragging young men from the Metro and forcing them to the draft boards to enlist.

Kirov District Soviet

Part of the Narva District's rebuilding was a new park. In the early 1950s, a statue was built here of Communist youth. On the flag they're holding is the only surviving graven image of Joseph Stalin on permanent display in a public space in any major Russian city, until the annexation of Crimea in 2014 saw a wave of new depictions of the despot. Here, it's like a little secret, the unacceptable face of the Soviet power that built this impressive, if decaying, square.

Backwards Through History on Vasilyevsky Island

One of the places foreigners were expected to stay in the late Soviet period, long before unobserved foreigners could get themselves a seedy room on Gorokhovaya, was the Hotel Pribaltiyskaya, at the furthest edge of the city, where Vasilyevsky Island meets the Baltic. This was an early bit of post-industrial regeneration, built at the far corner of an island which had since the early eighteenth century been one of Petersburg's working districts, home of the fleet, the shipyards, and much of the industry. The mammoth hotel is one part of a riverside ensemble built in the late Brezhnev era, a heavy, high modernist district of concrete and glass, set alongside locally specific things such as canals and the Gulf of Finland. The hotel itself is mammoth in scale, clearly expecting to deal with enormous quantities of tourists and so scooping them up away from the centre and putting them in somewhere where they can have a nice sea view and... not much else. How they were meant to get there is mysterious. On architectural grounds, the St Petersburg Metro is one of Europe's finest, from the heroic Stalinist narrative of Line 1, to the 1980s Futurism of Line 4; but unlike in Moscow, it is totally inadequate to the city's transport needs. So to get to the Pribaltiyskaya Hotel, you must first get yourself to Primorskaya Metro, then take a bus, a cab or, in the summer, walk. When you leave the station, you find something else that is no longer quite so obvious in Moscow – the effects of the "informal" commerce that arose out of governmental corruption and organised crime in the early 1990s. The station is in a collection of gimcrack little buildings crowding round

A Grin without a Cat

the station, some of them semi-permanent in appearance, others recognisably the impromptu kiosks they once were; there are Western brands like Burger King, along with opticians, pharmacists, and all the things a dense modern city needs, and which the Soviet Union provided only at spacious distances from each other. In a basement here is a Metro museum, which celebrates both the system itself and the many that St Petersburg's engineers have constructed elsewhere, in the USSR and in Central Europe – look closely at a tube carriage in Warsaw, Sofia or Budapest and you'll probably see the inscribed words "METROWAGONMASH-SANKT PETERBURG"

When outside the station, you can see what the Soviet economy and Soviet architecture did when it reached the level of mechanisation and standardisation that architects only dreamed of when they built Narvskaya Zastava. Around you is a wholly planned district of system-built housing, much of it by the in-house department in Leningrad.

Welcome to Vasilevsky Island

Many are examples of a relatively popular system, the ILG-600, known in these parts as the "ship houses", a model constructed in hundreds from 1965 to 1977, fairly sleek and elegant as these products went, with a strong horizontality that led to its nickname. According to Dmitrij Zadorin's catalogue of Soviet standardised housing, there was such incredulity that the Soviet building industry could produce something of this quality that it was assumed to be a mere copy of a Polish system (it wasn't).[7] Past the Ships, you find another ensemble, this one made up of one-offs, prefabricated again, to be sure, but designed only for this site and no other. Facing either side of an embanked canal, there are two distinct types, horizontal and vertical. The horizontal step away from the water, with shops on the ground floor and grand, Stalinist-style archways to the courtyards behind. Their Gothic monumentality marks them out as being from the very late Brezhnev era, when the domineering imperial aesthetics

ILG-600

of Stalinism made a comeback, even if in prefabricated form. The vertical part is much more interesting – a series of point blocks, strongly Brutalist – a style not that common in the USSR, given it involved exacting concrete work – and expressive, hauled up on angled little pilotis and faceted into a sculptural, zig-zag surface. Marching down the canal to the Gulf of Finland, they're strangely idyllic. In summer, people lounge around here with their clothes off, enjoying the opportunity to do in a city where autumn and spring is grey, and winter is punitive.

Duller prefabricated blocks lead to the hotel, which is in a similarly Brutalist, high-end manner to the canal-side vista, with a big statue of Peter the Great overlooking it. On either side of it is new development, and here you learn something important about Petersburg's urban geography. The concomitant of the lack of development in the worn but unimpeachable UNESCO-listed centre – a listing the city nearly

Brezhnev's Gotham

lost, when Gazprom proposed to build a skyscraper in the suburbs that would be visible from the Neva embankment – is intensive building in places like Vasilyevsky Island and further out. Here, given that the lack of a Metro connection means a bus can take you into town in fifteen minutes, property speculation has been especially rife. So if you stand on the high steps of the Pribaltiskaya Hotel and look down the Prospekt that leads to it, you can see the new Petersburg taking shape. It consists of high-density complexes with prefabricated "stone" ornament in such a manner as to look back both to the Stalinist city and to the imperial tenement type; they are oriented to the street and punctuated with towers, with little public space but car park courtyards, and are frequently gated communities. They're quite traditionalist in form, which puts them very close to the neo-Victorian "New Urbanism" movement advocated by Charles Windsor and the Walt Disney Corporation. Advertisements on the Metro sell these

The Canals of Leningrad

as the "Old Fortress", where the industrialised blocks are gazed at by cartoon nineteenth-century figures.

A walk around Vasilyevsky Island, though, is gratifying – everything has happened here at one point or another. When you're past the New Urbanism, you're in an extremely dense working-class district of very tall tenements, their seven storeys a sign of just how teeming this city must have been when the revolution happened. They're all a short walk away from the workplaces – the shipyard and the fleet. There is an oligarch's art museum round here, but more interesting is the Submarine Museum, where a large sub is suspended on a plinth, and you can climb into the "D-2 Submarine Narodovolets" and have a wander around for a small fee. Next to this is the Sea Station, where arrivals by boat from Finland and further afield still disembark; the porousness of this port was one of the things that kept the city unusually abreast of Western trends in the Soviet era, with pop records,

The New St Petersburg

for instance, coming through here before everywhere else. It is, like much of Vasilyevsky Island, an unusually strong building for Seventies Russia, Brutalist in form and Petersburgian in content, right down to the high and thin copper steeple.

Hidden within the tenements are several Constructivist buildings – not a whole planned space, as in Narvskaya Zastava, but scattered works. The elegantly bare tenements run along numbered, un-named streets, the projected sites of unbuilt canals, which then give way very suddenly, to more new Neoclassical high-rises, one with the subtle name of "Financier Apartments". In the shadow of these is the Kirov Palace of Culture, designed by Noi Trotsky in the early Thirties. Architecturally, it is another work at the exact midpoint between Constructivism and Stalinist Neoclassicism, something that seems to have been very common here, as an alternative to the opulent kitsch being built at the same time in Moscow (aptly, it is mostly limited to

Sea Station

the aptly named Moskovsky District, the city's southern entrance, a parade of giant streets, massive Neoclassical housing complexes and yawning ceremonial plazas). At the building's back, is crisp and clear modernism, and at the front, a complex composition indebted to the abstract painting of Kazimir Malevich has been encased in rustication, smothered in detail – but you can still recognise this as Constructivism – the asymmetrical massing and Suprematist interlocking planes are unmistakeable. It is also quite vast, with the tacked-on stone crumbling and some of the windows boarded-up. It faces a nice if scrubby green.

Across this green is a Constructivist Factory Kitchen, one of the three in the city designed by ASNOVA architects. In Richard Pare's monumental photobook The Lost Vanguard, he finds this building completely stripped, with straw reinforcement sticking out of the steel struts, with a group of homeless Petersburgers sitting round a bonfire made out of the building's remains. In that image, Soviet modernism collapses back into medieval Russia. I was so impressed by this image that I used it in my first book, and span some rash theories out of it. So

Rusticated Constructivism – the Kirov Palace of Culture

imagine my surprise to not find a tumbledown wreck, but a cleaned up and restored local centre. Needless to say, this has not been done with a great deal of historical care. The restoration of the actual building isn't too awful, but one wing of it has been covered with a metal screen, which promises a "Fashion Gallery" (in English) inside. On asking, it turns out a Fashion Gallery is a shopping mall. It's funny – as in, both depressing and ironic – to see a device like this used here. These metallic skeins were used by high-tech architects in the Eighties who were utterly in hock to Russian Constructivism – and now they're used to encase one of the few actual Russian Constructivist buildings left. Even so, it is a challenge to an idea about Soviet modernism that Pare's book was an early and influential example of, and which I compounded in my own.[8] Left as a ruin, it is an image which unites 1917 and 1991, Eisenstein and Tarkovsky, optimism and collapse, old wooden-built Russia and peasant futurism. Unfortunately enough, that interpretation was bollocks. Most "ruins" here are inhabited, and even those that are not, in cities where money is to be made, like

Not Actually Ruined

One Chernikhov Building, for sale

St Petersburg, can quickly be brought back into useful use. Ruins, at least when war and disaster hasn't taken place, tend to exist more in the head than in reality, a romantic idea of the effects of the Soviet collapse belied by the bright and tacky actuality.

Of all the architects the high-tech architects of the Eighties were in the deepest hock to, the foremost might have been the "Soviet Piranesi", Iakov Chernikhov. He has a building just round the corner from the Factory Kitchen, which is unusual. Most books about Chernikhov note that, while he was working on his incredible 1933 brochure Architectural Fantasies, he was designing several industrial buildings. The only one of these to my knowledge that has been positively identified is this, and one of his dynamic drawings of it survives. It's a factory just next to the docks on the Neva, and is the other side of Piranesi – those images of noble buildings overcome by various kinds of vegetation. It looks like one of H.G. Wells' Martian tripods beached on the Neva after catching cold, with its eyes boarded up, a quiff of green weeds on its head. The sign draped on the building when I first visited in 2010 said "For Sale", but there have been no takers. Unlike with the Factory Kitchen, repeated visits have only confirmed the ruination, with the building unsold and the trees growing out of its Martian forms only getting bigger. But just next to it is a working shipyard, with the cranes of the Neva that inspired Tatlin to create the Monument to the Third International still darting about, and the icebreaker Krasin docked underneath.

The Petrograd Side

While "St Petersburg" evokes autocracy and post-91 restoration triumphalism and "Leningrad" Stalinist leader-idolatry, "Petrograd" – the city's name from 1914 to 1924 – summons up images of the Petrograd Soviet, the city that called itself "Petrocommune" during the Russian Civil War, and perhaps the city that rebelled again in 1921. The Petrograd district itself, north of the Neva, meanwhile, is a mostly an art nouveau/eclectic area where you could easily be in any other big city of the late nineteenth century – Vienna more than Berlin, perhaps – as opposed to the oneiric Neoclassicism of the central canal-side areas. If you cross the river at the Troitsky Bridge, though, the first building you'll come to was once the Collective House of the Society of Former Political Exiles, built at the turn of the Thirties. It's International Style modernism rather than Constructivism, Gropius in granite style. Few of these former political exiles – usually Old Bolsheviks, sometimes Anarchists, Mensheviks or SRs – would survive the Thirties. The October Revolution emerged from some strange places. One such place, the Kshesinskaya Mansion, was designed for a ballerina in the Imperial Ballet by Aleksandr Von Gogen in 1904-6 – an iron, tile and glass Jugendstil jewel that just happened to be the headquarters of the Bolsheviks throughout 1917. The ballerina in question was subject of the "controversial" recent film Matilda, whose suggestion that Nicholas II indulged in extramarital sex scandalised

The Society of Political Prisoners

Samarkand on Baltic

the Orthodox Church, who venerate him as a saint. Next door is something originally named the "Railway Transportation Academy Named after Comrade Stalin", designed by G.A Simonov in 1931 – a projecting front and a long curve round the back. It's another instance of Petersburg's domestication of Constructivism, leaving it close to a kind of Scandinavian modernised classicism. Not that all the pre-revolutionary buildings around are so sober: the Central Mosque, designed at the same time as the mansion, combines thick, knobbly rustication and obsessively complex detail, in a manner that bridges the mosques of Samarkand and the Moscow buildings of the 1930s. This strange collection of buildings then gives way to a grand boulevard of eclectic edifices, a continuous nineteenth-century city of mass, grandeur and pomp. What is perhaps more interesting than the façades – some of which are indeed very pretty – is what happens at the back. As much rent as possible was squeezed out of the spaces, with long systems of courtyards within courtyards, in which you will find Seventies glass cage lifts, random lumps of

Mansion of Insurrection

Spring

ice (spring only), the ubiquitous broken pipes, and gigantic cracks running down the buildings. It's fascinating, a half-hidden seedy second city behind the grand frontage, and one which you can walk through almost continuously for some time, until you eventually find a courtyard that has been gated off. Up the road a fair bit from here is the Lensoviet Palace of Culture, another Petersburg building that began Constructivist and ended up a strange melange, with plate-glass walls and asymmetries under sculpture and stone. It's a very worthwhile accidental style, this, a forgotten form of imposing, compromised modernism maybe more akin to Auguste Perret or the Portland stone-modern of the Forties in the UK than the full-blown Stalinist fantasias you find in Moscow – there's a dialectical standoff between the openness and irregularity of the original plans and the brooding masonry they're wrapped in. The finest example of this "postConstructivist" architecture is the Collective House

Postconstructivist luxury flats

for Workers at the Lensoviet Palace of Culture, a luxury complex (including servant's quarters – you didn't get that at the Kshesinskaya Mansion in 1917), designed by E. A. Levinsohn and Igor Fomin in 1931, finished four years later. The space inside the housing scheme is full of sculptural games, with proper Constructivist ramps jutting out of it, and a pavilion at the back which is randomly bashed-up, with varying kinds of political and puerile graffiti all over it. The building's plan is like something by Lubetkin, all playful games with canopies, pilotis and curves, but the finished building is defined by a mix of granite and concrete (now spalling) which makes its games feel more Kafkaesque, deliberate puzzles in an authoritarian space. The writer who actually guards it, in a 1950s statue, is Nikolai Gogol.

Next to it, a more straightforwardly Constructivist office building – for the film industry, and originally going by the very sexy name Lenpolygrafmash – seems impossibly light and cheerful by comparison with all this murkiness. A longer walk to the west of here will take you to another postConstructivist scheme, the Svirstroy Housing Complex, finished as late as 1938, in bare concrete and red render. It has a notably un-Stalinist simplicity, but with lots of highly un-Constructivist monumental symmetry. Staring at this in 2010 I spotted for the first time a post-Soviet commonplace: the glass infilling of balconies, which is something done here, I was told, in order to create a free second refrigerator. At the corner of each of the building's wings there's a little abstract sculpture, a memory of Lipschitz or Gabo, stuck onto it. Finding public abstract art as late as 1938 on an apartment complex is unexpected, given how clear we like to imagine the divide between modernism and Stalinism to be. But the postConstructivist architecture of St Petersburg complicates those boundaries, showing ways in which the apparently distinct "cultures" of Soviet aesthetics could be reconciled. A mile or two from this (originally) bourgeois district is a redbrick industrial area of cotton mills and workers' housing, a fairly accurate reproduction of Ancoats, only with much taller houses. Even here, some of the mills have been transferred to property development – in one row, some are derelict, some are loft conversions. One of the mills has a little plaque outlining how the workers won some sort of award for heroic socialist labour in the mid-1960s. Although it isn't as inadvertently peculiar as the monument to children who died in the October Revolution – I had thought the unusual thing about the October Revolution was that nobody died in it (most unlike the civil war that followed). Sceptical local opinion has it that the lack of a monument to children just needed to be filled.

There's one main reason why anyone would come here for architecture. Erich Mendelsohn's Red Banner Textile Factory is merely one part of a giant textile works, but it's from an entirely different planet to the rest. It's often forgotten that the USSR invited projects in the Twenties from the most famous modernist architects – and while schemes by Marcel Breuer, Gropius, Perret, Poelzig, Lurcat and many others came to little, there are two enormous buildings by major

Textile cruiser

modernist architects in each capital – one in each, specifically, with Corbusier's Centrosoyuz in Moscow the other. Mendelsohn had the job taken away from him mid-way through construction in 1926, but the boilerhouse was completed entirely to his design. It is, like the De La Warr Pavilion in Bexhill or the Petersdorff Store in Breslau, one of Mendelsohn's sleek cruisers, a giant ship of red and yellow hurtling somewhere indefinable, far more massive than it looks in photographs. Even then, it's part of a larger entity. A classically Fordist grid-like daylight factory surrounds the boilerhouse, now derelict, with the odd room turned over to various ad hoc light industries. Oddly enough those hanging around there when I visited didn't seem especially surprised to see a fleet of English-speaking people with cameras descending upon it. Most unusually, however, just adjacent to the Red Banner factory is a decent new building, a moderate modernist sports hall and Jewish Cultural Centre – nothing special, just a decent small brick building which somehow managed to get built without explicit historical references or "gob-ons" of any sort.

There are two major historical museums on the Petrograd side. One of them is in one of those flamboyant bourgeois apartment blocks, though it concerns a man who was not himself bourgeois. In summer 2016 I walked to the S.M. Kirov Memorial Museum past election posters for the Communist Party of the Russian Federation, whose unabashed nostalgia and nationalism represents the official continuation, or terminus, of October round these parts. At 26-28 Kamenoostrovsky Prospekt is a handsome block of granite apartments, built in the early 1910s for an intelligentsia clientele of "government officials, celebrated writers, journalists and architects".[9] After 1917, the block was, like all other private apartment blocks, nationalised and turned into Kommunalki. In 1926, though, it was reorganised again as a block for... government officials, celebrated writers, journalists and architects. Among them was the head of the city government, Sergei Kirov, a street-fighting working-class Bolshevik who had been part of Stalin's personal circle in the Caucasus. He and his family got five rooms. The house-museum dates from the Fifties – originally, his artefacts were kept down the road in the Museum of the Revolution. Nonetheless, the artifice is not obvious – it looks in places like he's only just gone out for his fateful 1934 walk. You can see hunting paraphernalia and many stuffed animals, a prodigious library, a bourgeois sense of good taste, and separate beds between him and his wife. Now, how you assess Kirov's level of privilege depends on whether you assess him by the standards of the early Bolsheviks, eating gruel and burning their books to survive the Civil War,[10] in which case it is grossly opulent, or by that of world leaders in the 1930s, in which case it is modest. Judging by his taste, as exhibited here, Kirov – no matter how much avant-garde architecture was built under his rule of the city – was no Constructivist. This is a deeply bourgeois apartment, which you could imagine being owned by a particularly bookish French general. There are moments of bad taste that would

The revolutionary's drawing room

make a modernist wince, right down to the treated, sepia-toned photographs of Lenin and Stalin, looking like the dreamy, ghostly pics on an Edwardian Valentine's Day card.

There is quite some contrast between this matter-of-fact slice of Soviet bureaucratic life, and the depiction of the revolution now in Ksheshinskaya's Palace. When I first visited in 2010, you still had to wear plastic slippers and photos were strictly forbidden. The collection of revolutionary memorabilia had, at some point in the Nineties, been supplied with new captions telling you how awful the Bolsheviks really were. Currently, these rooms coexist with a more nuanced but still schizophrenic depiction of revolutionary events, after a recent expansion and restoration. Now, one room will tell you about Ksheshinskaya, another still replicates the Bolshevik Central Committee's offices, another gives a potted history of Soviet housing in the city. Most pertinent of all is a permanent exhibition on the Duma, the rigged parliament that Tsar Nicholas II conceded after the first of the "three revolutions" in 1905. It is aptly placed alongside the equally powerless current Russian parliament that bears the same name. You might, in all of this, miss the most important thing of all – the expropriation of the rich, their luxuries transformed into a base for plotting out the parameters of a new and better kind of society. The streets of Petersburg have abundant evidence of how that ended up; but they also show, still, why it was and is so very desirable.

Part Two:

DEBATABLE LANDS

ART AND REVOLUTION

KYIV, Kiev, Kijów, קיעוו

Kyiv is one of those cities that have a distinct upper and lower town. The lower, Podil, is based around a classical ensemble of market, theatre and the Kyiv-Mohyla Academy, one of the oldest and most venerable educational institutions in Eastern Europe. Podil today is an enclave of students shuffling around a grid of tenemented streets, whose combination of right-angled rigidity, gentle decay and mature trees feels like it could be in New York (and given the scale of Jewish migration from Kyiv to the east coast of the USA, the influence was going in that direction). In amongst the tenements is a diverse collection of very high quality and wholly non-bombastic architecture of every era – Byzantine churches from Kyivan Rus, seventeenth-century Baroque, Petersburgian classicism, post-revolutionary Constructivism, Seventies Expressionism. Sometimes, a speculative block of flats interrupts this harmonious townscape, but that's okay, because the developers have painted it in the national colours, blue and yellow. Podil has long been seen as the natural place for Kyiv's "creative class" to come to the fore and create a hipster district of bars, galleries and start-ups. In the centre of the square is Hostinny Dvir, an old trading hall gutted by developers after a long battle to turn it into a luxury mall. They lost, beaten by a "Right to the City" campaign, but the shell remains empty. In one square, a monument to the 1905 Revolution, a realist statue of a sinewy man about to pick up and throw a brick, was recently removed. Opposite is a building that has only just survived: Kino Zhovten, the October Cinema, which was set on fire in Autumn 2014. The fire started when a bomb was thrown in during a screening of *Summer Nights*, a French film on transgender lives. The fire was, depending on the politics of the observer, considered to be either a homophobic attack, a real estate-related arson, or both.

Kino Zhovten, though, is not any old fleapit, but an exceptionally rare Constructivist cinema built in 1931, and supposedly protected. After a petition and public protests, Kyiv's mayor, the former boxing world champion Vitaly Klitschko, pledged to repair it, and it is currently as good as new. But given that the city's newly appointed police chief is a leader of the openly neo-fascist Azov Battalion, it's hard to imagine the perpetrators being caught. Similar attacks on

The October Cinema

cinemas showing LGBT films followed, supporting the theory that the bombing was a homophobic attack. The arson attack revealed some things about Kyiv that make it unusual in post-Soviet cities, at least outside the Baltics. There are LGBT film seasons. If they are attacked, the people involved in these events are willing to go out onto the streets and shout. And there was an unspoken but clear collusion between the radical right and the government, with the latter often cleaning up after the mess caused by the former.

This is something I learned about Kyiv early on, something which made it hard for me to subscribe either to the simple narratives too many Western leftists indulged in, where a "fascist" street movement overthrew a democratically elected president, or that too many Western liberals indulged in, where a democratic street movement overthrew a Putin-backed dictator. The first time I was in the Ukrainian capital, in November 2010, I was tagging along with my partner at the time, who was taking part, funnily enough, in a roundtable on the writing of city guides.[1] A wry young leftist with a suspicious topknot invited us to an exhibition opening at the Visual Culture Research Centre of the Kyiv-Mohyla Academy, called "Court Experiment". In a barn-like room were a series of legal documents on the trials of opponents of the brutal and oligarchic government of Viktor Yanukovych and the Party of Regions, alongside shocking images of police brutality based on that testimony.

The work that drilled itself into my mind was a series of porcelain plates by Nikita Kadan, showing, in childlike detail, particular punishments and tortures that had been inflicted on young activists. After half an hour looking at these painful works, a smoke bomb was thrown into the room, and windows were smashed – everyone evacuated the building, and muttered about yet another attack by "fascists". It was an introduction, years before "Maidan", to a central problem of Kyiv. It has the most lively and intelligent activist culture of any city I've ever been to in Eastern Europe, and certainly in the former Soviet Union. But they're caught in an unenviable bind, between repressive governments (the most repressive of which most of them opposed on the streets, in the violent revolution of winter 2013-14), a far-right with which they've occasionally been on the reluctant same side with but which hates them at least as much as it hated pro-Russian governments, and their sources of funding come from Europe, seldom from within Ukraine itself. Not long after the "Court Experiment", Visual Culture Research Centre were thrown out of their room in the Kyiv-Mohyla Academy. It's currently used by an Institute of National Memory, headed by the Holocaust revisionist Volodymyr Viatrovych.[2]

I've returned to Kyiv at least a couple of times a year since then, and have written about it extensively elsewhere. What I want to write about here is those moments when the people there who I most respect – who have tried to carve out a left alternative in the city's culture, between the grim options of Soviet nostalgia and macho nationalism – have managed, even if for a couple of months, to impose their vision onto the city. Here, the links between art and revolution are not a sentimentally remembered figment of the Twenties or the Sixties, but something real and disputed. The first of these is a deeply atypical Biennale in autumn 2015.

The School of Kyiv

Lvivska Square is a small green space in the centre of Kyiv. On one side of it are some worn art nouveau apartments, from the Ukrainian capital's turn-of-the-century incarnation as a Tsarist boomtown, and a branch of the Austrian supermarket Billa. The three sides that are more dominant are Soviet, and modernist. There's an ambitious neo-Constructivist building of the 1970s, featuring a series of allegorical women holding buildings and art materials, decorated to the ground floor with multicoloured tiles. This is the "House of Artists". Facing that is an edifice that has been left unfinished since the early 1990s, whose brick, steel and concrete are caked in dirt and graffiti. This was to be the Kyiv Theatre Institute, and includes an entrance to a constructed, but never opened, Metro station below. Opposite that is a high-rise office block on a convex plan – the "House of Trade". Below it is a three-storey block with large plate-glass windows and marble cladding, with walkways leading to the street. Inside, it's what Americans would call a "ghost mall" – a ground floor features a Stolovaya (canteen) and a handful of shops selling various kinds of tat, but the escalators are permanently switched off. They're lined in the same burnished brown bakelite that you find in the Kyiv Metro.

If you choose to take the stairs, every level features pop-Mondrian abstract stained-glass windows, a different colour scheme for each level. On levels two and three, you came to the main venue for the Kyiv Biennale of 2015. It is not the Venice Arsenale.

Now, Kyiv does actually have the sort of prestigious, wealthy, oligarch-funded venues where you would expect such an event to be held, and indeed which have held Biennales before – Arsenal, a large space in a Neoclassical Tsarist barracks, or the Pinchuk Art Centre,

The House of Clothes

a typical oligarch's gallery that specialises in contemporary art. The reason why it was taking place mainly in a disused, if architecturally intriguing, Brezhnev-era shopping mall and fifteen other motley venues is the fact that the event had no major source of state or private funding. So the organisers, none other than the Visual Culture Research Centre, largely funded it via Austrian arts organisations, with the overall curation provided by the Viennese Georg Schollhammer and Hedwig Saxenhuber. The result was the "School of Kyiv", where essentially the city itself became the object of the Biennale. A series of "schools" (on "image and evidence", on "the displaced", on "realism", on "abducted Europe", and on "landscape", in which – full disclosure – I took part) took place around the city, with a bizarrely eclectic programme including figures of the neo-conservative right and others on the Marxist left, though seldom at the same time. But the city itself, and the route through it that the venues provide, is the best school, leading you through its grand spaces, housing estates, ex-industrial wastes and "aspirational" enclaves, to institutions where an A4 piece of paper with the Biennale's logo (or not) indicated its often seemingly reluctant participation.

In the House of Clothes, the works you find within the clean, clear lines and falling masonry were an interesting ragbag. Some were fairly typical Biennale fare, and some dealt with the cycle of revolution and war that has gripped the city since the uprising against Viktor Yanukovych and the resultant Russian annexation of Crimea and invasion of the Donbass. Of these, some, such as Yuri Lieberman's Odessa – Fragment 205, a film on the different sides taken by the city's ageing ex-dissident punks and avant-garde artists when the city was forced, for the first time, to choose a "Ukrainian "or "Russian" identity, were subtle and moving. Some, such as a cartoonish heroic painting of Cossack-coiffed thugs pulling down the Lenin statue in Kharkiv, were not so delicate. Others referenced the "Russian avant-garde", to which Kyiv has a legitimate claim, with parodic reproductions of work by Kyiv-born Kazimir Malevich; the spectre of decommunisation, and what it might mean for the city's iconography, is never far away.[3] An improving quote from Lenin still lurked on the walls near the staff toilets of the House of Clothes, though it might have been kept there because of its contemporary resonances: 'precisely because we are for the defence of the fatherland, we demand a serious attitude towards the defence capability and training of the country' (like most Leniniana, it's a meaningless truism torn out of context – it actually comes from a 1918 essay defending making peace with Germany, aimed against the pretensions of those advocating 'revolutionary war'). Beneath this temporary art museum, on one day the Stolovaya holds in the evening a meeting of the Ukrainian-Japanese society, and on another, a cross-bearing procession marches ominously by. Neither group, we suspected, was aware of what was happening above.

It is a long walk from here to the Kyiv Metro, but that network gave a good indication of the state of Kyiv and what "decommunisation" might mean. The Metro is, unusually for an ex-Soviet country, overwhelmed by adverts, products either of "wild" capitalism – the tatty ads for jobs and flats sellotaped to the inside of the carriages – or of much bigger business. At Maidan Nezalezhnosti, the beautiful upturned marble columns are obscured top-to-bottom by ads for Igor Kolomoisky's Privat Bank, and at Tolstoy Square, by ads for Samsung. Video screens play ads from above, projectors project ads onto the walls. It's a different kind of desecration to that called for by decommunisation, which has happened here in fragments. The giant Lenin head that looked over Teatralna station has been replaced with a naif painting of the Kyiv Opera House, and at Palats Ukraina, the stunning semi-abstract mosaic of a Red Guard from the January 1918 Bolshevik uprising at the Arsenal factory has been gingerly covered with a thin screen, as if the Metro's staff are hoping that, sooner or later, people will stop being so silly and they can take it off. Elsewhere, though, decommunisation hasn't happened at all – Vokzalna, the first station to be opened, in 1960, and one of the closest to the High Stalinist style with its bronze reliefs of Cossacks, Taras Shevchenko, the Red Guards of 1918 and the victory of 1945, has been untouched, despite its reliefs of Lenin and its hammer and sickles – the only intervention (still, at the time of writing in 2018) is a Cossack fringe and handlebar moustache added to Lenin's bald head.

On the surface, too, the record of this publicly funded and state decreed iconoclasm is chaotic. The monument to the workers' rising at the Arsenal itself has been defaced and is clearly not long for the world, yet until very late, the monument to the KGB survived at Lybidska Square, with its two giant granite heads of fearsome Chekists[4] sprayed and scuffed, but too large to remove at one go with anything other than explosives – not wise in such a densely packed area. Eventually a hugely complex and exacting process of scraping it away bit by bit took place instead. One friend at the VCRC got themselves a letter from the chic mid-century modern type attached to the monument. Even so, the density of all of these graven images was a reminder that decommunisation is a project which might actually be physically

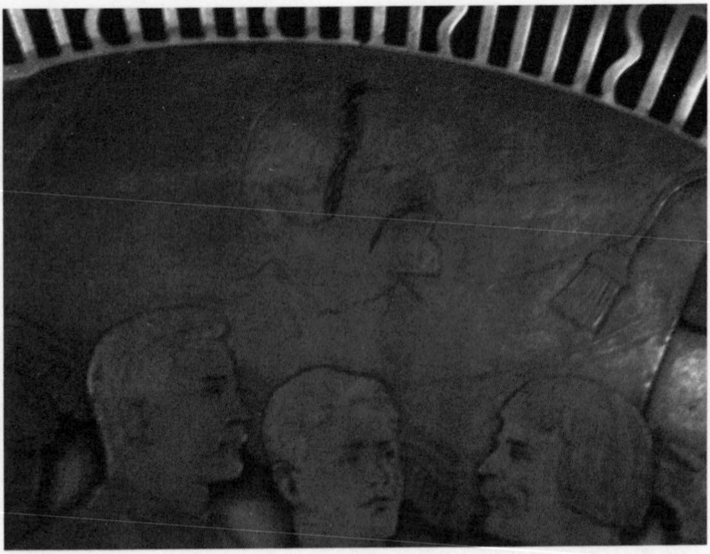

Cossack Lenin

impossible to execute in full, which hopefully poses the question – if Soviet Ukraine can't be wished away, what should be conserved, and what should be rejected?

There are a tiny handful of non-Soviet buildings serving as venues of the Biennale, three or four pre-1917 and just one post-1991. Among the older structures is the National Museum of Art, a very handsome, purist Neoclassical temple, just round the corner from Maidan Nezalezhnosti, the Stalin-era square which became the heart of the 2013-4 insurrection. Only a year before the School of Kyiv, the Maidan encampment still endured, even after Yanukovych's flight, with the piles of tyres, the barricades, and the tired men in fatigues still all in their places. By autumn 2015, all that was cleared except the photos of the dead left by ordinary people, and the propaganda billboards added by the city government. Inside the museum, William Kentridge was given the run of its remarkable collection of Soviet Ukrainian avant-garde painting, and selected two cycles by Anatol Petrytskiy.

Homemade monuments

One, "19 Ukrainian Intellectuals", consists of vivacious, imaginative, colourful sketches of the leaders of the Ukrainian Renaissance of the 1920s, when the Bolsheviks expressly promoted Ukrainian culture and the Ukrainian language. Next to these, pithy panels inform you who was purged, who informed, and who managed to avoid either. The other cycle is Petrytskiy's drawings of Ukrainian villages after their liberation from the Nazis in 1943 and 1944, a surreal picture of a real, lived hell. These rather overshadowed Kentridge's own films in between, which provide a commentary on the revolution, the avant-garde and the purges through animation and montage clips.

The most explicit engagement with recent history came with Nikita Kadan's installations in the National History Museum, a dour 1940s Stalinist temple dressed in the Brezhnev era with integral reliefs, tapestries and stained glass narrating from the Ancient Greek colonies of Crimea through Kyivan Rus to the revolution.

Past an exhibit on Ukrainian "warriors" (the fascist Ukrainian Insurgent Army and the Red Army placed on the same level, a stupid but not atypical attempt to keep everybody happy) and panels informing visitors why Ukraine should join NATO, Kadan's installation consists of fragments of shells fired in eastern Ukraine during the recent war, suspended from the ceiling. On the middle level of the museum, on the floor of post-revolutionary history, Kadan had two metal frames filled with loaded objects – one consisting of objects from the museum's collection, such as statuettes of miners from Donbass, maquettes of blast furnaces and souvenirs from Crimea, next to a similar frame full of objects from the war, whether from the "separatist" or "patriotic" side, or those from neither, such as a battered sign from the destroyed Donetsk airport.

It avoids any kind of commentary or heroisation, but it unintentionally led to a reconstructed tent from the Maidan encampment, and the new narrative of Ukrainian history, in which 2004 and 2014 are the new, unquestionable official story, as rigid as 1905 and 1917 once were, but with far fewer concrete results.

The Old New Ukraine

Shrapnel in the Historical Museum

Kadan's attempt at neutrality and sensitivity was almost battered into submission by different eras of jingoism.

Perhaps typically for a contemporary art Biennale, much of the "school" took place in industrial spaces, but there was not much in the way of post-industrial chic in most of them. A clever series of Isotype tapestries on Ukraine's disastrous economy and its exploitative trade links, by Andreas Siekmann, hung in the National Architecture Library, a neat modern building converted from a former canteen for printworkers. It was surrounded by the fragments of printworks and the former Bolshevik factory, a gigantic engineering works which originally gave its name to the sparky "Thaw"-era Metro station, renamed in the Nineties after the district, Shuliavska.

The machine sheds are looked over by clusters of luxury flats, on a gigantic scale, and the Economic and Financial University, whose Neoclassical pediment featured so far unvandalised stars, hammers and sickles. It stands next to a tank on a cantilevered plinth, and alongside

Hero Cities

are stelae of the "Hero Cities" of the "Great Patriotic War" (as it is no longer officially called in Ukraine), showing the monuments in each city to said heroism. Of the many stelae here, of cities across Belarus, Ukraine and Western Russia, only two, Moscow and Leningrad, have been vandalised. Graffiti and stickers show plucky Ukrainians beating up "Moskals".

One Soviet figure is, it seems, still likely to keep his name on streets and buildings – the great director Oleksandr Dovzhenko, whose films treated now utterly verboten matters such as the 1918 Arsenal Rising (in Arsenal) or the collectivisation of agriculture (in Earth) in a celebratory, albeit poetic and allusive way. The National Oleksandr Dovzhenko Centre occupies the eight storeys of a Seventies film processing factory. Like the Biennale itself, it's an ambitious operation clearly working to a minuscule budget, aiming to become Kyiv's cinematheque, but so far only partly able to make the space viable

Inside the Dovzhenko Centre

for public visits, with pipes and gantries from its original incarnation lurching through the concrete floors and asbestos roofs.

The first and eighth floors were the centre's contribution to the School of Kyiv, showing a huge selection of films, most interestingly the educational films of the 1960s–1980s documentary filmmaker Felix Sobolev, shocking, haunting investigations into autosuggestion, hypnotism and mental adaptation. They're instructively placed next to works on capitalist indoctrination by Harun Farocki on the eighth floor, where you get a good view of peripheral Kyiv, with Soviet apartment blocks crowded out by adverts and the spreading masses of post-Soviet "luxury flats".

After a spell in which they had premises in Kino Zhovten, the small offices of the Visual Culture Research Centre currently consist of one floor of a reclad light industrial building, in a post-industrial zone clearly in the process of being eaten up by high-rise infill flats, marked by billboards for the local elections being held at the time – fifteen or so oligarch-backed parties of the right jostling for position. It showcased the part of the school on "the displaced", with films on the migrant crisis in Europe, a useful corrective perhaps to the utopian image of the EU held by "Euromaidan". From the Visual Culture Research Centre, the pretty, unrenovated 1960s trams lead to Kontraktova Square. It was evidently not the intention of the organisers in any way, but the contrasts the routes through the city created could not but inculcate some nostalgia for Soviet Kyiv, if nothing else because the contemporary built environment, with its overbearing infill towers marketed to the affluent, and its clusters of kiosks crowded around almost every public space, is an increasingly desperate vision of extreme inequality. In a city where advertisements on the Metro try to sell you prefabricated high-rise flats as "Patriotica – the Traditional Generation", their attempt to restore some sanity to historical discussion in the city is desperately needed.

There is one really new space used by the School of Kyiv, and it is instructive indeed. That's the Vozdvyzhenka Art House, one of several rather luxurious art spaces in Vozdvyzhenka, an entirely new district of "art nouveau style" apartments, just off Kontraktova Square. Their concrete frames are decorated with thin, shiny and multicoloured approximations of the fin-de-siècle city – which, in its "real" form, is more than often rotting and dilapidated. Inhabited, it seems, mainly by enormous cars and construction workers, it is unnerving but remarkably complete, especially by Kyiv's chaotic standards.

The Art House's contribution to the Biennale was an exhibit by Pedro G. Romero on Les Checas, the abstract "psycho-technical" torture chambers developed by Spanish artists and NKVD advisers, used on Francoist prisoners near the end of the Spanish Civil War. Modern art and anti-Communism – even the Spanish Republic was evil too, you know, full of bloodthirsty Communists and anarchists who tortured priests – met here in an oligarch's fantasy of the wonderful world before the revolution of 1917, and in a city where 2014's popular revolution against a grotesquely wealthy elite became a nationalist purging of any traces of socialism from the landscape, leaving said elite more powerful than ever. Here, when most of the landscape was built under "Communism" decommunisation is a fool's errand at best, gross historical revisionism at worst. The School of Kyiv stood, with this one queasy exception, very clearly against this simple-mindedness. It provided those who chose to take its lessons a series of contradictory classes in one of the most fascinating, beautiful and conflicted cities in Europe. Lessons, not answers.

We Could be Lenin, Just For One Day

In spring 2016, the Mexican artist Cynthia Gutierrez staged an "intervention" in a public space in Kyiv, Ukraine. Called "Inhabiting Shadows", it was one of several alterations, additions and engagements that have been made upon the city's former Lenin statue, erected in the 1950s in a prominent spot at the end of the tree-lined Taras Shevchenko Boulevard, facing the late-nineteenth-century Bessarabian Market, across the city's Broadway or Oxford Street, the Khreschatyk.

Prefab patriotism

New Old Kyiv

The statue, sculpted by Sergey Merkurov in 1963, was one of two prominent at either end of Kreschatyk. The other, a far uglier 1970s construction, was destroyed immediately after independence; this Lenin, though, a small and relaxed realist statue, was left alone until late 2013, as its relative scale meant that Lenin just became another person influential in the history of Ukraine, less important than, say, Taras Shevchenko, Bogdan Khmelnitsky or Volodymyr the Great, but worth noting. A contemporary description of the monument runs as follows: "The leader of the world working class is portrayed at the moment of delivering a speech to the people in whose invincibility he profoundly believed."[5] It was eventually torn down by members of the Svoboda Party, a reformed fascist group, and hence the sort of people who would be entirely fine with having a basically identical statue with the beard shaved off and rededicated to Stepan Bandera.

Stand here

In the week before the Gutierrez's artwork was placed there, the plinth, still in place, was smeared randomly with blue and yellow paint; of the two quotations from Lenin embossed with gold on the black plinth, one, on "Soviet power", was scribbled out, the other, on how "a free Ukraine is possible with the united action of the Great Russian and Ukrainian proletarians. Without such unity, it is out of the question", was untouched. An impromptu plaque was nailed to the plinth, commemorating Sashko Bilyi, a fascist who was shot in suspicious circumstances in 2014. Gutierrez's project temporarily replaced all that with a lightweight construction that enabled members of the public to climb up to take the place formerly occupied by the bronze likeliness of Vladimir Ilyich Lenin. You could take in the view "Lenin" once saw (but nobody else could), you could emulate his imploring pose, you could shout to friends. For the time you were up there, you were the monument. For Izolyatsia, the formerly Donetsk-based gallery who commissioned it, this work was way of sidestepping the heated politics of memory in favour of asking another, more interesting question – what should an urban monument be today?

In the gallery's press release, Izolyatsia invited the public to "substitute the phantom" of Lenin, in order to "become new and diverse moving statues that head towards the light of a new horizon". In trying to express an "idea" (about democracy, openness, temporariness) rather than commemorate a man, this post-revolutionary monument is in the tradition of one of the first monuments proposed after the 1917 Revolution, Vladimir Tatlin's Monument to the Third International, which intended to symbolise the dialectic and revolution through its intersecting, spiralling parts. While that was a utopian proposal that could only feasibly be implemented after the "World Revolution" that Tatlin fervently believed was possible when he designed the project in 1919, here we had something much more tentative, deliberately short-lived and ad hoc. But the words used to describe Tatlin's project by the poet Vladimir Mayakovsky apply equally to Gutierrez's work – "the first monument without a beard". Perhaps, an approach like this could be taken to the other charged debates over statues elsewhere in the world – a ladder allowing people to occupy Cecil Rhodes's little niche in Oriel College, Oxford, for instance.

The way in which the project sidesteps the emotive debates over monuments in Ukraine has become crucial to Izolyatsia's work. They were forced to leave Donetsk at the start of the war fought between Russian-backed forces against the Ukrainian government; their gallery was used by the army of the "Donetsk People's Republic" for storage, the "pornographic" artworks in their collection used for target practice. But rather than wholeheartedly endorse the new politics of memory that has emerged after the Maidan insurrection of 2014, they've used their new platform, in a dockside ex-factory in Kyiv, to encourage a more sensitive approach. Recently, the Ukrainian government responded to a popular wave of toppling Lenin statues (known as "Leninopad" or Leninfall, a pun on Lystopad, the Ukrainian word for the month of November), and a scattered but influential enthusiasm for its wartime far-right, by passing a law that guaranteed all Soviet symbols, statues and names had to be removed (excepting those connected with the Second World War) and that decreed that Ukrainians "honour the memory" of any and all fighters for Ukrainian independence, including the openly fascist Bandera faction of the Organisation of Ukrainian Nationalists. Unsurprisingly, this has made an already heated situation worse, with residents protesting as some statues are removed, others making plans to honour the new official idols. It's a "nation-building" project of a classic kind, building in a compulsory conception of history through interventions into public space.

Izolyatsia are hardly sympathetic to the Russian-backed rebels who forced them out of their hometown; Internally Displaced People are, despite fleeing from the Donbass that Russian intervention has turned into a warzone, regarded with suspicion in many quarters. Instead of defending Soviet monuments as such, their work has tried to bring nuance to the debate, although even that is controversial enough. One of their first projects after moving to a post-industrial space on the Dnieper was to catalogue and conserve the polychromatic mosaics that were placed on many public buildings across Ukraine between the Sixties and Eighties.

This project saw people who have come of age in an era where contemporary artists are trained to be wary of objects and straightforward meaning, let alone of propaganda, engaging deeply with applied, figurative propaganda art. Mosaics were one of the few places where artists could combine propaganda and abstraction, but the fact remains that this was, when it was made, between the Fifties and Eighties, official art, part of an artistic culture that was built around centralised Unions of Artists working to quite rigid state commissions. One suspects that the fringe benefits of this – the free flats and holidays – would be quite appealing to the usually precarious workers at places like the VCRC or Izolyatsia, but the close state monitoring of content much less so. In the Ukrainian context, meanwhile, one of the effects of the winter 2013-2014 revolution and the subsequent "decommunisation" has been in forcing people to look at artworks that were habitually ignored, or not even considered to be "art" in any meaningful way. Statues were one part of this, but much less that the obsessive collection and documentation of mosaics, which were hardly exclusive to Soviet Ukraine. In parallel with Izolyatsia's carefully itemised database of mosaics, crediting their authors and trying to find as much information about them as possible,[6] were various projects on Instagram or Tumblr. One of these, by the Kyiv-based photographer Yevgen Nikiforov, was published in 2017 under the inevitable title Decommunised.

The Russian art historian Boris Groys recently argued that the official culture of the Soviet Union and its satellites is so incomprehensible in contemporary terms that it is better compared to that of a totally discontinued culture like ancient Egypt than to anything in the twentieth century.[7] Its official art – heroic sculpture, propaganda mosaics and reliefs, mass-produced architecture, children's books – sat for years in the dustbin of history, rejected in favour of work by dissident poets, underground conceptual artists, and visionary film-makers once marginal or censored. In their introduction to Nikiforov's book, Olga Balashova and Lizaveta German argue that these mosaics "were hardly ever seen", even when the ideology they represented and celebrated was unavoidable; they were just something you passed by. They argue that this is because the USSR's public sphere was inauthentic – "a totalitarian state playing at a welfare state, it imitated public spaces"[8], lacking the freedoms of a true agora. This is a peculiar argument about historical public spaces, given that most streets and squares anywhere were in "undemocratically" ruled cities until the twentieth century, but certainly, few would have imagined much outside interest in these artworks when the system collapsed in disgrace at the end of the 1980s. Much more decisive for the fate of the mosaics is the combination of the banality of their content combined with the shift of "urban spaces [...] into private hands without a chance of becoming public platforms" as the Soviet Union fell. Because of this, it is only really decommunisation that meant that the mosaics could be seen, brought into visibility by their illegality.

The most interesting Ukrainian mosaics are in smalti, a mixture made up of tiny tinted pieces of glass, creating strange and vivid effects of light and shade, used frequently in Byzantine art. They were often made part of monumental ensembles, especially on the post-war schemes where conventional architectural ornament was absent. In 2016 I went to hunt out a couple of these, just outside the immediate centre of Kyiv, where the modernist city starts. Both are on wide boulevards with names that probably won't be decommunised – Victory Avenue, because the Second World War is still just about officially an acceptable subject to name a street after, and Lesya Ukrainka Avenue, named after a socialist poetess who had the good sense to die before 1917. The former of these is more famous – probably the most prominent mosaic ensemble in Ukraine.

Each mosaic, designed in 1968 by the team of Valerii Lanakh, Ernest Kotkov and Ivan Lyotovchenko, is placed on the gable end of a residential high-rise. In a spectacular example of the lack of communication between departments in the command economy, the artists were not informed that the architects had decided during construction to add a shopping street below the towers, which blocked out part of the mosaics; they redesigned them in 1980 into their current form, so as to be visible above the shops.

They celebrate Peace, Labour, Space and Socialism, and though they're now doubly blocked by the insignias of Adidas, Sberbank Russia, et al, once you've crossed the street they're still stunning, the smalti glistening in the dim light, and the iconography a precisely calculated fusion of Ukrainian folk patterns and abstracted industrialism. But the symbols, the stars, hammers and sickles, are forbidden, and so they may well be gone by the time you read this book.

Slaying the Dragon of Intertop

There is a clear narrative that can be built up in these mosaics: Ukraine, originally the centre of the Orthodox civilisation of Kyivan Rus, is awakened as a nation in the seventeenth century; is explicated in the poetry of Taras Shevchenko; joins in the revolution in 1917; industrialises in the 1930s; and fights heroically in the Second World War. Then its perfectly gender-balanced population spends peacetime playing football, exploring the cosmos, and participating in an international friendship of post-colonial peoples. It is not *the* truth, but it is *a* truth about Ukrainian history. But then it is not meant to be truthful so much as an attempt to will things into existence. Its belief in human possibility and progress is touching, sometimes moving, especially when placed in a flattering context of nationalism and graft.

Walk round Victory Avenue, and you can see the schizoid nature of the Ukrainian capital's development. The problem with the city, according to those governing it, is that it didn't sufficiently reject Communism after 1991, with a "Communist mentality" keeping its hold on the masses. Yet what appears to be happening here to the untrained eye is a totally unrestrained capitalism, where cheap new towers arise in every empty space, next to 1960s housing that has been left to rot, its playgrounds unkempt, its concrete panels gooey and flaky, and with "Western-style" glass office blocks getting half-way to construction before being semi-permanently abandoned when it becomes obvious that investors aren't interested in anything remotely long-term. Knowing this city for eight years, I've not noticed much change since the "Revolution of Dignity", but for the slightly larger niche that people like the Visual Culture Research Centre and Izolyatsia have managed to carve out for themselves. The main visual change is that the neglect has intensified, as resources are diverted to the war in the Donbass, and a new official nationalism has joined Communist mosaics and cheesy adverts as the background mood.

Pecherska, where the group on Lesya Ukrainka Boulevard is placed, is less unnerving – as a less important area, it hasn't been subject to property speculation to the same degree, so the rigid and drab enfilade of 1970s blocks is relatively unaccompanied by developers' kipple. In this case, the mosaics are less obviously propagandistic, and are placed at eye level along the street, on the ground floor, alongside the shops. Designed in 1969 by Anatolyi Gaidamaka and Larysa Mishchenko, with a strict pink-white-black colour scheme, they mostly show you the things you can buy in the shops – joints of meat, fish, fruit and vegetables – alongside the peasants who made them. But after fulfilling that basic informational function, the artists have let themselves have fun, creating Miro-like abstractions and shapes floating around the wall surface, and throwing knights, penguins, aircraft and atoms into the mix.

It makes a wonderful streetscape out of something that would otherwise be rather grim, and while it is official art, it's not official fine art – the Unions of Artists would not have allowed the abstraction, distortion and spacey surrealism of either of these ensembles onto a canvas in an art museum. On the side of a building, it was

Protecting the Family, Protecting the Fatherland

Scientific Shopping

Abstraction and Abundance

acceptable. Freedom to do what you wanted in one place, and not in another – it isn't a predicament massively unlike that of the radical artists of today's Kyiv.

In both cases, there are things you can and can't talk about. Izolyatsia's temporary addition to the Lenin plinth ran alongside an exhibition at their gallery in Podil. It happens to be in one of the strangest places in central Kyiv, the sort of chaotic post-industrial playground that could have been found in Berlin in the 1990s but that has usually been cleaned away from Western European cities, a land of warehouses surrounded by railway tracks and freight carriages sunk deep in tall grass. This is the industrial section of the Dnieper, and the river is hard to find – you cut past the nineteenth-century grid, past a monolithic concrete grain silo, to a cluster of factories, and, should you want to cross to the river, an angular concrete bridge which has barriers telling you not to cross it, which are routinely ignored by the badass Podil hipsters.

The Presidental Shipyard

From this bridge you can get to Rybalskyi Island, which is home to one of President Petro Poroshenko's many holdings, the Lenin Shipyards, renamed as the Rybalskyi Shipyards in 2017, several years after a massive and bloody anti-oligarch uprising installed an oligarch as president. Beneath is the small factory Izolyatsia moved into when they were forced to leave Donetsk, and in front of it is a miniature war memorial to the deeds of its workers in 1941 to 1945 – boasting, of course, red stars and hammers and sickles.

During Izolyatsia's monuments exhibition you would enter, walk up the dusty concrete steps, and you'd find works by artists from Poland, Bulgaria, Russia, Israel, the Netherlands, Columbia, Mexico, taking critical, ambiguous, ironic approaches to the question of the authoritarian, grandiose monuments bequeathed to cities around the world since the first rise of nationalism in the nineteenth century. In the contribution by Luchezar Boyadjiev, for instance, plinths of horse-riding leaders and warlords stand with the human figures photoshopped out, their horses and thrones suddenly headless. The hope was, it seemed, that these sorts of critical commentaries and oblique interventions could show that conceptual art has something to provide that totally avoids the compulsory nation-building politics and retrograde sculpture that still besets Ukraine and many other countries. Maybe so.

However, underneath Gutierrez's Lenin intervention you could find another, perhaps stronger, albeit unintentional, conceptual work. Steps leading down from Lenin take you to a shopping centre, one of many crammed into every available space in the Ukrainian capital. At first, it seems like just any other of these, where the spacious thoroughfares of the Soviet city were filled in by people, then businesses, selling whatever they could. But go deeper in, and it opens out into a multi-level underground atrium, with a lift passing between floors, like a full-scale suburban shopping centre. This is a city where any and all public spaces are seized upon by parasitic capital. As an image of what power really is in Ukraine – and elsewhere – it serves so much better than the melancholy, anachronistic figure of V. I. Lenin. But these processes, so hard to treat in terms of symbols and semiotics, are uniquely hard to explain and understand. Unlike a sculpture on a plinth, you can't just knock them off and proclaim victory. But as I left the city for the last time as of the time of writing, passing the monumental walls of new apartment complexes, the half-developed infrastructure around them, the kiosks crowding around each Metro station to the point where you can't even see the Metro "M" sign, restaurants called "MAFIA", hasty plastic street signs renaming Lenin Streets of wooden houses and gas stations after previously obscure 1930s Galician nationalists, I came across an advertisement for a development called "New England".

The same prefabricated blocks, of course, but with the monumental pediments and classical detail apparently so common in ordinary English housing. Evidently there was no point in making art that satirised or criticised contemporary Ukrainian capitalism and its longing for Europe. It was doing that itself.

On the European path

НОВА АНГЛІЯ
ПОСПІШАЙ НА
АКЦІЙНУ ПРОПОЗИЦІЮ!
ТЕЛ.:
(044) 300-11-01
700 м до метро Васильківська
ROYAL
HOUSE

New England

OLIGARCHY IN ROCKET CITY

DNIPRO, Dnepropetrovsk, Ekaterinoslav

Trains journeys in Ukraine are a useful metric as to what sort of society it is. In Kyiv's gigantic Neoclassical station, built in the late 1920s and then ineptly extended in the 2000s, you have an obstacle course for the disabled, and a vaulted waiting room with Stalinist murals of the cities you could be going to, or of the collectivised countryside you would pass through. You have to pay extra and pass through a turnstile to use this, so most don't bother, and sit around on the stairs or in the corridors. I've travelled "hard class" across the country, and it's fine, so long as you can sleep easily – regular glasses of tea and uniformed staff keeping an eye on you – but the carriages, with their long dusty carpets thrown across lino, have usually not been upgraded since the Seventies. If you fork out for one of the fast intercity trains, you get comfortable chairs, TV and magazines. In November 2015 I made my way eastwards on one of these. The in-train TV interspersed its adverts with some astute historical trolling, showing a clip in Ukrainian and English on Vlasov's Russian National Army, a wartime collaborationist force rather larger than those recently extensively discussed in Ukraine. Upon arriving in Ukraine's fourth-largest city, you're at another hulking Neoclassical portal, this one designed by the Moscow Metro's greatest architect, the Kharkiv-born Alexey Dushkin. This leads you to a columned central hall, with a chandelier and stucco ceiling more rococo than Baroque. The waiting rooms, similarly to Kyiv, are segregated between those with plush armchairs, which you have to pay extra for, and more mundane rooms with plastic chairs. As soon as you're out, the steps lead down to Petrovsky Square, named after the Communist politician the city is no longer officially named after. Post-war "empire-style" Neoclassical flats loom vaguely over a small statue of the man himself, pointing eastwards. A wooden Orthodox cross had been erected in front of him, until his final removal in 2016. Before 1917 Grigory Petrovsky was a local worker, a Bolshevik organiser among the Ukrainian, Russian and Jewish steelworkers and miners of an area that was industrialised at the turn of the century; Ekaterinoslav, named after Catherine the Great, was renamed as a compound of the river that flows through it (Dnieper in English is Dnipro in Ukrainian) and Petrovsky in 1926. The cross was there because, as a member of the Ukrainian government in the early 1930s, he is considered to

Last days of Petrovsky

be an "organiser" of the "Holodomor", the great famine that killed millions of Ukrainians, many of them in the countryside immediately around the city named after him, while grain continued to be exported in 1932 and 1933. R.W. Davies and Stephen Wheatcroft's definitive book on the famine, *The Years of Hunger*, finds a horrified Petrovsky – more a figurehead than an active leader by this point – writing to the Politburo, demanding that they publicise the famine and ask for foreign aid.[1] These shades of grey are hard to find, in a time and place when the famine is usually either ignored and downplayed (in Russia – strangely, given how many Russians it killed) or, in Ukraine, turned into a nationalist myth. When I was in the city, the local government of Dnipropetrovsk had just voted overwhelmingly to change its name: to "Dnipropetrovsk", with the "Petro" officially referring to St Peter, who as we know has had only a benign influence on history. This wasn't good enough, and in 2017 it was officially renamed "Dnipro"; although this is a bit like calling a British city "Thames" or "Severn", it is at least the name of the local football club, so doesn't seem to have caused the same consternation as, say, the renaming of nearby Kirovohrad as Kropyvnytskyi.

Until very recently Dnipro would have been considered one of the major cities of eastern Ukraine, but the war has made it, among other places west of the Donbass, rebrand itself as "Central". Central it certainly is, in political and economic terms. Since the 1970s this was arguably the most important city of the Soviet military-industrial complex, and then became the centre of Ukraine's post-industrial elite. Aside from the steelworks and mines established under Nicholas II and then hugely expanded under Stalin, it became one of the main production centres of the Soviet space programme under another local boy, Leonid Brezhnev. There is some tedious controversy about whether he identified as "Russian" or "Ukrainian" – his Party card said the former, his passport the latter – but either way, Dnipropetrovsk was always his power base, and the city centre was substantially remodelled in the 1970s and 1980s. It then became the base for nearly the entire post-Soviet Ukrainian ruling class.[2] Here, on the rock of the asset-stripping of "Rocket City"'s factories, were established the fortunes of Leonid Kuchma (director of the rocket plant before he became President), Viktor Pinchuk, Igor Kolomoisky, Pavlo Lazarenko, Gennady Korban and Yulia Tymoshenko. By comparison, Donetsk hoods like Rinat Akhmetov, or the Bessarabian confectionery and shipbuilding mogul who is the current President, are fairly minor – and Donbass's ruined, war-devastated status means that Dnipropetrovsk is the most decisive city in Ukraine, something aided by the way that the city's "Anti-Maidan" was swiftly bought off or suppressed by Kolomoisky, the newly appointed post-Maidan governor, who then proceeded to funnel his money into often neo-fascist volunteer battalions and a panoply of astroturf political parties.[3] Dnipropetrovsk should also be an interesting place to see if any of the immense wealth made by Ukrainian oligarchs has managed to "trickle down".

The river the city is now solely named after is also the most interesting part of it, architecturally – the long river walk across the Dnipro that was, when these pictures were taken, still called the Lenin Embankment. Carved out under Brezhnev and opened to the public in the early 1980s, it is an unexpectedly lovely public space, lined with a panoply of impressive late-modernist structures, to which little has been added, but whose boardwalks and greens have been reasonably well maintained; it's the centrepiece of Dnipropetrovsk as the futuristic, industrial capital of Brezhnev's Age of Stagnation.

The first of these is the River Terminal. Most big ex-Soviet cities – including Kyiv – have one of these usually faintly Neoclassical palaces with spires, modelled on Moscow's elaborate Italianate Northern River Station, but Dnipropetrovsk's is totally different, a Constructivist volume extended out into the river. Past that is Parus, a high-rise hotel that steps down, ziggurat-like to the water. Designed in the early 1980s, it was never finished (structurally complex, it was left to rot as astonishing fortunes were made around it in the early 1990s), and has been a famous failure ever since, eastern Ukraine's own Ryugyong

Hotel. The rotting concrete is occasionally spruced up, sometimes with an advert for Kolomoisky's PrivatBank, and currently, with a big Ukrainian flag. Then there is a rotunda restaurant, also out on a pier in the river – originally modernist, it has gradually been turned into a tatty neo-vernacular wigwam, with a pointy tiled roof. Beyond a concrete bridge with heroic and illegal sculptures of heroic workers and peasants is the most impressive monument of the Lenin Embankment, Dnipropetrovsk Circus.

This enormous building commands its own square, and its tent-like design, capped by a little diorama of figures, in silver-painted concrete, is fairly obviously borrowed off Oscar Niemeyer's cathedral in Brasilia, with the goofy elements of that building desacralised and applied to the USSR's strangely persistent love for the Big Top. Next to it, a curved, expressionistic block of flats complements the design,

The Parus Hotel, overlooking the Dnipro in Dnipro

originally reserved for the workers of the Circus. Alongside that, in turn, is the more prosaic Hotel Dnipropetrovsk, a standard slab which contains within it some magnificent stained-glass panels, in an Intourist Pop Kandinsky manner, hotel décor being another one of those Soviet places where abstract art became acceptable. Fountains in the river splash away, and all this fascinating exotica can almost make you miss the other side of the Dnipro, where panel-built slabs extend interminably towards a skyline of red, rusting chimneys.

The Embankment No Longer Named For Lenin becomes a little less formal as it becomes Victory Embankment, and a steel bridge leads to a green island, with a golden domed Orthodox church and a truly colossal Soviet statue (the bald, moustachioed head peering out over the domes and trees is that of Taras Shevchenko, so is wholly legal). Then the Embankment stops altogether, and becomes, like in Kyiv, a messy space of highways and the verdant private spaces of

Apartments for circus workers

ponds and dachas. In amongst these is the Dnipropetrovsk Palace of Pioneers, which, though designed at the turn of the Eighties, being finished at the end of 1991, can lay a fair claim to being the last Soviet building. It stands in its own extensive grounds towards the river, with lots of green space and an amphitheatre for the pioneers to do their pioneering. It is unlikely anyone noticed this in 1991, but it shows just how strange and original mainstream Soviet architecture – in its "one-off" as opposed to the standardised variant – had become in the Brezhnev and Gorbachev years. This architecture links the never quite banished Stalin-era fixation with fine materials and decoration, with Postmodernism's preference for complexity and contradiction and a futurist commitment to what Gorbachev called "acceleration", expressed here in an wiry architectural language indebted to the Pompidou Centre or the Lloyds Building. All of this is encapsulated in a tiny building, a crescent enclosing a courtyard full of brightly

Abstract decor

coloured abstract furniture, with steel-mesh miniature skyways firing off into and above glass walls. Nearby, on the embankment railings, someone, a pioneer, quite possibly, has sprayed, in English, "I wanna fuck a dog".

From here, you have to go up a steep hill to get to the city centre, past the glassy headquarters of PrivatBank, and then some small, northern English redbrick houses from Ekaterinoslav, to the square housing Dnipropetrovsk's War Memorial, a very tall, flat red granite obelisk topped by a figure of victory waving a flag over the Dnipro, a (lit) eternal flame and the hammer and sickle. She's in very good condition, and from the upper level, the view is heart-in-mouth. In Kyiv, you never quite get to see just how beautiful this river is, but here, its commanding, snaking shape, lined by trees and then giving way to the endless flatlands, is something to behold. Victory's dominance on the skyline is reduced by flanking high-rise Postmodernist office

The Palace of Pioneers

Victory of capitalism

Papa Karla

blocks, whose ground floors feature "Bootlegger: Original Stylish Bar", and offices for some of the post-Maidan political parties. These are a vacuous bunch, and it helps to list their names in English: Petro Poroshenko Bloc "Solidarity", People's Front, Our Land, Renaissance, Opposition Bloc, Dill, Fatherland, Freedom. With the exception of the last two, each has existed for mere months, yet have offices and billboards everywhere. Politically, each of them is right-wing, with minor variants – Fatherland are mildly economically populist, Freedom are rebranded fascists, "Solidarity" and People's Front are the government, and the most "European" in outlook. Most are funded by Kolomoisky, who has specifically stated the only parties he doesn't fund are Opposition Bloc (Akhmetov), Fatherland (Tymoshenko) and Petro Poroshenko Bloc "Solidarity" (Poroshenko, obviously). Renaissance, Our Land and Opposition Bloc are all rebrandings of the formerly governing Party of Regions, whereas Dill is "patriotic" and accommodating to neo-Nazis. The mayoral election in 2015 went to a run-off between Dill and a Poroshenko-backed Opposition Bloc candidate, with the former winning. This is not the political system anyone could possibly have had in mind as they held their vigils in the freezing cold and fought the riot police, but their inability to create an alternative to it is still mindboggling.

A short walk from victory is what was Dnipropetrovsk's main drag, Karl Marx Prospekt, and is now Dnipro's main drag, Dmitry Yavornytsky Prospekt, after an important local historian and folklorist (mercifully, the city successfully fought off suggestions that the street be renamed after anyone from the OUN or the UPA). Still there, if Google is any guide, is a cafe named after the old man, Papa Marxa, whose sign features Marx dressed in a smoking jacket, sipping a cup of tea. This extremely long boulevard is a low-rise mix of classical, Gothic, Constructivist and Stalinist empire-style buildings, with lots of cafes and shops, and a strip of parkland though which a tram runs in the middle. With the exception of the thumpingly banal Stalinist Lenin Square (Heroes of Independence Square, rather), it's very pleasant.

One part of it adjoins a park featuring the pretty, St Petersburg-style Transfiguration Cathedral (the architect was Andreyan Zakharov, and the central spire is clearly modelled on the famous spike he designed for the Admiralty in the northern capital), the Battle of the Dnipro Rotunda and the Museum of the City of Dnipropetrovsk. The Rotunda is quite straightforward tub-thumping Soviet jingo, housing a big painting of the pivotal crossing of the river by the Red Army in 1943, with sound effects – I watched a group of schoolchildren have it all explained to them. This has been left unchanged, but I can imagine what has happened to the adjacent Museum of the City of Dnipropetrovsk. It is an exemplary Soviet museum, beginning with Homo erectus, who through dioramas, relics and sculptural reliefs, evolves and ascends through slavery, feudalism and capitalism to the construction of socialism and victory in the Great Patriotic War. Almost nothing had changed, it seemed, between the 1980s and

A Mini-Admirality

the winter afternoon in 2015 when I visited. A continuous mural and an incredible collection of revolutionary memorabilia covers a large hall on October 1917, and the room on the early 1930s borrows heavily from El Lissitzky to create a dizzying panorama of socialist construction. *Something else* happened here in the early 1930s, but it is not mentioned. The only room that had been changed was that on the space programme – important here, given it's where the satellites and spacecraft were actually made. Lonely spacemen, part of the building's 1980s decoration, look out over exhibits on traditional Ukrainian folk culture. The rocket factory still exists, and at the time of my visit I discovered it hadn't paid its workers for four months. Just round the corner is a monument to ninety years of the Komsomol, the Communist youth league. It was erected in 2010.

When you explore round here a little you uncover a secret. For the proponents of decommunisation, like Holocaust revisionist

All You Need to Know About Ukraine in the 1930s

historian Volodymyr Viatrovych, Russia is a dictatorship today in large degree because it didn't de-communise, and if Ukraine does, it will be inoculated against the bacillus inculcated by Communist street names and monuments. However, Dnipropetrovsk in November 2015 had far more of these than Moscow or St Petersburg (and far fewer, incidentally, than fully decommunised dictatorships like Uzbekistan and Turkmenistan). From 1991, the Russian capital had no streets named after the Cheka's founder Felix Dzerzhinsky, or Stalin's right-hand-man Kliment Voroshilov, nor has it recently erected monuments to defunct Communist youth organisations – and the sculptural plaque on the residence of Leonid Brezhnev was removed, although it was restored in 2013. Dnipropetrovsk, until 2017, had all of these things, although it should be noted that it also boasts a plaque for anarchist leader Nestor Makhno, whose "Free Territory" briefly encompassed Ekaterinoslav. The lack of de-Sovietisation was more profound than in metropolitan Russia, and it appears most likely to have been a means not of enshrining dictatorship, but of creating an appearance of continuity for the workers of Rocket City, as the Rocket Managers made themselves into billionaires.

You can see some of where the money went, in and around Karl Marx Prospekt. The two pyramid skyscrapers named The Towers, clearly modelled after Canary Wharf, in the city where this lot put their money, are useful examples. So too are the many high-end shopping malls, such as the Passage, Soho, the Europa Center and Most City Center, and the many brick apartment buildings, with stepped sections and grids. What is notable about all of these is that architecturally, they are far closer to their European models than anything you will see in Kyiv or Lviv. The Ukrainian capital's architecture for the last twenty years is mostly indistinguishable from that of Moscow – masonry clad high-rises with vaguely Neoclassical detail and bulky massing, rammed pell-mell to maximise profit on small sites. But in Dnipropetrovsk, architecture is much more laconic, with regular façades, high quality stone or glass façades, and reasonably

Brezhnev Was Here

Dnipro's Soho

sensitive massing on the street. They could be in Germany. Most peculiar is the Menorah Center, a pet project of Kolomoisky, a "Jewish-themed" shopping mall topped by a stepped skyscraper hotel, in a classical-modernist style similar to that of Berlin's Potsdamer Platz. No "New Russian" kitsch round here. You don't have to walk far to find redbrick houses with no windows, covered in vegetation, but it's still unexpectedly neat for Ukraine. They've splashed their billions on some really nice hotels, office blocks and malls, good for them.

To see where the money did not go, take the Dnipro Metro. Or rather, take the tram to the Dnipro Metro, because it has never made it to the city centre – although finally, around twenty years after schedule, work is underway at the time of writing on an extension that will; the works obscure the plinth where the city's Lenin statue used to stand, around what is now Heroes of Independence Square. The stations stretch from the main railway station out into the panel

The former Communard Metro Station. Infrequent but fully decommunised

suburbs, and the plan and construction time – and even the trains – are very similar to the Warsaw Metro, begun in the early Eighties and opened to the public in 1995. The differences between Poland and Ukraine, comparable in 1989, can be seen in the two systems. One now has twenty-seven stations, the other, just the original six. Both were originally planned around lines taking workers from factories to housing estates first, and more leisurely journeys second. The centre wasn't a priority. The differences between "Western-leaning", "normal" Poland and Ukraine since 1991 could be summed up both in the fact that a Metro in a Ukrainian city that is the equivalent of, say, Katowice, got built at all, but also that after that, development stopped almost totally. No wonder Poland is considered the "road not travelled" by many Ukrainians. Nothing to envy, it would seem, unless you have the opportunity to explore the architecture of the Dnipro Metro.

It is jaw-dropping. The stations are reached by deep escalators with funereal uplighters, in the Moscow Metro style. The ticket halls are

Metallurgists Metro Station

lined in various kinds of marble, with patterned concrete ceilings, and the signs, pointing you the direction for the Ilyich Palace of Culture, Kalinin Street or Dzerzhinsky Street, are chic and simple. But the underground halls themselves resemble anterooms for intergalactic travel more than waiting rooms for the daily slog to work. Two, Kommunarivska (just renamed, now Pokrovska, as presumably a new name is just as good as a new station) and Vokzalna, are Moscow-style, with ornate lamps and deep red marble, and concealed lighting creating a grotto-like effect, respectively. The others are all of a standard type, with gigantic barrel-vaulted halls where lampshades in the shape of metal blobs light ceilings lined with curved plastic panels in some very un-Nineties colours – sharp, metallic purples, blues and yellows. Appropriately for Rocket City, it evokes the Mir Space Station, a late moment of cosmic confidence. These are structures somewhere between cathedrals and psychedelic laboratories, although it is very much best to photograph them when the uniformed women who flag the trains by aren't looking, lest you be hit with their red lollipop. The signals appear to be played on an analogue synthesiser, as if Kraftwerk were moonlighting to create public transport jingles. The trains run every fifteen minutes, and are half empty in rush hour. Around a third of the lights in the stations are permanently switched off to save electricity. The shops and kiosks in the underpasses, a chaos of informal commerce in Kyiv, are nearly all empty. This, in a city that plays home to some of the richest people on Earth.

Hooligan Lenin

THE END OF COMMUNISM IN EASTERN UKRAINE

ZAPORIZHIA, Aleksandrovsk

The statue of V.I. Lenin in Zaporizhia was the last major edifice of the Bolshevik leader left standing in the centre of a big Ukrainian city. I had the pleasure of seeing it mere weeks before it was taken down. The first notable thing about the bronze likeness of Vladimir Ilyich was what he was wearing. Draped over his suit was a large yellow bib, like a high-vis jacket, which features both the Ukrainian coat of arms and the logo of Ukrop (Dill), an oligarch-sponsored nationalist party, and his outstretched hand was carrying a Ukrainian football scarf. This actually replaced the first new outerwear V.I. received post-Maidan, when a traditional embroidered Vyshyvanka was lowered by crane onto the giant figure. The gesture of that was an unusual attempt in Ukraine to create genuine consensus – the wishes of those who would defend the statue weren't insulted, as it was neither defaced nor demolished, and those who would tear it down could see it wasn't allowed to stand inviolate, but was draped in Ukrainian symbols. In fact, given Lenin's role, pointed to by none other than V.V. Putin, of bringing Odessa and Donbass into a unified, sovereign Ukraine, against the objections of many Bolsheviks, the costume had some historical justice. The replacement with the sponsored jacket and scarf is a little more derisive, though as Oleksiy Radynski of the Visual Culture Research Centre told me, "it's actually more appropriate – he's wearing football gear and he has who is sponsoring him on his jacket, so he looks like a real worker". Anyway, this was until recently one of Zaporizhia's less controversial statues – in 2010, a new statue of Stalin was erected by the local Communist Party, although it was removed after some unsurprising vandalism. As for the statue itself, it had it all – the gigantic scale, the heroic scowl, the red granite plinth (given a dressing of Ukrainian embroidery) featuring a crowd of smaller workers crowding around the feet of the giant leader. Lenin makes the "look here, see what we have wrought!" gesture common to many of the tens of thousands Lenins, although this specific one is not one of the standardised Lenins that were churned out in factories. The significance comes in the inscription and the thing to which he is pointing. The Ukrainian-language inscription is the famous slogan "Communism = Soviet Power plus Electrification of the Whole Country", a slogan which is more complex than it appears; it didn't mean "cables plus one-party state" so much as that the direct democracy of workers councils connecting with the decentralised nature of a national electrical grid would create the new society, an earlier variant of the Fully Automated Luxury Communism young folk in the West like to make memes about. But this was to be enabled by the sort of big, state-sponsored heavy industrial tech that the great man is pointing to – that is, the structure officially called DniproHES in Ukrainian, but most famous just as the Dnieper Dam, one of the largest Dams ever constructed. Lenin is pointing right at it, across the gigantic square, and the pylons, wires and gantries around the structure poke up into the air around him, as if he's the dictator of electricity. The Dnieper Dam was so famous and so publicised in international Soviet propaganda of the 1930s as to have been specifically sniffily mentioned by Orwell as a cult object. In the USSR, and not just in Soviet Ukraine, it was completely ubiquitous, featuring on countless reliefs and mosaics, on stamps, on

Mastering Electricity

badges. It was – though this was seldom mentioned – a major project of Leon Trotsky's, who campaigned for it after his demotion from the Politburo, and similarly inconveniently, its technology, engineering and senior personnel were almost entirely American, largely courtesy of General Electric. After it was opened, it generated more power than the entire infrastructure of pre-1917 Russian Empire; the industrial base of the city was expanded further by Zaporizhstal, a large, and also American-designed steelworks.

First the foreign engineers and experts, and only then the workers who built all of this, were housed in an extension of the small industrial town of Alexandrovsk, which was renamed post-1917 – the new name means "beyond the rapids", referring to the currents that power the dam's generators. The new city was masterplanned by Viktor Vesnin (who also designed the dam's long, ribbon-windowed power-house) along Constructivist lines as a "Sotsgorod". After

Dnipro Dam Administration Block

destruction in the war, the dam was extended, and later, a futurist administration block was built alongside and a flyover was built on top – a spindly construction that rattles every time a bus or a lorry goes across. To actually get a full view of the dam, you have to go down to the riverbank, or go to the other famous thing here – Khortytsia Island, known as the base of the Zaporizhian Sich, a self-governing Cossack state dissolved in the eighteenth century, then claimed by every conceivable political trend in Ukraine in the succeeding three hundred years. It has one of those typically Soviet "folk architecture museums" approximating what their encampment might have looked like, and a full view of the monumental curved concrete wall of the dam. The likely replacement for Lenin will, apparently, be a Cossack hetman, but at the time of writing the plinth is empty.

The planning of the city, however, will still be around the dam. Zaporizhia centres around a typical Stalinist magistrale, an example of Soviet imperial Baroque at its most stupefying – a long, wide boulevard which begins near the railway station and then after several miles terminates at Lenin. This is no longer called Prospekt Lenina on Google Maps (where it has reverted to its original name of Prospekt Sobornyi, Cathedral Prospect, though there is no cathedral), but it is on all of the street signs, many of which are built onto the buildings, and decorated with golden swags. After a couple of days in Zaporizhia it becomes clear that the only way to "decommunise" a city such as this would be to raze it to the ground.

A tour of Lenin Prospekt might begin at the other end to Lenin, at Central Square, in front of the Hotel Intourist, as it is still called. This is a large and dour plaza, flanked mostly by government buildings and two symmetrical, fortress-like precast concrete blocks of flats for the better class of Zaporizhian. Government buildings stand on the other side, in the slightly classicised, stone-clad Soviet variant of International Style modernism, and a mural shows a muscleman heroically harnessing the power of DniproHES. A small monument of molten steel being poured stands in one corner of the square, with the

A street sign on Lenin Prospekt

legend "GLORY TO WORK" on one side and a sheaf of wheat on the other. Along the Prospekt, there were, when I when I was there, posters reading "FOR PEACE AND STABILITY – ZAPORIZHSTAL". The post-Party of Regions Opposition Bloc easily won the elections here last autumn, and Zaporizhstal's chief engineer was elected as mayor. It's a post-Soviet company town. Zaporizhstal's assets are held by a company headquartered in Guernsey, and not much of its wealth has made its way to the rusting, crumbling city where the steel is actually made. It's a story which could be told anywhere in Russia or Ukraine, and no political force seems to be willing or able to challenge it.

Much unlike Dnipro, only two hours west by train, you can count the new buildings in Zaporizhia on one hand, and none are notable. The Stalinist USSR was also a profoundly unequal society,

Glory to Work

but trickle-down there meant at least the swaggering grandiosity of Lenin Prospekt, built up largely in the early 1950s. Every Baroque trick of perspective and symmetry is brought in, with towers, urns, archways, turrets, spires, fluffy stucco hammers and sickles and burly male and female steelworkers in the place where there should be cherubs and angels. It's thug Baroque, with heavy columns, beefy pediments and abrupt portals. You can see here that the Khrushchev critique of architectural "excess" had a point, given the proliferation of superfluous details – on one corner, two Roman temples flank each other on top of two blocks of tenements. Step into the courtyards, and though the scale is maintained, everything else is more informal – brick and stucco replaces tile and granite, and there's as much green space as in a post-1956 modernist *Mikrorayon*. Neon signs reading "HAMMER AND SICKLE" are unlikely to be switched on again.

Hammer and Sickle for sale

The Putinist-Tsarist Eagle

There's plenty of amenities, cinemas, theatres, concert halls, mostly Neoclassical – the Dovzhenko Cinema features a lovely metal bust of the film director and relief sculptures of workers and peasants; it also features a patriotic poster commemorating the "heavenly hundred", the most explicit sign of Ukrainian patriotism I came across in the city. Graffiti, always a good measure, is conflicted – "white power" on one tenement courtyard is crossed out and replaced with "USSR", "ATO" (Anti-Terrorist Operation, the official name for the counter-insurgency in Donbass) is crossed out elsewhere, there are stencils of Shevchenko, and a stencil of a Tsarist eagle seizing Crimea, holding a nuclear bomb in one talon and a bottle of vodka in the other. A bridge over the railway, offering views of Zaporizhstal in full blast, spewing out into the atmosphere (and you can taste it) and a tiny memorial to the Great Famine of 1933, leads to the Sotsgorod, or Sotsmisto in Ukrainian; both mean "Socialist City".

This is a complete late-Twenties/early-Thirties modernist housing estate, comparable in its completeness and scale to the Berlin estates of Bruno Taut from the same era, which are UNESCO-listed and restored. Some of Sotsmisto was reclad after 1945 to make the design heavier and more monumental, but you can still see what it is clearly enough. One part consists of a dozen or so free-standing, low-rise, deck-access blocks with curved, glazed stairwells, and pedestrian space around. These blocks have faced a variety of treatments, some classicised, some left alone, some given plasticky reclads more recently, but their architectural expressiveness is still clear. If they were anywhere west of the Elbe they'd have a preservation order, a DOCOMOMO listing and a commemorative book – though the Urban Forms Centre in Kharkiv have tried to popularise the area as "Bauhaus Zaporizhia". The centrepiece of the Sotsmisto is a crescent, clearly recalling the Horseshoe Estate in Berlin, but with open colonnades, a simple garden filled with trees, and an advanced state of dilapidation, with balconies filled in and extensions added. It also features the only poster for a political party I've ever seen in Ukraine that is on someone's flat

Bauhaus Zaporizhia

Somewhere in here is a Modernist masterpiece

Vote Communist

rather than on a billboard; a faded image of the Communist Party leader Petro Symonenko. At the parliamentary elections of 2012, his recently banned party got 21% here; in 2014, just under 10%. Like the fraternal Communist Party of the Russian Federation, the KPU were little more than an Orthodox Christian nationalist party, and had taken part in several coalition governments since independence. It's surely the case that capitalist Ukraine determined the fate of the Communists, not vice versa.

Sotsmisto too has its amenities. "Citizens of the USSR have the right to work", reads the pompous Russian inscription opposite the Kirov Palace of Culture, unpromisingly. They had the right to other things too, and concerts and suchlike are held here. Appropriately, then, someone has put a baton in the hand of the statue of Sergei Kirov that stands in front of this Neoclassical temple, so that he looks either like a conductor or a magician. This sort of gentle pisstaking, seen also in the changing outfits of the nearby Lenin, seemed a much more genuinely democratic, "anti-totalitarian" approach than pulling down monumental statues, soon to build new ones. This history is remembered with a certain critical distance, but it isn't stripped away – in a city so totally Soviet as this, how could it be?

However sensible the city's relation to its past, especially in comparison with the hysteria elsewhere, its status in the present is less clear. Obviously, this mainly working-class city is not made up of nostalgic Stalinists (though there are clearly some), not Banderites (of which election results and political actions suggest there are very few), and not of liberal democrats either (of which there may be still fewer). There was never much question of this Russophone city becoming part of the "Novorossiya" Putin dreamed of, and while pro-Russian protests did take place, they were small, just as Maidan here was negligible. The example of Donetsk, very nearby, was clearly not terribly persuasive about the virtues of trying to join the Russian Federation. Beyond that, it's hard to say what the future could be for this place. Communist iconography is built into the fabric of Zaporizhia, and will remain so; but voting loyally for the representatives of a company which keeps the fruits of your labour in Guernsey doesn't suggest an acute class consciousness.

Conductor Kirov

STREETS OF CROCODILES

CHIȘINĂU, Kishinev, קעשענעוו

As you approach the capital of Moldova from the airport, you face a bracing prospect. A previously featureless road up a shallow hill brings into view two enormous, symmetrical triangular apartment buildings, like great white wings closing the vista. Their mass is

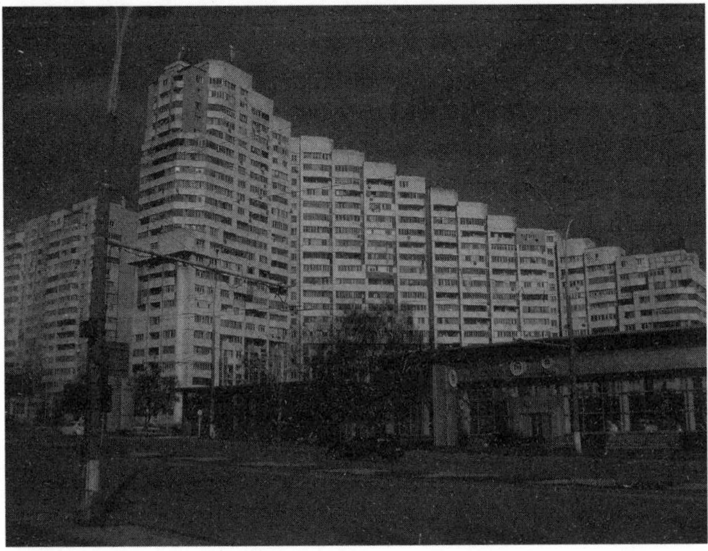

One half of the City Gate

prodigious – thirty storeys and around sixty bays, stepping upwards towards the street. These are the Chișinău City Gates, and they're one of the most ludicrous and impressive urban sights of the post-Soviet space, an image of Baroque city planning achieved in the early 1980s for the purpose of public housing. What this announces, or rather bellows, at the driver or bus passenger, is that you're in a very, very modern country, and one which considers the provision of mass housing to be the most important thing worth displaying on the skyline. At night especially, this is still an exhilarating sight. If you were to get out at this point, you'd find that image tarnished somewhat. Like most Soviet apartment buildings, these were assembled from factory-made concrete panels, and these were from the last generation of Soviet "micro-districts", when the building blocks were arranged into complex shapes and silhouettes. This hard image of monumental, concerted planning fades as soon as your feet are on the ground. In front of the "Gates" someone has placed a cross, as if to affirm that the church might be more important than housing or the glory of the Moldovan Soviet Socialist Republic; public paths are poorly paved and scrubby. Newly built car dealerships stand in front of the ground floors of the blocks. A legless man on crutches hops along the middle of the road, between cars stuck in traffic, but doesn't seem to be asking anyone for money. Above, giant adverts for Western goods are suspended across the lampposts and power lines. A wide street of monumental concrete apartment blocks, often pulled into similarly domineering shapes, proceeds from here; you can see, looking at them – or looking at contemporary photographs from the decade when they were built – how this could once have been a highly dramatic broadway, with the integration of shops on the ground floor and gesturing, repeated towers resembling Kalinin Prospekt in Moscow or Edgware Road in London, but the all-pervasive shabbiness and disorder to which the buildings were subjected, as the state abdicated their upkeep and businesses large and small parasited onto the low-rise pavilions, is inescapable. As a promenade, it retains some charm, with tree-lined pedestrian streets running on each side to shelter the walker from the noise and danger of the traffic. Street art, helpfully donated by Poles, takes up some of the blank spaces on the sides, with a large mural of Lech Wałęsa all the way up one, gazing out at the property ads, computer repairs, and EU Partnership billboards. Through the underpass that takes pedestrians across this boulevard, you can see a tangle of graffiti – anime characters, Masonic signs, "404 not found", Romanian and Russian language declarations of love, and in English, "Fuck the Police". This is Botanica, the largest micro-district of Chișinău, and to say that its monumentality provides a misleading impression of the rest of the city is only part of the story. You'll soon find, when your bus drops you off at the city centre, that this is a capital turned inside out – apart from a handful of prestige towers for government or (more seldom) business, central Chișinău is low-rise and undemonstrative, looking every inch the Shtetl that it once was, a forgotten small town that has acquired the paraphernalia of the capital of a peripheral, deeply impoverished country. Moldova is blessed or cursed, depending on your view, with a strategically insignificant geographical position. On the week that I spent there in March 2016, the parliament – a fairly nondescript modernist municipal palace, in front of a pretty park and the more convincing classic-modern synthesis of the National Theatre – had a tent city in front of it. As in Kyiv in the winter of 2013/2014, people were protesting at a spectacularly corrupt government, seemingly bent on squandering and squirrelling away the assets of a country slipping at great speed from the "Second" World into the Third. Moldova is the poorest country in Europe (on any definition of "Europe"), and on most indicators, it is on the level of much of sub-Saharan Africa.[1] Chișinău is its richest city, but the poverty here is acute.

Unlike in Ukraine, it could be argued that this doesn't represent anything new – whereas the Ukrainian SSR was economically one of the USSR's most successful republics industrially, educationally and scientifically, Moldova was relatively poor even within the Soviet

Union, a largely agricultural province swiped from Romania in 1940 soon after the Nazi-Soviet Pact. It has been alternately under the suzerainity of the Ottoman Empire, then annexed by the Tsars, then for twenty years in the interbellum in Romania, then for another forty-five or so years in the Soviet Empire. Its population, historically, has always been mixed – dominated by Romanian-speaking Moldovans, but always with large minorities of Yiddish-speaking Jews, Russians, Ukrainians and Gagauz, all of whom still inhabit what is still a pleasingly multicultural capital city, though those of the city's Jews that didn't manage to escape eastwards were massacred by the Romanian army when they re-occupied Moldova after 1941. Until recently, Chișinău was mainly in the history books for the Kishinev (the city's Russian name) Pogrom of 1903, when over forty Jews were killed, and nearly a thousand injured, by their neighbours, an event which led to widespread migration, for instance, to East London. After 1991, the more Russophone slither of the country east of the river Dnister, which had never been part of Romania, declared independence as "Transnistria", backed by covert and overt Russian forces. Yet apparently puzzlingly, the dominant party in Moldova from the late Nineties until recently was the Communists, who won several elections and were pivotal in orienting the country towards the EU rather than Russia, in punishment for which Russia imposed a blockade on wine exports. The current subsequent Liberal Democratic Party government is dominated by oligarchs, and widely despised; its recently elected President comes from the Socialist Party, a pro-Putin split from the Communists.

So far, it's almost a mirror of Ukraine – Russian-backed separatism, economic collapse, corruption. But there was no international furore when Moldovans took to the streets in their largest protests since independence, no "I am a Moldovan" viral videos of pretty blonde women telling Westerners about freedom. The EU this time backed the government (who signed the sort of Association Agreement with the EU that was at issue in the first place at Maidan) rather than the protesters; Russia was indifferent, branding the protests as yet another "colour revolution", even though many of the participants were strongly pro-Russian.

Some of the contradictions in all this can be seen in the way that the tent city is literally spatially split in two between the sort of pro-European, anti-corruption liberals whose slogans aren't a world away from those at Maidan, and supporters of the Communists and the Socialist Party. Their symbols, red stars and red flags are unabashedly Soviet. Each part of the tent encampment can count on widespread public support. The Socialist Party, whose Putinophilia extends as far as supporting a ban on "homosexual propaganda" (not a conspicuous problem in Chișinău as far as I could see), have the greater number of stickers around town. One of them reads – in Russian, not the usually more dominant Romanian – "IT WILL BE BETTER WITH US". The two groups actually united at various points in the

It Will Be Better With Us

protest, including on the storming of parliament a few weeks before I visited. Their positions are probably genuinely irreconcilable, and on previous form (or Ukrainian precedent), there's no reason to assume they'd not be much the same in government as the people they're challenging. Though very probably they wouldn't be quite so venal as the incumbents, who managed to avail themselves and their oligarch backers of $1 billion from the state reserves, which "mysteriously" disappeared into banks in Hong Kong and London, making up an incredible one-eighth of the country's entire GDP.

The cityscape of Chișinău is a fairly acute example of the popular stereotype of a post-Soviet city, in its combination of crumbling, kitschy space-age modernity, utterly ruthless and almost comically seedy gangster capitalism, and the semi-rural remnants of a turn-of-the-century market town on the borders of the Russian and Ottoman world. Fans of linguistic-cultural determinism will find little to support their theories in this easternmost outpost of the Romance languages. I stayed while here in the "Soviet, space-age" part of this equation, in the Hotel Cosmos. Like most of the more interesting buildings in Chișinău, its façade is a pattern of concrete panels, concave and convex, giving a rippling effect. From the upper floors you get a view of a cityscape shrouded in yellow-brown dust from construction works. An inept square, mainly consisting of wayward traffic, oscillates around an equestrian statue of the Moldovan-born Russian Civil War commander Kotovsky. Next to the hotel, a folksy mosaic shows a male and female figure in national costume in front of a stylised cityscape of Orthodox churches on one side, and rural crops and herds on the other. On the other side, the hotel has grown various new appendages, such as the Grand Hall shopping mall and the Napoleon Palace Casino with its neon-lit Ionic colonnade. Further on, another mall, "Atrium", with a high-rise business centre on top, whose rather Soviet-modernist castellated silhouette houses a bizarre Postmodernist interior, with columns shaped like vases, flowing green neon suspended ceilings and a central pink trumpet sculpture resembling a jollier version of

Cosmic Horseman

Mafia Classicism

Better than the Arcelormittal Orbit

Anish Kapoor's *Marsyas*. Here, you can get a decent panorama of the Moldovan capital, with a cliff of prefabricated high-rises encircling single-family houses, car repair and light industry.

Walk up Yuri Gagarin street and turn onto Stefan the Great Boulevard, with its travel agencies ("work legally in Poland") and dubious-looking pubs, and you soon come to another show-piece, where a monument to Victory in the Great Patriotic War stands inbetween socialist realist classical palaces and crumbling Soviet modernism, with the Hotel National gutted of its rooms, its outdoor pool drained. Opposite, the Constantin Brancusi Exhibition Centre occupies the ground floor in a cruiser of 1980s Soviet luxury flats, with allegorical metal sculptures of "the arts" represented by women in flowing drapery. Inside, an awful exhibition of the sentimental Moldovan landscapes of some 1980s hack shares space with the more interesting collages of a young artist, neither of which are quite what you expect from the main art gallery of a European capital. At this

Stalinist Kishinev

point, I turned off the main road, on the lookout for the House Museum of the Russian architect Alexey Shchusev, born in Chişinău. Shchusev replanned his hometown after the war, and Stefan the Great Boulevard became its grand boulevard, with the main government buildings concentrated here, as a Romanian provincial city became the capital of a Soviet Republic. The style used is not dissimilar to the fruity eclecticism of the 1900s City Hall, by the architect Alexander Bernardazzi, whose work appears to have been taken as a model, a distinctive style to much of the southwestern periphery of the Tsarist Empire – a bit Moorish, a bit Gothic, a bit Orthodox.

But just off that street, which does indeed have quite a lot of impressive socialist realist blocks, often designed with a decorative repertoire borrowed from Byzantium, you're in a city of one and at most two-storey villas, the somehow preserved houses of the early-twentieth-century petit-bourgeoisie. After a little exploration off the main streets, you find that most of the centre of Chişinău is like this.

Borderland eclectic

Detail of Capitals in the Shchusev Plan

Battered rows of bungalows, some with their roofs seemingly sinking, others with plasterboard roof extensions, some with no roofs at all; some, especially the nearer they get to shopping malls, have multi-storey tenements of trespa and fibreglass mounted onto them. Private health clinics, the preserved house of Pushkin on his brief stay here, the glass outgrowth of the local offices of Lukoil, the big red sign of a phone repair shop spread out across a dusty shed that looks like it'd fall down in a strong wind. Fragments of high-rise schemes from the 1980s stare out at them incongruously, leftovers from a modernisation that never fully took place.

In his 1970s study of housing policy, *Urban Inequalities Under State Socialism*, the Hungarian sociologist Iván Szelényi found that for reasons of land ownership and constructional simplicity, Soviet-style economies preferred to build huge estates on virgin land on the outskirts for skilled workers and bureaucrats rather than develop the often privately owned "transitional zones" in the inner city.[2] In, say, Prague or St Petersburg, this is one reason why you have some of the best preserved historic cityscapes in Europe, or anywhere; in Chișinău, the result is considerably less delightful. It is constantly interrupted, though, by outbreaks of sudden modernity, something in which both the Soviet and post-1991 periods seem to have specialised in without any noticeable overall plan. At the very least, the Soviet mosaics and murals still on the sides of many buildings, with their images of goofily optimistic modernity, are a little more charming than the giant adverts that drape the stone and mirrorglass façades of the handful of new office blocks, or the gimcrack Vegas classicism of the new apartment blocks that have emerged where some enterprising citizen has built on the site of one of those one-storey villas. The clearest difference is that the Soviet spaces have some modicum of unity, built around obvious squares and streets, often in ensembles of little classical tenement blocks around monuments, such as a tall, pathos-ridden monument to the Komsomol; all the 1990s and 2000s have really done with this is eat away at it: neoliberal urbanism as a parasitic growth.

The transitional zone

Walk down Strada Columna, and you'll find a diffuse street market, extending along each side of a pavement which looks to have just suffered from an earthquake, jagged and sharply angled so as to make shopping into a balancing act. A factory alongside is covered in an elegant, op-art concrete screen, as if Oscar Niemeyer got a job designing components for the prefab factory – these experiments in panels do a lot to enliven Chişinău's bleaker corners. With some interruptions for traffic-choked roads, this market extends all the way to the railway station. In front of its large, Shchusev-planned, tree-sheltered plaza, is a section of the market which obviously has a bit of an eye to tourists – while most of the markets sell useful goods, the usual Chinese-made consumables, this one also sells old books, postcards, cameras, and miscellaneous Soviet tat. In the middle of the square is a monument to the Moldovans who were deported to Siberia with the Russian reconquest of the city in the 1940s – they're

Socialist City Mirage

depicted as a collective body of huddled, hunched, headscarved figures with bundles and bags. The station itself is, maybe unexpectedly, glorious, its colourful, richly decorated arcades the most impressive example of post-war Chişinău's Soviet-Byzantine style. Here's where you can get the Moscow train – easily and simply – to Ukraine and Russia, and can take the more complicated route to Romania, which, although in the European Union, evidently does not have the same magnetic, this-could-be-your-future role that Poland plays for western Ukraine. Here, the "better place", richer, more stable, possibly even less corrupt (although given the breathtaking scale of the Moldovan elite's corruption, that's relatively speaking), may actually be to the east. Here, it is hard to believe in the alleged civilisational battle between the freedom and democracy of the EU and the despotism and obscurantism of Eurasia. Chişinău is caught between the two yet receiving the benefits of neither.

The way out

Part Three:

THE CENTRE

WHERE THE GAUGES CHANGE

BREST, Brest-Litovsk, Brześć-nad-Bugiem, בריסק

Travelling to or from Belarus is a useful lesson in the political, rather than geographical nature of borders. The city of Brest – Brest-Litovsk, to history students, Brześć-nad-Bugiem to Poles nostalgic for when this was part of Poland's *Kresy*, its eastern borderland – is 200km from Warsaw, about the distance between London and Manchester. In six years regularly staying in the Polish capital, I don't think I ever met more than two Poles who had visited their immediate eastern neighbour, although it is far closer than Berlin, Vilnius or Prague. The train is slow, and makes several leisurely stops – waiting for around thirty minutes at Warsaw's East Station, and then for forty-five minutes at each side of the border so that the guards can check your credentials and make sure nobody is smuggling anything, before they then change the rail gauges so your train can go on to Moscow. Even then, the journey takes just under five hours, not a long journey in Eastern Europe, though the Pendolino that travels between Warsaw and Krakow would make it in an hour and a half. The border is the river Bug, a geographical cipher that purports to stand in for the divide between the Catholic and Orthodox, the nationalist and the Soviet, and now the European Union and the Eurasian Union, which the likes of Timothy Snyder have imagined as the cleavage in a contemporary "clash of civilisations".[1] Even so, you're still some distance west of Vilnius, Riga, Tallinn or Helsinki, and Brest is the only major city in the former USSR where you can leave the train before the Central European gauge under your train is exchanged for the Russian wide gauge (you have the same bumpy experience going from France to Spain, but that's of less geopolitical significance). Once you've gotten over the many bureaucratic hurdles the country's visa regime will throw in your way,[2] it's a good place to explore the degree to which Belarus, the "Last Dictatorship in Europe", an "outpost of tyranny", as it was once described by the US state department, is different from its neighbours. Belarus has had only two free and fair elections in its history, and the results of both were landslides; one, in 1991, was the referendum Gorbachev held on the maintenance of the Soviet Union, where the result was 80% Yes; the other, in 1994, saw the election of an anti-corruption campaigner promising to restore the historic links with Russia and the Soviet symbols a brief nationalist government had rejected after an unrequested independence, with another 80%.[3] Alyaksandr Lukashenka, for it is he, has been president ever since, and after forcing through a dubious referendum in 1995 giving himself sweeping powers, it would be apologism to call Belarus anything other than a dictatorship. Unlike others who have made enemies of the USA, such as Hugo Chávez, who struck up an alliance with Belarus, Lukashenka has never faced truly competitive elections, and protests after the elections of 2010 were heavily repressed. Opposition candidates were jailed, and one has plausibly claimed he was tortured. However, even that election was not comparable to the situation in Ukraine in 2004, where ballot-box tampering made a genuine difference to the close Yanukovych/Yushchenko battle. Even opponents estimate Lukashenka's actual share of the vote to have been well over 30% above his nearest rivals, something replicated at the polls in 2016, though a couple of opposition MPs were elected to Belarus's rubber-stamp parliament.

The first building in the land of the Soviets

Lukashenka's success has been put down to many things – strong economic growth until very recently, relative equality, full employment which critics consider to be an "artificial" meddling with the market's infallible invisible hand, and of course, repression, censorship and the closing off of the country as much as could be possible in contemporary Europe. On my way in, a young border guard took a good look at the books in my bag, "Any *political* books?", she asked, smiling sweetly. I smiled back, not sure if this was a shared joke or a serious question.

In 1939 and again in 1945, annexed as part of "Western Belarus" or "our beloved *Kresy*" depending on who you're talking to, Brest's function shifted from a garrison town in eastern Poland to the major border city of the Soviet Union, the first piece of Soviet territory that a traveller on the trains from Amsterdam, Berlin and Paris would see. This would at first seem to be the reason why this small city has a railway station of such splendour. The vaulted roof of the main station hall – redesigned at the start of the 1950s – with its gilded, shimmering chandeliers, above terrazzo floors and plush, well-kept benches, shames the stations of cities ten times its size. The main façade is modelled on the Stalinist skyscrapers of the period, an open colonnade of granite columns on either side of a genuinely Baroque clock-tower that is still surmounted by a Soviet wreath and star. However, if you arrive, as I did, at midnight, coming in from Poland, this isn't what you'll see at all, but the earlier, nineteenth-century station building, based on a standardised vernacular classical design that will be familiar to many Poles, and a vague street of single-storey houses. The most likely conclusion, given that this is what travellers going east see first, is that the spectacle of the station's main façade was not intended for the visitors to impress upon them that they're entering the USSR. It was for Soviet citizens, as a sternly impressive gate, standing at the point of departure.

I stayed in the Hotel Intourist, as is wise – "invitations" are taken seriously here, and a Western European will have to book a state-run hotel first before they will be given a visa. It stands in the south of the city, and gives a view of the skyline and of the extremely close proximity of Poland, the country Brest was part of for longer than anywhere else. Intourist, like everything around it, has been meticulously painted, in a bright orange and white. Next to it, past a drained fountain with bronze Soviet sprites dancing around, is the Brest Univermag, a multi-level department store designed in the 1970s as the city's main shopping centre. In old photographs, this is a Brutalist scheme, with shuttered concrete walkways and a jagged clock-tower. None of it has been demolished but its current incarnation is painted lime green, in the pastel manner popular just over the border when post-war buildings get renovated. It houses a supermarket, travel agencies, cafes, and just round the back of it, where you're not meant to be looking, is an ordinary but small post-Soviet market of makeshift buildings and puddles.

Compared with any city of similar size in Ukraine, the relative cleanliness and affluence is noticeable; compared with any Polish equivalent, it is the lack of cheesy adverts you miss, both the giant canvas ads for Western cars and lingerie that would be draped over the bulk of the buildings, and the messier efforts of smaller traders that would crowd around the spaces left empty. Their absence doesn't make it feel like a Soviet time-warp, as the buildings are made to look as new as possible. Freshly arranged flower patterns run alongside the walkways. Everything is neat and ordered, and that is the least one should expect from a dictatorship. Family values posters and "I Heart Belarus" looms down from the billboards as often as Western brands.

From here, you can see the city's main attraction, in Soviet times and today – the Brest Fortress, whose entrance is marked by a huge concrete slab, with a hole in the middle shaped like a five-pointed star. You can't walk there very easily, as Prospekt Masherova – named after the former Partisan leader Pyotr Masherov, who became Belarus's Communist Party boss in the 1960s – is currently being dug up, presumably so its pavement can be as impeccable as that around the Univermag. So instead, you'd have to improvise a route through a new housing estate of utter banality, prefabricated slabs around surface car parks, with ingratiating little details to mask the fact that this is nothing more or less than Soviet housing without the green space or the social planning – identical to mass housing in contemporary Russia and contemporary Ukraine, with dictatorship in one, "managed democracy" in another, and an oligarch-dominated democracy in another, all creating seemingly identical urban results. There are Soviet blocks on the other side of the road, not as dilapidated as in Russia or Lithuania, not as nicely renovated as in Poland, a large power station, and then a dual carriageway cuts you off from the Fortress entrance – this is the main route from Paris to Moscow here, you don't cross it lightly. But when you do, you're in another world.

The Soviet Union named several "Hero-Cities" for their deeds in the Great Patriotic War – Moscow, Leningrad, Kyiv, Odessa, Volgograd, Sebastopol, among others – but Brest is the only "Hero-Fortress", a title bestowed not upon the city, but upon a large military

Post-Soviet Standard

complex constructed during the Tsarist Empire.[4] A system of bastions and concrete outposts around a redbrick Gothic core, it was one of several in eastern Poland, useful both for military purposes against an invasion from the west and to repress the restive Polish population. It became particularly notorious after Polish independence when re-used by the government of a former Tsarist political prisoner – the Polish dictator Józef Piłsudski, who imprisoned his centre-left opponents there in the run up to the rigged elections of 1930. The opposition press nicknamed it "the Brest election". In 1939, the fortress was taken by the Nazis, who then transferred the town and its environs to the USSR as part of the Molotov-Ribbentrop pact; the ceremonies on the day are unsurprisingly remembered by many Poles as a Nazi-Soviet joint victory parade. Barely a year and a half later, Operation Barbarossa started here. The fortress held out for a week until it was crushed, and the commander, Yefim Fomin, was immediately shot, perhaps the first victim of the "Commissar Order" that mandated the killing

Socialism and the New Life

of Jews and Communists. The memorial there now was designed in the mid-1960s, and opened on the thirtieth anniversary, in 1971.

The Brest Fortress memorial is one of the most stunning Soviet monumental spaces I have ever seen, and I have seen many – a masterful, authoritarian manipulation of the emotional possibilities of architectural space. What you see from the road is the long, rectangular concrete slab (painted – no bare concrete allowed to be seen here) with its cleared star-shaped space. As you move towards it, you can hear a metronome ticking away. Inside the "star", and you notice on either side that this concrete star-as-absence is actually twisted into several polygonal parts, an anticipation of the belief held by Daniel Libeskind among others in the 1990s that non-orthogonal geometry and war had some natural affinity (and not the only time Soviet memorial architecture has shades of a less tasteful precursor to "DeConstructivism"). The crushed concrete volumes are cantilevered out across the remains of one of the Fortress' brick gates; you can see

The Endless Sacred War

the empty rooms and corridors inside, in enfilade. The outline of the star, suspended above you, frames perfectly a steel obelisk, and the giant concrete bust of a seemingly growling soldier, so deranged in its scale you don't know whether to laugh or shudder. The metronome stops, and turns to a recording (reconstructed?) of the Fortress' garrison calling Moscow, and then, the ubiquitous, terrifying marching song of the Great Patriotic War, "The Sacred War", calling to the hairs on the back of your neck.

Like so much in the iconography and self-justification around the Soviets' war, it is hard to regard any of it with equanimity and acceptance, let alone the total submission that it demands. The giant figures – the snarling bust, and, just out of view to the left of the star, a concrete soldier reaching his helmet out to the moat, called "Thirst" – are so literal and domineering that they almost neutralise the moving effect of the scattered ruins of the Fortress complex, and the smaller plaques to its defenders. A plaque to Yefim Fomin is on the

The remains of Brest Fortress

Fortress' original main gate. The gate is so riddled with bullets and potholed by mortars that it tells the story the architects of the complex want to tell you – about astonishing violence, astonishing fortitude – without needing to spell it out as the statues do. Young conscripts stomp in formation in the very large square between the star and the giant head; and behind the latter is a tacky, reconstructed version of the nineteenth-century garrison church that was previously left as a ruin. Fomin and the other multi-racial defenders of a state based on a harshly atheist ideology might not have been happy.

A small museum inside the Fortress' barracks has one room on the nineteenth century, one on the interwar years when this was in Poland (curiously missing the propaganda own goal provided by Piłsudski's use of it to jail Communists and Belarusian-Ukrainian nationalists), and half a dozen rooms on the Fortress' defence, and its defenders. As always with these places, propaganda and real horror and heroism intersect, inextricable – a ludicrous painting here, a set of haunting photographs of victims there. The gift shop features fridge magnets, plates and a variety of other Red Army-themed consumer goods featuring the complex; you know you're *not* in Russia largely because of the absence of images of "Krim Nash" and Vladimir Vladimirovich, and the interesting absence of the Orthodox, Tsarist iconography that, in Great Russia, is now conflated with that of the USSR. The Museum of the Fortress is careful to credit its defence not to "Russia", but to "the people of more than thirty nationalities". As it was.

Nothing else in Brest can compare with the experience of visiting the Brest Fortress. Gogol Street leads from there to the centre, through some more poor-quality new housing, much of it evidently on post-industrial land, and then a delightful tree-lined prospect, whose central avenue works as a linear park, fresh, spick and span; in Poland or the Baltic states, you'd assume this was funded with EU money, here it's the astute use of Russian subsidy, to much the same pretty and conservative effect. Compared to the real economic failures of the "transition" – Ukraine, Moldova, Georgia – the evenness of the streets

Lenin...

and the cleanliness of the buildings is something of a marvel, though head off the main road and you'll find a relative shabbiness, with un-renovated panel slabs shadowing interwar Polish houses, their modernist lines hidden by ivy. Eventually the street becomes a park, and then Lenin Square, with a standardised statue of the leader of the Great October Proletarian Socialist Revolution pointing to a twin-towered Catholic church, another little piece of Poland standing as the odd man out in a square of monumental classical offices.

Around Pushkin Street, you're in a small-scale city that could be absolutely anywhere between Łódź and Smolensk, streets of little houses and two-storey tenements, with unfussy 1950s additions in a delicate classical style. New buildings are uniformly hideous, with new constructions in an eternal Nineties of mirrorglass shards and stone-clad "references" to the historic past. Then you come to Brest's main drag, Soviet Street, heralded by the glass rotunda of Kinoteatr

...and the Catholic Church

Belarus. Its free, Khrushchev-era modernist plan is actually dictated by the shape of the foundations of Brest's Great Synagogue, destroyed by the Nazis. Brest's Jewish population in 1936 was over 20,000, which then made up 41%; nearly all were killed.

Oddly enough given the circumstances, the recent reconstruction of Soviet Street aims at a weird Disneyland Shtetl style, with fibreglass candelabras, *Fiddler on the Roof* street furniture and a plethora of inept approximations of picturesque pre-war architecture, housing cafes and boutiques. It is strange indeed to see pretty wood-effect street signs with curlicues and gilding which, just a few miles away would say "John Paul II Street" or "Józef Piłsudski Square", here reading "Komsomol Street" and "Felix Dzerzhinsky Street". In Belarusian, everything has changed but the nomenclature. As in Russia, or anywhere else, nostalgia has been incorporated into consumerism. At the Brest Fortress this takes on unusual forms, with Soviet memory perpetuated

Synagogue turned Modernist cinema

on an enormous scale, because that is what Belarus has to hand, its useable past. Looking at Soviet Street, the retained names that come with that memory are the only things that tell you you're not in the European Union. All those brutally enforced borders, immortalised by a monument right at the border crossing – and this is what you find on the other side.

Simulacra Shtetl

TIME, BACKWARD!

MINSK, Miensk, מינסק

Minsk doesn't have much in the way of branding or the names of Western corporations. You can walk for miles, in the centre of the Belarusian capital, before you find one of the giant advertisements for a brand of Western car draped across a semi-derelict building, that ubiquitous feature of almost every post-Communist capital city of similar size – Kyiv, Yerevan, Riga. What this city – conventionally described as the land of eternal Sovietism, with Lukashenka as its impossible-to-dislodge Brezhnev – does have is a Hilton Hampton hotel, just behind the back of its large railway station. Minsk is a stop on Europe's main east–west route, so this is very much a through station, with niceties like ticket offices and restaurants located in a very Nineties, strongly symmetrical complex of marbled cladding, atria and pink-tinted glass pyramids. The front end leads you to the pre-planned arrival vista of the City Gates, which we will come to presently; but the back end is another matter. Tunnels lead through a passageway with a Stolovaya that sells sausage that is in no way fit for human consumption, to the construction works for the third line of the Minsk Metro. Outside are narrow paths for pedestrians through fenced-off works, muddy expanses around station outbuildings and a shabby bus station. There are various little kiosks selling products, and those products are something to behold. Mostly – though not exclusively – available from behind the counter, rather than from the

Consumerism in Minsk 2017

shelves, "Western-style", these silvery tins of Kasha and sour milk appear not to have changed their design since 1980, a little museum of faded Seventies photography and cutesy Soviet graphics, but one which seems unaware of its own retrochic. Past the hotel itself, part of a small cluster of recent, and also visibly "Western-style" office blocks, and past the bridge over the railway, you come to the market – a typical one in this part of the world, where people spread out on canvas, card or an item of clothing various bits and bobs for sale – cheap Chinese-made consumer goods, sometimes second-hand, agricultural produce. If I hadn't been staying in this relatively posh hotel, I wouldn't have seen any of this, and the sleight of hand that Minsk performs – a showcase of the Last Soviet Republic – would have worked on me entirely, and I might have believed they really had built an egalitarian, affluent society genuinely different to that of contemporary Ukraine and Russia. *From the Ruins.* Whether hostile

The back of the station

or complimentary, all accounts of Belarus will mention the extreme Sovietness of its capital, and the equally extreme cleanliness and lack of commercial pollution and/or vibrancy.[1] This leads to some interesting errors. Historian Andrew Wilson, in his otherwise convincing critique of the Lukashenka regime, *The Last European Dictatorship*, describes its dominant style erroneously as "Brutalist". Nothing could be further from the truth.[2] Minsk is arguably the greatest Neoclassical European city of the twentieth century, with most buildings in the city centre resplendent with colonnades, Baroque archways and romantic skylines of spires, obelisks and heroic sculptures, all on an axial plan integrated with landscaped parklands around the river Svislach. This is the direct result of one of the least known episodes of the Second World War – the intensity of resistance in Soviet Belarus to the Third Reich, which deserves to be as well known as that of Poland or Yugoslavia, but isn't, largely because it isn't useful to anybody much, save perhaps Lukashenka's unpleasant government. The Soviet Partisan movement was at its largest in Belarus, beginning almost immediately after the

You Don't Know How Lucky You Are, Boys

Nazi occupation of the country. Helped by the close proximity of the forest to the capital, partisans were able to save thousands of Jews from the Holocaust that began here; and the attempts to create a Judenrat in the newly designated ghetto failed repeatedly, as the appointed leaders defected to the resistance; by 1943, partisans already had several "liberated zones" in the forests and marshes. Reprisals, however, were unbelievably brutal – proportionally, more Belarusian citizens were killed than any other nationality in the war. Hundreds of villages were destroyed and all their inhabitants exterminated; and the capital, Minsk, was destroyed, for the same reasons as Warsaw: as a symbolic gesture to punish resistance.

In her history of the resistance in the ghetto, Barbara Epstein argues that the relative lack of a strongly defined nationalism in the country – something for which it is usually considered somehow "backward "and "incomplete" – and a less horrific experience of Soviet power than nearby Ukraine (the famine of 1932-33 did not reach Belarus) meant that Soviet internationalism was taken seriously by Belarusians, and many acted heroically when their Jewish neighbours began to be deported and ghettoised.[3] It is puzzling, then, that it is exactly this absence of a national consciousness which is usually considered the cause of Belarus' eternal dictatorship. Equally, it could be the result of – as Wilson somewhat reluctantly acknowledges – the sheer unpopularity of nationalism, as represented by the Belarusian People's Front that emerged under Perestroika. Belarus briefly, from 1991 to 1995, used the flag of St George, initially used by the relatively benign German puppet regime of the Belarus People's Republic in 1918, and then used again by the Nazi puppet regime of the Belarus Central Rada, in 1944. Among the measures that made Lukashenka popular was replacing this with a faintly redesigned Soviet coat of arms; you see it everywhere in the capital. The opposition use the St George flag, something which, given the experiences Belarusians had under it, seems to an outsider like an act of pure self-sabotage. But the partisan experience was initially repressed in Soviet Belarus, too, as

Epstein points out; when the Party leaders who fled into the Russian interior in 1941 came back, they demoted or jailed many partisans, whose experiences were embarrassing; it wasn't until 1956 that their narrative became the dominant one, and Lukashenka has made it a central plank of history as his government conceives it. Again, this should not be surprising – nobody is puzzled by the ubiquitous nature of plaques, murals and monuments to the Warsaw Uprising on seemingly every street corner in the Polish capital, and nor should they be in Minsk. In both the Jewish experience, however different it was in the two cities, is similarly minimised.

One important difference, though, is that while the Polish narrative focuses on victimhood, martyrdom and betrayal (as it has every right to), the Belarusian one, like the Russian, focus on victory and triumph. The rebuilt city, the most complete example of socialist realist architecture in Europe, works as one gigantic victory monument, and accordingly, it requires a strong stomach for vainglory, pomposity and heroic grandeur. Within those confines, it isn't at all unattractive. Imagine an entire, complete city centre built like Berlin's Karl-Marx-Allee, Warsaw's MDM, Kyiv's Kreschatyk, Sofia's Largo, and that's what you have here. Because of this, the Belarusian government has put the entire city centre up for consideration on the UNESCO World Heritage list, St Petersburg style. The application is currently on hold, largely because the government have belatedly realised that UNESCO status means a moratorium on any property development within the area (a revised application for a more tightly drawn area is apparently set to follow). The best place to begin a perambulation of it is the other side of the Central Railway Station, the opposite end to the muddy building sites between the bus station and the Hilton.

UNESCO Stalinism

The City Gates are two blocks of symmetrical flats, culminating in stepped eleven-storey towers – a model used elsewhere, like at Constitution Square in Warsaw, Strausberger Platz in Berlin or

Gagarin Square in Moscow, or indeed in reconstructed towns like Zaporizhia in Ukraine, but none of them have quite this level of imperial bombast. The usual paraphernalia of spheres and spikes surmount the tops, with an ornamental clock on one and the Soviet coat of arms on the other. Symbolic statues of workers and peasants rise at the peaks of the towers, which were of course luxury flats, always intended for the elite. There is a McDonalds in one of the towers, but more unusual is the plaque, recording that this "Soviet architectural monument" was built from 1947 to 1953, and restored in 2000-2005. These sort of developments are often part of the "Potemkin City" style so common to the Stalinist era – thin façades, leading to courtyards where you can easily find traces of an earlier, shabbier city – but the traces are harder to find in Minsk, though the courtyards are drab as anywhere.

Bombast

A certain emptiness is noticeable, but the buskers are good – one young hipster out of 1960s Soviet central casting, playing the *Godfather* theme on a clarinet (a good Kremlinologist would note here that a Russian documentary series about Lukashenka aimed at adversely influencing his re-election, was called *The Godfather*). The City Gates lead past a grand crescent to Kirov Street, where another pompous Stalinist block has become a Crowne Plaza hotel, opposite the Dynamo stadium; walk along here a little bit and you come to the green esplanade of Komsomol Street, its tree-lined path culminating in a bust of Felix Dzerzhinsky, and in front of it, a Neoclassical block with tall metal doors. It is topped by a Renaissance lantern, with tall

The House of Government

windows so the inhabitants can, symbolically, see all the goings on.

This is the headquarters of the KGB, which, as every article on Belarus since the 1990s will tell you, is still called the KGB.[4] Its placement here supports the contention by the Belarusian artist Artur Klinau that Minsk is (as much, if not more, than St Petersburg) the fulfilment of the Enlightenment dreams of the "City of the Sun", as the Italian utopian Campanella called his ideal Renaissance city. A perfectly organised metropolis defined by an *architecture parlante* based on Roman and Greek precedent, a close integration of buildings and nature, and the constant presence of power – here, the extreme panoptic gesture of having this almost Parisian little prospect end at the outlook tower of the secret services. "The Communist project", writes Klinau, "was not only a project of the Soviet Union. It's a European project [...] therefore, 'The City of the Sun' is a European monument, and only we in Minsk have it. There are only a few imperial style cities in Europe: Paris, Berlin, St Petersburg, Vienna, Rome and then... Minsk!"[5]

The KGB headquarters is on Independence Avenue, the most recent name (previously: Lenin, Stalin, and Skaryna, after an early printer in the Belarusian language) for the centrepiece of the city's post-war reconstruction. This street actually begins a quarter of a mile away, around some salvaged fragments of the pre-war city – a curiously stark redbrick Catholic church, a couple of art nouveau tenements, and two modernist buildings – Minsk University, hauled up on pilotis and shoved between thick and domineering classical wings, and the Constructivist House of Government, designed in the early 1930s by the architect Iosif Langbard for the governance of the Belarusian Soviet Socialist Republic. The House of Government has some similarities with the famous Gosprom, the earlier governmental buildings for the Ukrainian Soviet Socialist Republic, in its combination of high-rise scale, symmetry and a minimal, laconic Constructivism; it appears like a postConstructivist design from a distance, with its glazed stair towers like grand pillars, but closer up the cubistic geometry of the flanking wings roots the building back in the Twenties. It is a stylish design that deserves to be better known, but the gigantic square it commands is harder to admire.

The House of Government, and the flanking buildings of the University and the Brezhnev-era tower of the Metro headquarters look out at what is usually an empty, albeit incredibly clean square, surrounded by freshly painted buildings. What makes it amusing is that glass domes protrude out of the pavement, just as they do in Kyiv's Maidan Nezahelzhnosti (another "Independence Square") and in the Republic Square in Almaty, Kazakhstan,[6] and for the same reason – there is an underground shopping mall beneath. Unlike in Kyiv, the revolution attempted here in the 2000s – not fortuitously called the "Jeans Revolution" – quickly fizzled out from repression and indifference. Now, gatherings around the Lenin statue that still stands here are discouraged. As I took photos of it on my first time

Totalitarian Money Shot

in the city, a lone security guard slowly made his way to me and told me to stop, but I'd already taken half a dozen of them, one of which you can see here. The statue was sculpted by Matvey Manizer in 1933, and shows the Great Leader of the World Proletariat speaking from a frame-like platform which looks distinctly like tumbrils about to slam down on someone's head. The smaller high relief figures teeming around the leader hold aloft pitchforks. It is unmistakeably an image of revolutionary violence, of Red Terror. The square itself, though, is a useful reminder that Soviet urbanism, when it is genuinely Soviet – clean, upkept, largely uncommercialised – is a different matter to its more commonplace and casual current state, when the axes and formal ensembles have been allowed by dilapidation, decline and the absence or disinterest of a secret police force to be roughed up a bit and used.

The similarities and differences with Kyiv are especially indicative. Minsk looks richer and better managed, much less lively, a lot less

The KGB is watching you, unironically

Convivial Minsk

desperate, and a great deal more controlled. You can walk for miles before finding overbearing oligarchs' residences, giant ads, dereliction and dilapidation – though they're all there to be found – and the relentless cleanliness of the streets and buildings is a genuine shock for anyone used to Kyiv or even Warsaw. A few particularly impressive things stand out – the Post Office, florid, Piranesian and Roman, the domed Circus. The House of Books, with its Seventies ceramic abstract reliefs and its shrine to Lukashenka (this is the only thing I found of its kind – there is clearly a personality cult, though it is nowhere near on the scale of Putin, let alone a Nazarbayev). The local GUM, with its preserved atrium of stained-glass windows, frosted-glass uplighters and discounts for Heroes of the Soviet Union, is nice enough, but better is the Tentralny Store, with its marvellous open public colonnade of kiosks and stools, where Minskites hang out over shots, beers and pastries, under ceramic reliefs of peasants labouring to produce the grain liquors, sausages and fermented drinks we're consuming.

Socialist and capitalist liquids

The street entrance to the October Metro station also has an open public gallery, with meticulous mosaic depictions of the revolution, the Five Year Plans, the war and the conquest of space. There is a memorial here to the 2011 bombing of this station that followed one of Lukashenka's "elections", about which conspiracy theories unsurprisingly abound.

If Klinau's argument is to be taken seriously and we are to compare this planned city with St Petersburg or Vienna or Paris, the most obvious change has been the increased heaviness of the architecture. Not only in comparison with Petersburg's delicate classicism, but also with the already lumbering and graceless bulk of nineteenth-century imperial architecture. There are chubby columns and great sheaves of plaster wheat everywhere, the architectural equivalent of over-eating good stodgy, sugary food – fun for a while, but eventually leaving you somewhat bloated.

Large squares punctuate the street along its immense length. There is the *rond-point* of Victory Square, around the Victory Obelisk, framed by pretty classical buildings with open colonnades, lots of trees, and gateways to the local Gorky Park, and with a subterranean eternal flame for the Partisans. A permanent message across the tops of the curved gateway buildings tells you of the deathless deeds of the war. In one of the attractive blocks of flats here, Lee Harvey Oswald stayed on his journey to the USSR – there is a museum inside. I would learn on my second visit to the city that this was the most popular square with younger Minskites. Similarly relatively relaxed is Jakub Kolas Square, where again the Stalinist symmetry and ceremonial towers and gates manage to accommodate a fairly civilised urbanism, with people relaxing and sitting around. When I was here a young Ukrainian photographer told me that Belarusians, unlike their southern brethren, don't welcome conversations with strangers on park benches, a problem which, being English, failed to scandalise me.

Both of these spaces are most unlike the genuinely rather chilling October Square. It has two buildings: the Stalinist-Greek splendour

Entrance to October Metro Station

of the Trade Union Palace of Culture, with its pediment stuffed with proletarian giants, and the much later Palace of the Republic, a late-Soviet design not completed until the 2000s. Its stripped classicism is stern, mean. Nothing is allowed to disrupt the emptiness here, with any attempt to fill the space regularly refused, a permanent blast of abstract air, an abstracted and cinematic space for contemplation, rather than use. Most people, when placed here, would assume that they were in a dictatorship without needing to be told so. Although, as I later realised, it is actually the parallel streets nearby where you ought to be careful – the Presidential offices, and the tacky neo-Stalinist hotel alongside, are those where you should not be taking photographs, lingering or doing anything suspicious. Even here, what is and what isn't official can be confusing; in the basement of the stiffly Postconstructivist Military Club, with its tank on a plinth outside, is a student cafe selling hipster burgers. There is also one building so

Part of Victory Square

Proletarians of Mount Olympus

October Square

superb that it's worth risking wrath for photographing it – the terrific Constructivist National Library, replaced after independence with a building on the suburbs which we will come to, but regardless of its demotion, an avant-garde building of real rigour and drama.

My first impression was that Independence Avenue wasn't the *real* city street that the parallel post-war showpieces have become in the capitals of Germany, Ukraine, Poland, Russia, but that, like a showpiece still, it was to be admired more than used. This is only partially true – it is not a street for everyday business, but people have a great deal of attachment to it, and to the project of which it is a part. In a recent paper on the current usage of city's Stalinist centre, British-based Belarusian scholar Nelly Bekus argued that many of the activities of Minsk's "civil society" (to the extent it exists, which it does, in a sense) have involved trying to stop unsympathetic renovations to these buildings, such as a petition that successfully stopped the owners

The Constructivist Counter-Tradition

of a confectionery store from remodelling their 1950s interior – and an unsuccessful campaign against a hotel built next to the Circus.[7] In both cases, Soviet planning regulations were held up as a model that the city government hadn't measured up against.

The Prehistory of Minsk

The other aspect of Minsk as enlightenment metropolis is the "Green Diameter" of designated public space that runs through the city along the heavily engineered river Svislach. Independence Avenue crosses this at one point, and steps will take you down to Jakub Kolas Park, with its axial paths through the trees and a lovely, if strange landscaped river path. The buildings around have their towers and turrets arranged so as to exploit this sylvan scene, and stone spheres and urns punctuate the embankment. This is where Klinau's Sun City feels comparable to a genuine Renaissance town: in fact it's peculiarly French, owing much to utopian eighteenth-century architects like Boulee and Ledoux. Its only jarring note – although its planners would have found this appropriate – is the tall radio mast placed on one of the porticoes. Here, you can find one of the very rare salvaged buildings of the original city – a small wooden house which just happens to have been the building where the Russian Social Democratic Labour Party was founded. This is a particularly extreme example of utopian town planning as the shaping of a historical narrative – though it is not, as we will see, the only major historic building to be preserved in the city, it is, aside from the Church at Independence Square the only one to have been retained in the City of the Sun, as if to say "nothing much happened here, except the founding of the Party that eventually became the Bolsheviks (and the Mensheviks, of course)".

It is a totally ordinary but pretty clapboard house of the sort you can find absolutely anywhere between Kaunas and Vladivostok, set in a little fenced garden, its gates decorated with stylised hammers and sickles. It is still officially the House Museum of the Founding Congress of the Russian Social Democratic Party, but it doesn't seem to take that role particularly seriously. At the entrance are drawings of typical Victorian folk with their top hats, corsets and canes. Inside, I was told that the main exhibition is undergoing "remont", so all there was to see was an exhibition on prehistoric man. This consisted of waxworks of various Neanderthals and other Hominids, pulling dramatic facial expressions in plastic and paper undergrowth, accessorised anachronistically by a couple of dinosaurs, and a squirrel, like those that scurry around in the park outside. It is not entirely clear what this is doing here, presumably a reference to the fact that capitalism, as Marx once claimed, is humanity's prehistory.

You can keep going from here up Independence Avenue for more classical boulevarding, if you so wish, but if you turn onto Kuibyshev Street, you'll go past some of what Belarus has instead of adverts for European or Russian companies – happy families, with the legend

The Museum of the Founding Congress of the Russian Social Democratic Labour Party

"I Heart Belarus", and posters warning you against cybercrime, where masked baddies are ready to steal your password – until, on a disused factory, you'll eventually find your first giant advert for a Western corporation (a big Renault car, draped across a concrete walkway). Just past here is what can only be described, despite its inner-city location, as a *leafy suburb*, made up of a different class of socialist realist housing – two storeys with decorative pediments, more or less on the same scale as semi-detached houses, although they're actually flats. Like most things in Minsk, they are, as the architectural historian Dmitrij Zadorin points out, standardised, and we've already encountered some of the same type in Sillamäe. But added up together in the laid-back way they have been here, they make for a very pleasant townscape, usually arranged in a U-shape around little gardens. One of the streets curves around towards the Green Diameter, ending in the spire of

Minsk as a Neoclassical Village

one of the riverside Stalinist blocks. Some of these things, which we could call "house-flats", have obviously gone up in the world and become boutiques or offices for architects, others have very obviously not been renovated for a while. It was sad to hear from Zadorin that these are currently slated for demolition; not so much because they're great works of architecture, but because their earthy intimacy gives something to the city it wouldn't otherwise have.

One of these house-flats that obviously won't be demolished is the one redesigned into the Embassy of the Bolivarian Republic of Venezuela. Under Hugo Chávez, the country struck a cheap oil deal with fellow anti-American populist (although not fellow democrat) Lukashenka; Chávez visited Minsk, and spoke very highly of it, as you might expect – it is most of all from somewhere like Caracas that the order and (apparent) equality of Minsk would seem genuinely utopian.[8] After this villa district, you come to another pre-war remnant

A Bolshoi Ballet

– the Opera House, designed in the late 1930s, again by Iosif Langbard, this time in the postConstructivist fashion. It sits at the centre of a park, and is on a Cyclopean scale – a series of concrete cylinders rising one above the other, like a truncated Palace of the Soviets, and with yet more allegorical figures, this time of various arts as well as the usual workers and peasants. On my second visit to Minsk, I went with friends to the opera, to see Tchaikovsky's *The Queen of Spades*. I'm not entirely qualified to speak of its quality as a production (I was *told* it was good), but what I did notice was that in a capital where the cost of living – food, transport, and other essentials – is actually rather high, a good seat at the opera is outrageously cheap; most unlike behaviour at the same places in Western Europe, children wander around the chairs, and people whisper conversations to each other, with no reverent hush. What you get is a straightforward classical production in a lush hall, no innovations, no fuss, no development, with a heavy public

The advert marks this 1920s building for death

subsidy. This was the Brezhnev cosplay of Lukashenkism in a nutshell, the eternal preservation of the late Soviet Union, including its better aspects, but nothing more, nothing beyond it. Other friends went the same night to see a dissident theatre group performing in a private home, a phenomenon which is doubtless much part of this game of preserving the age of Stagnation forever as anything else.[9]

Standing on the steps of the Opera House, you can suddenly see a pretty little Baroque skyline, which the town plan has nowhere emphasised. From here, past the wasteland on which, until early 2017, a Constructivist office block stood, steps lead down from this giant object in space to what purports to be the only fully preserved piece of old Minsk. This is the Trinity Suburb, an area which partly escaped the destruction of the city in 1944, and which was partly reconstructed. It is puzzling why it was this place which was decided worthy of being pieced back together, and the effort is in no way convincing – no

Skyline of "European Minsk"

Modernist Minsk

Warsaw Old Town. First, the most genuinely picturesque part of the suburb, a row of classical houses, all painted in different colours, with delicate window details, is on a dual carriageway, and fenced off by metal bars, so that there's no way of appreciating it visually. Inside, cobbled courtyards enclose nondescript little houses, overpainted and buffed to such a sheen that those of them that are genuinely old are indistinguishable from the reconstructions. They market this place to tourists, hilariously, but even the most credulous would find the place's lack of atmosphere or history uncomfortably obvious.

From here, when you reach the Green Diameter, which becomes a river promenade, you can see that the preservation of the Stalinist capital which goes along a west-to-east axis does not extend to a similar care for the subsequently built modernist one along its green north-south axis. The major part of this modernist city, Victory Prospect, is a series of repeated towers, like a miniature, riverside version of

Modernism on the Way Out

Moscow's New Arbat, which has been clumsily supplemented by Minsk's stabs at Western business skyscrapers, whose height kill the attempted illusions of the Trinity Suburb. On either side of the river are – or rather were – the Brutalist Palace of Sport, and the crystalline box of the Exhibition of Economic Achievements, demolished in 2017. Presumably, its lack of *weight* marked it out for erasure in a city where even the best architecture is stuffy and stodgy. Barging into the river view here is a horrible block of new flats, courtesy of a developer nicknamed "Lukashenka's Wallet". Conspicuous largely because there is so little like it in Minsk (in Moscow, you wouldn't notice); it dominates everything around it as by far the largest single building in the city. It has been heavily criticised locally for doing damage to the Soviet ensemble of the Green Diameter, but rather shockingly, among the residents of this breathtakingly authoritarian edifice, is none other than the dissident conscience of Belarus herself,

Lukashenka's Wallet, Alexievich's Apartment

Svetlana Alexievich, who bought a big new flat there with her prize money after winning the Nobel.

On the other side of the river are further fragments of Old Minsk, a little less tawdry this time – Freedom Square, which is the source of that Baroque skyline. The towers belong to two Baroque counter-reformation churches of the eighteenth century, in a recognisably Polish-Lithuanian style (these churches are one of Belarus's claims to be genuinely "European", whatever that might mean in this context). Their twin spires and domes can abruptly appear in your view as a complete city-picture, which is of course the point, given that so little else – until very recently – has been allowed to obstruct them. Souvenir stalls do a quiet trade around a reconstructed City Hall, and something calling itself the Hôtel d'Europe. What is interesting here is that the "Old Town" is obviously expanding, with new construction of "Old Minsk" houses going on everywhere.

It has even expanded into the modernist areas of the city, as a stairwell

If there had been skyways in Pushkin's day

next to KFC leads up to a concrete walkway that has been redesigned into a Shtetl street in the sky. Under here, the Nemiga Metro station can lead you out into the suburbs.

The Minsk Metro is a quite typical Soviet Metro – in so far as this extraordinary typology is ever typical – of the 1980s, without the ultra-deep escalators that mark Kyiv, St Petersburg or Moscow, but with a later spin on their use of underground system as continuous artworks. Nizhny Novgorod has the most similar system, although unlike it, Minsk Metro has been constantly expanded since it was built, given that the command economy that made it possible has never quite been dismantled here. Signs are in Belarusian and English (with older, Russian signs visible in many stations), and announcements are in Russian – there seems to be no unified system of priority between Belarusian and Russian in the city, though the former predominates on signage, the latter on adverts. The trains are fast and frequent, and some of the stations are genuinely special – marble uplighters like torches at October and Victory Square, Sovietised folk art figures at Jakub Kolas, grand hangars at Tractor Factory and Vostok, and a hammer and sickle set into a globe shaped like a football at Lenin Square. The latter boasts a bust of Lenin set into a niche in its underpass, very like the one recently removed from Teatralna Metro station in Kyiv. Much as people rub the nose of the dog in Revolution Square station in Moscow for luck, here, passers by rub the nose of Lenin himself. It has been worn yellow by rubbing, and I watch a couple of people do it on their way out. It's the sort of superstition that would have utterly horrified the revolutionary leader, but it strikes me that this domestication of Soviet symbols might be a little bit more healthy than the government-sanctioned Leninoclasm in Belarus's southern neighbour.

There seems to be a dozen members of staff at any station at any one time, and they are cleaned, judging by the amount of times I saw people sweeping and mopping, almost constantly – that "artificial" system of full employment. Less encouraging is the evidence of the country's militarism; I see hundreds of soldiers in my two trips to the

Lenin's Nose

city, thin young men and women on military service, crammed into uniforms too big for them. More soldiers, in fact, are visible than in Kyiv or Dnipropetrovsk, in a country which was recently invaded.

Accidentally Fashionable

Minsk's Gallery of Art is part of the post-1945 Stalinist ensemble being hawked to UNESCO, just round the corner from Dynamo stadium and the KGB. To the outside, it is staid classicism, with statues in niches so similar to those in Warsaw's Palace of Culture and Science that I wouldn't be surprised if they were by the same sculptor. Inside is, first, an incredibly tedious exhibition of Russian art exactly like that you'd find in any medium-sized Russian provincial city, a dusty reminder of just how much the Soviets – at least in the Stalin era

Tractor Factory Station

– resembled the Victorians, with their jingoism, kitsch and liking for awful narrative painting. But, at one point, when you're annoyed at wasting your Belarusian roubles, these drab galleries give way to a Postmodernist extension, which has one of the best Soviet picture collections I've ever seen, along with a great selection of glassware and ceramics, all in a free style more often associated with Poland or the Baltics. The paintings tell a much more interesting story of the city than the one-dimensional Victory roar of the "City of the Sun". A Jewish-Belarusian-Lithuanian-Polish city with cobbled streets and tumbledown cottages appears in many of them, as do reminders of 1917 – a still life with jugs, a chess set and a copy of the futurist journal *Art of the Commune*. The Stalinist epic painting is of mainly historical interest, but the work of the Thaw was truly fascinating here, much of it, as in Yugoslavia, concerned with the Partisan war; the stand-out is Leonid Shchamialiou's "My Birth", where a newborn child is cradled by the swaddled figures in an abstracted snowscape. This is the kind of work which, in MOMAs from Berlin to Warsaw to Vilnius to Riga, is being rediscovered by hot young curators dabbling with the forbidden fruit of socialist realism; here, it is on the walls because it always has been.

The walk from the Academy of Sciences Metro station to the Centre for Contemporary Art provides an interesting insight into how Minsk is managed. These are humble, working-class streets, either in an attenuated Stalinist style with pitched roofs or simple brick *Khrushchevki*, many of which are being renovated – the surfaces are stripped off and then reapplied, mostly leaving residents' balcony extensions in place. But what is unusual here is the way that graffiti is treated. Graffiti is an ever present thing in Kyiv or Warsaw, and it can be nasty: the permeable line between the boasts of football ultras and anti-Semitic sloganeering. It's hard to know what the graffiti would be saying here, because it is all scrubbed off or blanked out; there is a law about insulting the president, after all. In the centre, the scrubbing is seamless, but not out here in the residential areas, where you notice

The Artist

The Gallery

that almost every tenement has one, two, three or four white or green rectangles painted onto its render or brickwork. The result is as if those bars that censor words or body parts in old newspapers were applied all over the city to its naughty bits and nether regions; an abstract image of a population silenced. You can see that the local sprayers are aware of this, so they do what they can – tags and stickers are on many of the street signs, which of course can't be painted over, and the eyes of the parents and children on a "SCHOOL" sign are blacked out. The gallery itself is in a redbrick 1980s building, and its exhibitions are excellent; October 2016 was "Minsk Photography Month", so these were photo series, one of them on the street markets of the region, another on the evergreen topic of "concrete", with some great work by young photographers. It was all very low budget indeed, mostly consisting of colour printouts sellotaped to the wall.

That's about as much unofficial culture as I managed to find in the capital of Belarus, I'm afraid. Official culture is best represented

...

by the National Library of Belarus, a nation-building monument for a country pejoratively without nationalism. A friend had taxed me with the task of finding a Lukashenka magnet for him during my stay, but I couldn't find any, just dozens of magnets and other trinkets featuring this extraordinary building, the only genuinely post-Soviet construction in the city of any significance. It is a giant, opaque blue glass cube with a tapered top and bottom, a 2001 monument dropped on an immense square in the Vostok district, opposite a *Mikrorayon* whose blocks are each decorated with Soviet frescoes. Designed in the 1990s by architects Vinogradov and Kramorenko, finished in the 2000s, and intended as a monument to Belarusian independence, the Library is undeniably impressive – flirting with kitsch, which doesn't make it particularly unusual among Minsk's earlier monumental architecture, it will doubtless become as much of a slightly ironic cult object as its Soviet predecessors. Next to it is a building site, with a large nearly completed shopping mall, covered in the usual "Happy People of Belarus" advertisements. At the bus stop next to the Vostok Metro station entrance is a long, straight queue of people in single file, waiting for transport to the further suburbs. Looming behind the library and the half-finished mall are dozens of new prefabricated tower blocks, a new *Mikrorayon* emerging.

The Lukashenka regime's censorship, its lack of any meaningful democracy or autonomous institutions, its conscription, and its alleged suppression of the "true" national identity of the country, all only partly explain its longevity. According to Bekus, Belarus has long been unusual in the region for maintaining a public housing system, with waiting list, subsidies, public ownership and suchlike; but these are private. The social settlement that has kept Lukashenka in power for all this time is coming apart, as Russia demands its pound of flesh for its years of subsidy; in some government circles, dismantlement of the Belarusian welfare state is being proposed for the first time. From only having provincial "minigarchs", its system may begin to resemble Russia and Ukraine: the monstrous tower barging into the Green Diameter

At least you can admire the mosaics while waiting for the bus

The Icon of Belarus

is a little preview of what might be to come. What will happen then? Belarusians have certain things that, however much they're criticised, are rather attractive when compared with Ukraine, Moldova, Russia, even Poland. A more detached relation to the recent past, a relative lack of the xenophobia, obsessive victimhood and cultural aggro that mar so many post-Communist countries, some retention of certain aspects of a Soviet culture of social planning – none of these are things to be embarrassed by. Could they ever be combined with genuine democracy, a free public sphere, freedom to protest, and an end to the petty bureaucracy, thuggery, militarism and arse-kissing that Lukashenka has continued from the Soviets? It seems unlikely, but then stranger things have happened here.

Eternal Return

I don't want to put words into their mouths, but this seemed to be part of the project of the sixth Minsk Architectural Forum, an annual workshop for young architects organised by the Belarusian Association of Student Architects. Its organisers, Stefania Soich and Arzu Mirzalizade, had – as is usual for the forum – little financial assistance from the official Union of Architects or Minsk's architecture schools, and what money there is was raised from the sponsorship of a paper manufacturer. I was invited to the forum in March 2017, and got to spend another fortnight in the city. While I'd spent my first week there six months earlier in a swish Western hotel in the city centre, this time I was placed into a very, very different area, one which made the alternately admirable and infuriating things about Belarus acutely obvious.

The Hrushauka district was laid out in the early twentieth century, on the wrong side of the railway tracks. Until a couple of years ago, it would have consisted only of wooden houses and some scattered *Khrushchevki*. The wood of the houses is painted and treated, and gardens behind make it feel deeply rural, although you're actually only a couple of miles from the centre. The pre-revolutionary bungalows were supplemented during the 1930s with an equally sleepy and only semi-urban new plan, where wooden barracks, a few very low-rise tenements and a little House of Culture stand in the densely wooded streets. There's a plaque to say that the "legendary hero of the Civil War", General Shchors, lived round here, and until the Metro station was built a couple of years ago, he'd have probably found little to surprise him here, though he would otherwise have been disappointed by the world a hundred years after the socialist revolution he fought for. This is the sort of place all of Minsk must have been until the war and until the City of the Sun was built, a strange industrial Shtetl. But the Metro has brought development here, and there's intensive building of new high-rises all over, just behind the wooden houses (not, thus far, replacing them). I spent my two weeks in one of these, and got to see others being built, where you could see the panels being lifted into place by crane as if it were still 1980. Hrushauka is Minsk on brand.

Second Shchors Street

Modernisation

I used the opportunity while back in the city to try and confirm some suspicions and hunches. Going to the microdistricts of the 1970s and 1980s were evidence that Minsk really did treat its mass housing better than any comparable city, with complete Styrofoam and render programmes making these arrangements of prefabricated jigsaw shapes bright and shiny. Many of them were already architecturally interesting. An exemplary ensemble is at the far end of Victory Prospect, which must, judging by the plaques for film directors, have been high-end at the time, jagged and rectilinear, with sharp asymmetrical balconies at the corners. The Minsk ghetto was here, not that you would know it. If you search long enough, you can find a monument in one of the ravines where the dead were thrown. One of the paradoxes of Minsk is that while cities whose record during the Holocaust is vastly worse trumpet everything anybody did for the Jews, here the extraordinary events recounted by Barbara Epstein in her book on the ghetto are just ignored, as if they're just not interesting. This could be because of anti-Semitism – Lukashenka, typically, has

Microdistrict on Ghetto

said some highly unhelpful things in this regard, asking for "rich Jews" to visit the towns their grandparents came from – or it could just be a continuation of the Soviet narrative where the murdered Jews were just "Soviet citizens". So they were, but it's not enough.

Over the river, there are towers in Op Art patterns, though they're in part of a plan that shows the limitations of these places – empty, desolate, with huge and useless public spaces and few facilities, with the propaganda posters mocking the vacuity. The one that looked most actually livable was in the Komarkovka district, where the panels are twisted and twirled into tubular edifices around a vaulted market hall, giving it a focus that these places too often lack. Nearby is an extraordinary piece of junkspace, with warehousing and light industry turned into the centralised shopping centre that Independence Avenue is so obviously not, selling all the essentials, whether second-hand hand-knitted folksy jumpers or Chinese-made underwear with labels

I Love Belarus

Propaganda and 4G

saying "ART "or "MANTEGZ". There's a "Windmill" in the middle of it. It is still as spotlessly clean as everything else.

The other confirmed suspicion was about the city's big new building project – the Museum of the Great Patriotic War of the Republic of Belarus. The design is a remix of several other buildings, a monument in Riga and the Great Patriotic War Museums in Moscow and Kyiv, except with a shattery-effect thing going on, like a mall designer had tried to do Danny Libeskind. It's an awful, awful piece of architecture – tacky, vacuous and patronising, and much the same is true of the exhibits, which have a huge quantity of hand-holding edutainment – big aeroplanes, reconstructed huts and trenches – and neo-Brezhnevite propaganda, which as always, crowds out anything on the partisan warfare that was so crucial here. The unique, extraordinary things that happened in Belarus and pretty much only in Belarus, downplayed in favour of the war experience that every

Children's story

Soviet citizen knew – the giant battles, Stalingrad, Kursk, Bagration, all of them obviously important to any telling of the war, but here supporting the proposition made by scholars like David Marples that what Lukashenka's cult of the war is really about is cementing the world as it appeared to Soviet citizens in the first half of the 1980s as a new national narrative, bolstered with all the paraphernalia and pageantry of nation-building. But when you make it to the room on the Partisans inside this blustery, empty place, it's shattering. The laconically related stories here, and the simple photographs of ordinary working-class people who decided to risk their lives to fight against fascism and for their persecuted neighbours, are extremely moving, especially because they don't tell you too much – it's hard to read them without welling up. But you could almost miss it, and never mind – there's a reconstructed Partisan hut in the woods next to these panels to fill in the gaps for you.

Teaching Minskness

The format of the Architectural Forum is that four groups of students work on a project on a chosen theme, which in 2017 was defining *Minskness*, and its expression in the city's many, often large and formal, public squares. I wasn't expecting the scene when I arrived at the forum's venue: the Zair Azgur Museum, dedicated to a mediocre Stalinist-era sculptor. On steel shelves reaching all up to the ceiling of a triple-height space, in a tiny redbrick building in a housing estate, are dozens of busts and statues of notables, writers, revolutionaries and dictators. Mao, Churchill, Thomas Mann, Immanuel Kant, Khrushchev, Kim il Sung, Stalin, and around twenty different Lenins. Usually the place is open to the public, but presumably interest in it is so low that some architecture students could take it over for two weeks without anyone asking to see their favourite bust of Taras Shevchenko. It was an ingenious place to choose for the students – most of whom have lived all their lives under Alyaksandr Lukashenka – to confront the question of Minskness. The way in which they sat around casually when surrounded with this (literal) overpowering weight of authoritarianism was striking – they didn't look like they were constantly oppressed by the legacies of totalitarianism. They looked like they thought it was funny, which, given it includes, for instance, a statue of Felix Dzerzhinsky cradling a small child, it is, in its dark way.

The forum happened to coincide with the anniversary of the beginning of the Russian Revolution. In March 1917, women's day protests spiralled into a strike wave that brought down the Tsar. Minsk's response? A poster campaign celebrating "100 Years of the Belarusian Police". Downplaying the revolution, even given that this revolution founded the Soviet state that is venerated here, was not so strange, given that a protest wave – against a tax on the unemployed, given that full employment here is finally collapsing under the weight of the financial crisis – was spreading, quietly, around the

The Zair Azgur Museum

country; many analysts were surprised that it wasn't the usual suspects anymore, the nationalists and liberals who turn up to get arrested every independence day, but people who had never been on protests before. The public squares that are so well suited to protest, so open and available, yet so obviously a showcase of power and planning, that the students were supposed to focus on. Ukrainian sociologist Natalia Otrichenko's students developed a series of metrics and graphs to find out how well these spaces were used (don't be disabled in Minsk, was one obvious lesson); Dimitrij Zadorin's group proposed turning the shabby, ignored courtyards behind the grand Stalinist façades into community spaces.

My students researched two squares of different eras: Station Square, of the crenellated twin towers, and Freedom Square. The idea was that the two would apparently contrast with each other, in that one is very post-Soviet, with cramped underpasses full of people selling flowers, pies and lottery tickets, while the other – as the students informed me, to my surprise – has become the city's main hipster district, with craft beer and homemade blinis under those ersatz heritage façades. But both of them, they found, were state projects. In fact, Freedom Square's start-ups and small cafes are carefully managed by a city-run, profit-making Minsk Heritage Company. The students produced a critical brochure for the two squares, where the enticing gateways open out to show a much more complex reality of state capitalism and constantly manipulated heritage. I can say this without fear of exaggeration, having taught in various Western European cities – these were excellent students, largely because of their conservative education giving them superior technical skills, and the internet, and the proximity of far freer architecture schools in Warsaw and Moscow, making them fully aware of what else is out there. All four groups were sharply satirical in their work, but satire has to be subtle here. Cynical comments on the authorities are normal, but nobody ever mentions the president. Anthropologist Michal Murawski's group decided to put all the things they don't like about the city – anti-social interactions, ubiquitous kitsch, surveillance and policing – and throw it into a bowl of borscht, with the Dynamo Minsk stadium as the bowl. When they unveiled the project to the public at the end of the forum, the students – all dressed in matching borscht-coloured outfits – were keen to distinguish between the Sovok, the remnants of Soviet attitudes, especially to authority, and the Soviet, which they thought could still mean something different to the deeply conservative policies of Minsk's contemporary rulers. The protests were eventually suppressed – a straggling demonstration in the snow on Jakub Kolas Square was rounded up into vans, and that was that, for now. But protest will be back, and when it is, those Soviet public spaces are going to be crucial. To see them being approached with such humour and nuance made me think that Belarusian architects might, one day, do something unique, when they're allowed to.

More than this, there is nothing

LIFE IN THE TWENTY-FIRST CENTURY

MOSCOW, Moskwa

The Capital of Capitalist Realism

Another first impression: Moscow, spring 2010.

Welcome to Moscow

The Hotel Kosmos, an oversized brown glass crescent surrounding a statue of De Gaulle, stylised into a cylindrical moustachioed hat-wearing tube. A lobby full of sex workers, bored, waiting for you to catch their eye, at which point they would be sure to hold it. A Chinese restaurant that charged around a week's wages for sweet and sour pork. In front, an elevated flyover, with a constant churn of traffic, above and below. Just beyond it, two monuments, one of them, the "Worker and Kolkhoz Woman" by Vera Mukhina, familiar to anyone who has ever watched a Mosfilm, the other, the Space Obelisk, describing a skyward sweep, both of them clad in shiny, silvery titanium, and placed as if to be visible from the cars speeding past, each of which seemed to be belching out lead of a density that could almost make you nostalgic. At ground level, a chaos of kiosks selling everything from socks to pies to maps to porn. Beyond the motorway, past the Metro station, a Stalinist theme park – the Exhibition of Economic Achievements, whose spires and domes I could see through the traffic fumes from my hotel window.

Walking around it the next morning, this park, with an asphalt pedestrian boulevard at its centre, was lined with the most disgustingly exquisite Stalinist architecture. A metal dome for the Kosmos, with a space rocket outside, was placed on axis with a miniature version of one of the seven Moscow skyscrapers that were built, like this Exhibition of Economic Achievements (the Russian acronym is VDNKh), in the decade after the war. Most were national pavilions, all around a golden fountain, watched over by golden women representing the various Slavic, Baltic, Turkic, Caucasian peoples of the empire, sorry, Union. An open latticework for Uzbekistan, a delicate piece of Orientalism, seemingly designed for some ornate tea ceremony. A patterned entrance for Kyrgyzstan, like a Stalinist magic carpet. A thick wooden pediment with whole wooden figures for Karelia. A little Neoclassical temple for Armenia. And most stupendously of all, an extraordinary palace for Ukraine, dripping with intricate ornament, gold, bronze and marble. But if you went into any of these you found… not much. Kebab stalls. Pet shops. Bric-a-brac. Or, just nothing at all.[1] None of it made any sense, nothing was being used, and nothing was being valued, although the wealth on display was enough to make the average "dictator's home" look like a *Khrushchevka*.

I had never been in a city so apocalyptic, so cruel. I found it disturbing, and, guiltily, I found it thrilling. I have been back at least once a year since, but the last time I visited was in May 2017. By this time, VDNKh was undergoing some sort of restoration. The buildings were inhabited by something close to their original functions, with the Kosmos pavilion having stuff about the cosmos in it, for instance – though what exactly the government that was busy dismembering the non-architectural Ukraine was proposing to do with its pavilion was unclear. Retro-Fifties burger stalls occupied the space that seven years ago was taken by real estate ads and cat exhibitions. The grass was cut, the buildings clean – the only thing that hadn't changed was

The Ukrainian Pavilion

the horrific traffic around the site and the overpowering air of being out of time, by now consciously and ironically.

The attempted transformation of VDNKh is part of a wider project that aims, among other things, to change the capital of the Russian Federation and former capital of the Union of Soviet Socialist Republics into what is called nowadays a "liveable city". This is a fairly impressive thing to attempt, because the overwhelming first impression that a newbie must have to this city is of its extreme inhospitality, something which is now often caused by the intrusive roadworks that are meant to eventually make for a more hospitable city. There are pockets where you can get some idea of how Moscow was once a very pleasant and rather irrational city of winding paths, fascinatingly complex churches with onion domes and twisted confectionery skylines, but they have been supplemented with a harsh city of enormous wide streets, ultra-authoritarian classical architecture, and hideous traffic.

Much of this can be blamed on the Soviet Union itself, obviously.[2] There are some planning decisions that are genuinely baffling, that create spaces of staggering inhumanity. By this I do not necessarily mean the sort of widescreen axes by which the Stalinist capital created a setpiece city, particularly through the erection of seven skyscrapers at strategic points around the city – yes, these make you feel incredibly small, yes, this is the pure expression of despotic power, but after a certain amount of time architecture that does this is unironically adored the world over, from Washington to Delhi to Rome. What I mean is things like the picture on this page, showing the traffic intersection that leads past one of those seven towers, the high-rise apartments on Kotelnicheskaya Embankment, at the confluence of the rivers Moskva and Yauza. There is a pedestrian crossing here somewhere, but it is hard to work out exactly where it is quick enough to avoid being beeped at by the most malevolent drivers in Europe, who have decided, for their own reasons, not to use what is arguably its best Metro system.[3] What makes it all the worse is that this is actually the point where a decent bit of nineteenth-century planning, the continuous parkway of the Boulevard Ring, meets the river – that is, it should be one of the most pleasant and most important parts of the city, but instead, it's a terrifying wasteland. This is just one example, but the USSR provided around a dozen of these around the city. But rather than reforming this, and creating a more pleasant, more humane city, the mayor elected in the early 1990s, Yuri Luzhkov, concentrated on making it, if anything, nastier, meaner, and more hostile to pedestrians. The difference is that this time, a few people (Luzhkov included, who was married to the city's biggest property developer) were making a *lot* of money.

Rather puzzlingly for a city that was supposedly enjoying its

Why did the chicken cross the road?

newfound freedom and democracy, what seemed to define Luzhkov's rule was an embrace of the aesthetics and architecture of Stalinism, and a total crushing of public opposition. As Anna Shevchenko, who worked as an architect under Luzhkov and a journalist during the rule of his successor, tells me, "There was no public participation in Luzhkov's city whatsoever (nor was there in the late-Soviet one), final decisions were made behind closed doors. Technically there was the Urban Planning Council, where all major projects had to be presented", but it was easily dominated by a "mayor known for his great passion for architecture and very specific aesthetic views. Sometimes there were public protests in most outrageous cases, but those were basically ignored." The resulting architecture was dripping with bling, and defined once again by domes, spires, and ziggurat-like proportions. Much of it was built by more or less the same institutionalised architectural firms that had been designing modernist ensembles a decade or so earlier;[4] but whereas they had their maybe chilling, maybe authoritarian public squares and places of shelter and repose, here everything was shoved into everything else, in much the same way as the cars were often to be found parked on the pavement. New towers were dripping in bling, in sculpture, in spires and in references to the buildings of Stalin, and to the bizarre style of the VDNKh. Many of these could be found in the city centre, poking out at random; the tallest, at the time of writing the tallest residential building in Europe, the Triumph Palace, was in a post-industrial backyard lot in the city's northern suburbs.

It's hard to pick out one in particular from these examples of Stalinist architecture minus planning, but the tower which most encapsulated the open malevolence, the almost gleeful embrace of evil and avarice, was something called the Patriarch Building, just next to the ponds which readers of Bulgakov's *Master and Margarita* will know well. Luxury apartment blocks are not a new typology in Moscow, but in the 1970s and 1980s, they would, unsurprisingly given they were built in what claimed to be a classless society, be careful

The patriarch

not to make too much of a show of themselves – Muscovites can spot them by their brick façades, applied to quite restrained ten-storey buildings. The Luzhkov generation of buildings didn't want to hide that they were housing a new ruling class, they were screaming it from the rooftops. So, designed in the early 2000s by Sergei Tkachenko/SPAT Architects, the Patriarch Building hogs every plausible inch of chargeable rent on its plot of land,[5] rising to twice the height of every other building on the street, on a corner site. It is for most of its elevation a fairly normal Neoclassical apartment block, but on the roof it has a protrusion of heroic statues, very much on the model of the heroic workers and peasants who stand on top of each pavilion at VDNKh. These are in the likeness of the property developers who sponsored the building. Then at the very top, is a model of Vladimir Tatlin's Monument to the Third International, hauled up as the severed head of the dream of liberty, equality and fraternity. The Patriarch loomed over Patriarch's Ponds, constantly visible over the trees, something which even the beefy Stalinist luxury flats built round here between the Thirties and Fifties considered to be bad manners, but it was always possible to change the old architecture, to make it be more in keeping with the new.

Throughout the 1990s and 2000s, developers would frequently add a few extra storeys onto a historic building, listed or otherwise. Classical palazzi that had survived post-revolutionary iconoclasm, Stalin, and the aggressive modernisation of the Brezhnev era, suddenly sprouted three-, four-, five-storey extensions, in an approximation of their original styles. The efforts of the civic activists that were widely expected by liberal observers to have more influence in a capitalist than a command-socialist urban economy were almost entirely in vain, constantly appealing abroad for funds in order to help them fight the barbarism of their now freely elected representatives. Probably the culmination of this, almost comic in its corruption, was the reconstruction of the famous Hotel Moskva, which enthusiasts for high-quality hard liquor will know as the building on the Stolichnaya bottle. This hotel, designed in the mid-1930s by Alexey Shchusev, was famous for its two contrasting (though equally Neoclassical) wings, something sometimes ascribed, although sadly without any evidence, to be the result of Stalin unknowingly signing off two different drafts. Rather than restoring it, its owners, with the full enthusiastic support of Luzhkov's administration, decided instead to tear it down and then rebuild it in replica, this time with a multi-storey car park underneath it, something the original foundations would never have been able to handle. The contrasting wings, of course, were faithfully reproduced. The saddest sight of all was the Narkomfin building, a collective housing project designed at the end of the 1920s by the Constructivist Moisei Ginzburg. Here, the lobbying of the conservationists stopped it from being destroyed, but was unable to do much else, as one of the most important buildings of the twentieth century, the blueprint for Le Corbusier's housing complexes, literally fell to pieces, shedding

Pomo vulture waits for Narkomfin to die

pieces of concrete and render, held together with bits of tin and wood. Looking over it constantly was a repulsive Stalinist-Vegas edifice by the son of the eminent Stalinist designer Mikhail Posokhin, lurking as if waiting to devour its corpse, and then erect a granite veneer and gold glass oligarch's castle in its place.

The Other South Bank

It is hard to praise what happened after Luzhkov was dismissed from office by the decree of then-President Dmitry Medvedev and replaced with Sergey Sobyanin, as someone will inevitably assume that what you're doing is endorsing the Putin narrative, whereby an anarchic "chaos" in the 1990s was followed by a return to normality and order under his rule. In most respects, Luzhkov and Sobyanin are the same beasts. Both members of Putin's United Russia Party, both have repressed protest, banned Pride marches, and both have embraced, in their different ways, the Stalinist legacy. But the fact is, Moscow is a more pleasant, better run city now than it was in 2010. It is not Barcelona, it isn't even London, but it is considerably easier to walk around it, it is less obnoxious to look at, and something resembling viable public space has been created. As Anna Shevchenko points out, this was part of how Sobyanin tried to differentiate himself from the "chutzpah" of his "autocratic" predecessor. The means by which this has occurred are frequently dubious, aggressive and predicated on the outright dispossession of small businesses. I find the regime that is based in this city repugnant, a rapacious, socially conservative government that is both corrupt and corrupting, and which has covered itself in blood in Chechnya, Ukraine and Syria. Saying that town planning here is better than it used to be may, I hope, be appreciated as damning with faint praise

The best way to approach what has changed is to begin at Kropotkinskaya Metro station, and cross the bridge that connects the emetic Cathedral of Christ the Saviour, a fusion of Luzkhov's "creative" approach to architectural heritage, megamall kitsch and ingenious property development (another underground car park!) to the House on the Embankment, a sprawling, early-1930s housing complex, and then walk for a mile along the south bank.Part of what has happened here is the consequence of Soviet planning, particularly the development of the south bank of the river between the 1930s, when Gorky Park, the prototype for the distinctive Soviet version of the Victorian municipal park, was first laid out along with a public embankment to the river, and the 1970s, when the Tretkayov Gallery on Krymsky Val was built in a parkland setting. The gallery very roughly represents the Brezhnev-era equivalent of the Tate Modern, to the original art nouveau/neo-muscovy gallery's Tate Britain. Curatorial accident – inheriting both an extensive official Soviet collection and half of collector George Costakis' haul of marginalised and ignored avant-garde work – has meant that this place easily has one of the best collections of modern art in Europe, and from Perestroika onwards, it was actually able to show it off, rather than keeping it in a basement beneath fifth-rate landscapes. The 1970s building is a laconic,

The home of the government, from the House of Government

slightly staid modern block, its clear International Style lines clad in marble, and given highly Seventies Soviet futurist bling chandeliers. In the Nineties, it was supplemented with Moscow's equivalent of the various statue graveyards which are so popular in the Warsaw Pact countries, though its scattered Lenins, Brezhnevs and Dzerzhinskys are a superfluous gesture in a locale where an actual monumental Lenin statue is just outside Oktyabrskaya Metro station, a short walk away.

Next to this is the Strelka, a "spit" jutting into the river, which was densely covered with factories in the late nineteenth and early twentieth century, mainly the redbrick storeys of the Red October confectionery works. Here, the by now traditional manner in which "creative class" regeneration takes place, has done so, with various start-ups, museums and galleries using the open-plan spaces of the old factories. Noting that this was an "artistic" place to be, the Luzhkov administration made its own contribution in the form of a colossal

Fallen monuments and Luzhkov architecture outside the new Tretyakov

'eter

work by his favourite sculptor, the Georgian muralist turned bronze kitschmeister Zurab Tsereteli, depicting Peter the Great atop a specially created artificial island in the river, an extremely complicated piece of engineering embarked upon for no perceptible good reason. It was originally refused by St Petersburg, and so foisted instead on the city that Peter hated for its irrationality and backwardness, and which hated him for moving the capital to a Swedish village on a poisoned marsh in the Gulf of Finland. By now, it has joined the fallen monuments as an example of ludicrous, flatulent sculptural folly, but also as a peculiar bedfellow for the so much more cultured, so much more Western, Strelka School of Architecture. Here, the usual consortium of oligarchical investors commissioned a group of prominent European architects and critics to set them up a proper architectural school, one that would offer scholarships to post-Soviet students and train them in the sort of architecture that Nineties/

Strelka

Noughties Moscow didn't do: civic, modernist, logical. Certain things about "Luzhkov's Moscow" would continue – the Strelka bar is insanely expensive, for instance – but the opposition of these ad hoc looking, lightweight buildings, with their open public terraces, to the kitsch, heavy and relentlessly privatised city around, is real rather than imaginary.

Along the riverfront, further experiments in this elegant, public-spirited, hipster urbanism continued. Gorky Park, so the narrative goes, was, before the Strelka-trained architects and enlightened oligarchs got to it, a place of street drinking and street sleeping, decaying Ferris wheels and a ubiquitous air of naff commercialisation, sadness and decline – which very much describes VDNKh as I first encountered it, though I never visited Gorky Park at the time so I can't comment whether this is exaggeration for the purposes of smoothing over the purposes of development, though it does not strike me as implausible. The first stage of the redevelopment of the park was a temporary home for the Garage Museum of Contemporary Art, founded by the asset-stripper and Chelsea owner Roman Abramovich's (ex)-partner, Dasha Zhukhova, as something to do with her immense fortune; it gets its name from its first temporary home, a Constructivist bus garage in the inner suburbs. Their first purpose-built home made clear how different this was going to be from Luzhkov architecture, but also the staid modernism of the 1970s represented by the New Tretyakov (which, around this time, escaped being destroyed in favour of a Norman Foster scheme in the shape of a glass tangerine in the process of peeling itself). No marble, no gold, no bronze, no statues, no ornament. In fact, the new building was made of paper, the trademark material of Shigeru Ban, whose semi-temporary buildings in disaster areas such as post-earthquake Christchurch are constructed from cardboard tubes. It's hard to express just how strange this image of lightness, ecological scrupulousness and recyclability appeared in this pompous city. Of course what it did was the same as what happens at these places everywhere else – a good-to-indifferent series of exhibitions, a gift shop, a cafe, but this shift was nonetheless huge.

Following it a couple of years later was the permanent building for the museum. The designers here were the Office for Metropolitan Architecture, whose most prominent partner, Rem Koolhaas, was involved in Strelka from early on. Created out of the shell of a derelict club built in the 1960s, OMA have created the new building with a delicacy and wit barely imaginable ten years ago, taking obsessive care of the original fabric while building a smooth, crystalline new pavilion around it. This deference is unsurprising from architects who have always, from their first efforts in paper architecture in the 1970s, regarded Soviet modernism with a semi-religious awe, as the moment where a progressive technocratic society and an architecture to match met in an impossible utopian moment. "Modernity is our antiquity", runs a current artworld catchphrase, and OMA's Garage Museum is the Soviet modernist Palace of Knossos. A mosaic of a woman floating

Shigeru Ban's cardboard garage

OMA's Palace of Knossos

The art of an ancient civilisation

through some sort of abstracted parkland in the 1960s cafe has been revealed and restored with the sort of reverence Arthur Evans gave towards Minoan frescoes of women gymnasts. As in Crete, the actual ruins have been supplemented by new construction techniques into an imaginary idea of what the past might have looked like that most archaeologists would baulk at. There is none of the clunk and thud of so much Soviet modern architecture in OMA's additions, which transform a workaday building into something sleek and glamorous.

The gallery's gestures may be questionable, but the park and embankment had by 2017, become a hugely successful space, easily comparable in its density of posing people in their twenties and thirties to the South Bank of the Thames, which is appropriate given that the development of that embankment as London's cultural centre at the start of the 1950s was modelled on the example of Gorky Park. There shouldn't really be anything impressive about this – a city of

Virgin Mary, chase out Putin

twelve million people having a nice, central public place where middle-class young people go is not particularly unusual, nor should it be specially applauded as if creating it is some sort of special achievement. But in Moscow it really is a real leap in quality. As if recognising this, the current theory is that young Muscovites have been allowed this thing as a way of stopping them from protesting – after all, Bolotnaya Square, where the protests against "Managed Democracy" began in 2012, is near enough to Gorky Park. The Cathedral of Christ the Saviour, whose lumpy excrescences look over all of this as a mockery of any attempts at good taste, was the target of the action that landed three members of Pussy Riot in prison. That's as may be. The fact remains that if these places had been created in Saakashvili's Tbilisi, or – fat chance – Vitaly Klitschko's Kyiv, we would hear endlessly about how they were great examples of civil society-led normal European urbanism. Maybe normal European urbanism isn't always created by democratic means. Certainly, that's the lesson provided by what Strelka and the new Moscow urbanists did next.[6]

Civilise My Street

Strelka shifted around this time from influencing society via teaching and publishing into straightforwardly advising the Mayoralty of Sergey Sobyanin in a semi-official capacity, as he set about using the blunt and deeply corrupt instrument that is Russian state power to achieve the school's stated aims. A green city, a walkable city, a city that respects and preserves its architectural heritage, a city with breathable air, a city which commissions world-class architecture – large chunks of central Moscow has become this at the hands of essentially the same people who made it barely liveable twenty years earlier. In addition, the means to make this liveable city were the same harsh and legally opaque means that Luzhkov used to personally enrich himself and his circle. There has been much criticism of one of the major parts of the Sobyanin programme, known as "My Street", for the constant roadworks and pavement reconstructions they have meant, but then the scale of the problem was, in fairness, enormous.[7] But in my case I was in the enviable position, as someone that doesn't actually live in Moscow, of being able skip all of that and, first, see the bulldozers have a go at the surface of Tverskaya – the former Gorky Street, the main north-south ceremonial axis that runs from the Belarus Railway Station to Red Square, built mostly in the second half of the 1930s – and then to see the results.

And the results were very good. Like most of central Moscow's main streets, Tverskaya had been choked by traffic, turned essentially into a runway for dangerous driving enthusiasts, and its street life defined by that particularly Muscovite combination of gimcrack kiosks and obscenely expensive restaurants. What "My Street" did here was repave the pavements, double their width, add maps and directional information for those unfamiliar with the city (quite a leap in Moscow) and the addition of new benches and seat furniture to encourage people to hang around and linger here. It's simple enough, but there it is. The squares along the street have been changed as well: at Triumfalnaya, an elevated square next to a statue of Mayakovsky that was an unofficial Speaker's Corner during the 1960s, that ultimate faintly infantile hipster gesture has been added – swings, along with the seats, for the young things to pretend they're even younger things. The contradictions all come out especially sharply at Pushkin Square. This 1920s-1960s Soviet creation entailed taking a typical bit of old Moscow – two storey houses, churches, etc. – and first building a Constructivist office block for the Soviet newspaper *Izvestia*, then demolishing a historic monastery, then adding two later modernist buildings, the pop-futurist Rossiya Cinema and a clumsy extension to *Izvestia*, all around a statue of Pushkin at the centre of a green square.

A few years ago, the original 1920s *Izvestia* housed a KFC and was usually covered by a giant canvas advertisement, and kiosks ran the way down the extension. It was still very much a place to meet people, but it was shabby. Now, the Constructivist headquarters, designed by Grigori Barkhin in 1926, has been restored as scrupulously and closely

Making sense of Moscow

Capitalism restores Constructivism

to the original as possible— a rare restoration of a building of this era that follows the highest international standards. This was, not long ago, simply unimaginable – Luzhkov seemed to reserve a particular animus for Moscow's unrivalled heritage of interwar modernism, and even when buildings did get restored, it was usually at a price, as with Konstantin Melnikov's Svoboda Workers Club north of the centre, where the exterior was reasonably accurate, but the investors managed to transform the inside into a neo-Tsarist palace. But now, these buildings, these products of the least hidebound and outward-looking period of the Soviet Union, when it led the world in planning and architecture, are actually being decently treated.

I nearly spat out my Piroshka on a tram passing the Rusakov Workers Club in 2016, seeing a building I had assumed would always be a vague shadow of the astonishingly ambitious, internationally pivotal structure Konstantin Melnikov designed in 1927, restored

Rusakov Club, 2011

to the point of even using its original typography, and reinstating windows that had been blocked up for most of the building's existence. An Azeri restaurant that had nestled itself in the corner had been unceremoniously removed, and the building used as an arts theatre. Similarly serious restorations had been carried out at the Communal House of the Textile institute, and at the ZIL Palace of Culture, and at the time of writing, it is, apparently, about to happen to the most famous ruined modernist building in the world, the Narkomfin. And yet. There is something queasy about this. The pugilistic, punched-out volumes of the Rusakov read "TRADE UNIONS, SCHOOL OF COMMUNISM", in a capitalist country that represses trade unions. At *Izvestia*, the sexy 1920s typography reinstated at the top of the block refers once again to the USSR, a country that does not exist. I was reminded that a Moscow preservationist told me around 2011 that their strategy was shifting to convincing oligarchs of the value of this apparently uninteresting heritage – they were perpetually embarrassed, it transpired, at parties in New York, London and Paris when asked if they collected the Constructivists, because they didn't know who they were. Well, they do now.

Look a bit more closely at Pushkin Square, and you'd notice some more additions and missing pieces. A sentimental gravestone, lamenting the destruction of the monastery that was once here. Attractive flower stalls and cafes, lightweight and temporary looking, like contemporary eco-architecture, are reminders of what else is not here – the kiosks, which have been cleansed from the streets of central Moscow. In what was nicknamed the "Night of the Long Bulldozers" in February 2016, a staggering 104 kiosks were destroyed in the city centre, overnight. Whereas the results of "My Street" seemed, after the work was done, basically positive, the results of "dekioskisation" were unnerving. The first de-informalised place I saw in 2017 was Chistye Prudy Metro station, which had been supplemented by two flanking wings selling the usual bits and bobs. They were gone, and in their place was open space, benches, air. I felt dazed.

Rusakov Club, 2017

Where was all the chaos?

There was another puzzling consequence. Educated Muscovites, like many East Europeans of their class, would often complain about how their city wasn't fully "European", but was instead defined by a distinct and local kind of mafia capitalism, philistine and violent. The way that public spaces were so often full of cheaply made, clip-together "parasitic architecture" was one obvious facet of this, brightly coloured pods selling useful things at a reasonable price appearing in places where Soviet planning rules would not have allowed them to be. This informal commerce, a small-time capitalism made up of many small entrepreneurs (of course, all paying much bigger "entrepreneurs" for protection) was everywhere in, say, Warsaw or Budapest, in the Nineties and 2000s, and has since been replaced by "normal" chain store and/or hipster commerce. The same process has now happened in Moscow, but instead of years of these places being run down and dismantled, it all happened in one night. The constructions were classed as "illegal", which they probably were when built – though many owners had since managed to obtain documents that legalised them – and that was the city's casus belli. Given that practically the entire Russian ruling class has emerged out of illegal activities and opaque businesses in the 1990s, for them to be picking on these very small-time benders of the law was hypocrisy in the extreme. But the fact remained. This was giving the hipsters what they said they wanted. And when they'd got it, they maintained they never wanted it at all. Which is untrue, they just didn't want the violence of the replacement of small business by larger ones to be made quite so horrifically manifest.

But Moscow really does now look more *European*. More honest observers have noticed this. Anna Shevchenko points out that "architecture and urbanism has improved aesthetically in the sense that it became possible to build a European-like contemporary architecture and public space, which was very difficult under Luzhkov given his hatred for any kind of modern aesthetics". This isn't just at the level of surface. "There wasn't any public discussion in Luzhkov's city on what public space could be like, all those Jan Gehl and Jane Jacobs axioms of the importance of a good walk emerged here after his dismissal, and actually changed the attitude towards city life greatly, which again wouldn't have been possible back then. In terms of neoliberal development practice there's not so big a change. It's still developers who determinate the face of the city". But the problem with the "the Nineties were corrupt chaos" narrative being pushed to justify Sobyanin's actions is that it's true. "Luzhkov was a local autocrat, who exploited the city, destroyed about seven hundred historical buildings and left Moscow uglier than it was. Although there're still enormous problems with real public participation, Luzhkov's city had even fewer options to affect the decisions." Nostalgia for the venality of that era won't help combat the harsh nexus of business and state power in the Moscow of today. But sometimes it reveals its real face of its own volition.

The truth behind all the churning civilising of Moscow that was going on between 2012 and 2017 was revealed to me by accident in May 2015. I was walking with friends down Tverskaya, only to find that the pavements were rammed full of people, all evidently waiting for something. Then they came: the tanks, the missile launchers, the armoured cars, the rockets, rumbling past the chain coffee concessions. In front of them was a line of plastic portaloos, as if this was a music festival. This was the dress rehearsal for the Parade for the 70th Anniversary of the Victory in the Great Patriotic War. All of a sudden, this street, with its boutiques, chain stores, staggeringly overpriced restaurants, oligarch's residences and luxury hotels, was bedecked with red flags and the hammer and sickle. Given that Russia was and is fighting a real, albeit low-level war against its fellow former Soviet republic, Ukraine, it was hard not to find it chilling. It's also a reminder of what nostalgia for the late USSR is actually nostalgia *for*. Although the route was complicated by the rebuilding of Red Square's gates in the 1990s, and although this is now a street in one of the most unequal

Here come the tanks

cities on Earth rather than one of the most egalitarian, the spectacle must have been exceptionally similar to that which was experienced in the Brezhnev era. So too, from the look of some of the hardware, were many of the tanks. This street was made for promenading on, and it was made for tanks to go down. Restoring it to its original form has two different meanings, and here, they are both fulfilled.

The Five-Storey Building Defence Squad

The next frontier of Sobyanin's Civilising of Moscow is the erasure of the humble Khrushchevka, and after the kiosk, it is the latest previously unloved Moscow typology to face an unexpected wave of public defence. It's moot as to how serious that is. People who work on the history of Russia and especially of the Soviet Union know that a failsafe way to get people interested in your particular corner is to use the word "resistance". You might be interested in poetry, clothes, furniture, ceramics, whatever, from the Soviet period, but just writing about that in and of itself, on its own terms, is seldom enough for the funding bodies and the popular publishers. Instead, what you do is say that the length of skirts, the design of kiosks, the precise form of lyric poetry, was a way in which the wearer or designer of the skirt, the kvass vendor or the lyric poet could contest the "regime" in a way that didn't involve directly engaging in active "dissidence". In that way, a society which saw only the most sporadic and scattered public protest between the early 1930s and the late 1980s could be redeemed, and the historian could get a bigger readership and some money to live on. Few would ever have guessed that one day, *Khrushchevki* could become a form of "resistance".

At the time, *Khrushchevki* were a humane and much-needed response to the strange architectural priorities of Stalinism, which had, for twenty years, squandered a huge amount of Soviet resources on vanity projects – opulent skyscrapers for ministries, crenellated and majolica-clad luxury flats for the nomenklatura, grand prospects and magnificent Metro stations – rather than workers' housing for the alleged ruling class of this "workers and peasants state". Soon after Stalin's death, Khrushchev announced the cancellation of this Neoclassical "excess", in favour of mass production to rehouse the millions forced into overcrowded housing (or worse) as a result of Soviet industrialisation and enormous war damage. The results were quick, cheap, simple, and intended to be temporary – and within a couple of decades, became one of the most obvious emblems of the squalor and homogeneity of the Soviet landscape. Sixty years later – roughly their intended lifespan – the Moscow city council has announced a massive demolition programme of its "five-storey buildings", as they're euphemistically known. The result has been a wave of protest from residents and others.

Compared either with the high-ceilinged, parquet-floored Stalinist blocks that preceded them or even the equally mass-produced Brezhnev-era towers and slabs that followed, *Khrushchevki* are not particularly good housing. Uninspired design, tiny rooms, shabby materials and messy balcony extensions make them a fixture in, for instance, the "Ugly Moscow" Instagram account. For the elderly or infirm, the lack of lifts makes them either unpleasant to impossible to live in. What they have in their favour is large green spaces and a small scale, which make them relatively intimate and pleasant in a city that can be overpowering and monolithic. More importantly, perhaps, the city's plans focus on what are, roughly, the inner suburban parts of Moscow, those just outside the maniac prices of the city's central zone, Moscow's equivalents of, say, Tottenham or Woolwich. Given their management of the city up to this point – an increasingly pleasant if gentrified centre, and increasingly demented overdevelopment of high-rise flats just outside it – residents are wise to be suspicious of the plans. Even so, there were unexpected ironies of the Khrushchevka self-defence campaigns. To see the *Economist* praise the results of Soviet mass-production and public housing was especially peculiar.[8] It's not hard to imagine how complimentary they would be about a proposal for a new wave of decent public housing in the extremely unequal and uneven Russian capital – but then, no Russian government will be advocating that any time soon. But what are these suburbs actually like? Are they as worthless as the government insists? And what can we expect the *Khrushchevki* replacements to be like? A tour of the Moscow suburbs where the project began could offer some answers.

The Elimination of Excess

The public square just off 60th Anniversary of October Street in the 9th District of the Moscow suburb of Novye Cheryomushki ("New Cherry Town") is a very ordinary, although unusually placid place. Trees, playgrounds, benches, mothers pushing prams and the odd middle-aged boozer circle around a small statue of Lenin.

The four-storey flats are a little worn, and the owners of apartments

Cherry Ilyich

have built extensions or glazed in their balconies – mass housing, originally let at token rents by workplaces to their workers, was privatised equally en masse after 1991. The sense of quiet torpor here is fitting given that Russians call the suburbs "sleeping districts", not much more than cubicles to come home to at the end of a day's work. If so, this is definitely one of the more attractive places to sleep, with low-rise buildings, lots of social facilities and a Metro station nearby. But this one is different. Novye Cheryomushki is the common ancestor of every *Mikrorayon* ("micro-district"), as they're officially known; the parent of thousands of prefabricated districts, the forefather of nearly every suburb in Moscow. This square was the site of a competition between seven blocks of flats. The winner, supposedly, would be built everywhere.

Each of these seven blocks, built in 1958 at record speed, uses a different prefabricated construction system, usually of concrete panels, slotted into place like toy building blocks. Each was assessed

K7

on expense and speed of construction, and then one lucky block of flats, codenamed "K7", was chosen as the winner.

It was then constructed in thousands of copies – though structural problems with it has meant that many of these have in turn been demolished. Nonetheless, this site was where began the largest experiment in industrialised housing in history, where homes would become mass-produced commodities like cars, fridges, TVs. In one respect, this was a fulfilment of a long-held modernist ideal. When he was the director of the Bauhaus, Walter Gropius declared his intention of becoming "the Ford of housing". Houses, he insisted, must become machine-made, serial products, as efficient, clean, cheap and essentially disposable as cars. Like so many twentieth-century dreams, this would eventually be realised in the Union of Soviet Socialist Republics, and with notoriously mixed results. For every Model T, there might be an Edsel, and bad things happen to disposable products when they're not replaced.

In the contemporary context, however, there is something quixotic and heroic about this effort. Those of us born since the late 1970s, in Britain especially, but to varying degrees in the west and east (and south) of Europe, have seen staggering levels of inflation in the price of housing, and a seemingly corresponding sharp decline in the price of consumer goods, from cars to food. It's almost a reversal of the Soviet situation, where by the 1980s, the need for cheap and decent shelter (and full employment, and a functioning, if rickety welfare state) was widely met. Currently, we have a society where housing is a constant source of worry, anxiety and cost for much of the population, but the goods the Soviet Union had such trouble manufacturing – particularly, the consumer durables most subject to fashion – are both abundant and extremely cheap. Because of this, if nothing else, it is worthwhile to examine this experiment, the ideas behind it and how it proceeded. In doing this, we'll focus on a particular area of Moscow – three large suburban districts that emerged in the hinterland of Moscow State University between the mid-1950s and the late 1970s.

There is Novye Cheryomushki, the country's first, built in the 1950s and 1960s; Belyayevo, an apparently generic example from the 1960s; and the more ambitious late-Seventies Severnoye Chertanovo, which tries to break from standardisation. Each offered stable, free or near-free housing to workers both white-collar and blue-collar until mass privatisation in the early 1990s re-introduced profit and insecurity, as more desirable locations were snapped up by investors. Each has also been infilled with new prefabricated housing in the 2000s and 2010s.

As well as the possible lessons they give of a means of solving the housing crisis seemingly endemic to neoliberalism (certainly, to Moscow), these housing projects reveal the way in which the USSR in this era attempted to return to the "utopian", technocratic vision of full Communism which was common in the 1920s, and fell into abeyance in the Stalinist era, with its showpieces and spectacles. It saw a re-engagement with the idea of revolutionising everyday life, an embrace of futurology and specific prediction, and also, something new – an extensive discourse over automation. Unlike in the Stalinist era, the Khrushchev "Thaw" saw a return of science fiction, and very blurred lines between that and actual policy. Two books of policy prediction written near the end of the 1950s, both of which were later translated into English, show this particularly well. M. Vassiliev and S. Gouchev's 1959 *Life in the Twenty-First Century* is a compendium of predictions by planners, scientists and economists, presented for a popular readership. The chapter on the "Moscow of the Twenty-First Century" focuses on the territory around Novye Cherymomuskhi.

> Nearly a third of the New Moscow was covered with green and blue patches representing the parks and hydro-electric reservoirs, arteries radiating from the centre. Yevstratov took out a metal stick and pointed out many of the details of the new town planning. "In the next five years Moscow will expand to the south-west behind the University..."

However, the planner points to "another characteristic of the Moscow of the future: each zone will be completely different from the next and differently organised." That is, the New Moscow, which will be dominated by greenery, electric cars, an extensive metro and garden suburbs, will be "beautiful" as well as functional.

> Most beautiful of all will be the façades of the four and five storey houses partly hidden by trees and shrubs. Let us enter one of these houses and ask permission to visit an apartment. Brightly lit, air-conditioned rooms with huge windows. Radiators have been replaced with heating in the walls and ceilings [...] If we go out onto the flat roof we will see a curious winged machine. It is an air taxi.[9]

The air taxi, and depending on taste, the "beauty", may not have been realised, but much of the rest was, and a long time before the twenty-first century at that. Largely, this was because of the extremely fast pace of construction enabled by building with concrete panel systems.

These were not new in themselves; the most influential system was the French Camus panel construction system, which formed the basis of Soviet practice from the mid-Fifties on. Some efforts had been made to combine industrialised construction and Stalinist luxury in the 1940s. Nonetheless, the story begins with Nikita Khrushchev's decree On the Elimination of Excess in Design and Construction in 1954. In a speech to architects and engineers the same year, the General Secretary made the following statement:

> 'We must select a smaller number of standard designs – and conduct our mass building programme using only these designs over the course of, say, five years... and if no better designs turn up, then continue in the same way for the next five years. What's wrong with this approach, comrades?'[10]

The vast territory of the USSR was divided into three climate zones and three soil types, and an often dysfunctional system of numbering and classification emerged, giving a (sometimes deceptive) impression of rationality. Room sizes, block heights and lengths were decided on the basis of mathematical calculation, not landscape or context. However, the system didn't remain the same from 1955 to 1991, but had three distinct moments, which Philipp Meuser and Dimitrij Zadorin divide into three games. "Chessboards" in the Fifties and early Sixties, somewhat more spaced-out "Dominoes" in the Sixties, and the final complexities of the "Tetris" arrangements found in the 1970s and 1980s.[11] Standard blocks which were identical in layout, height and flat size in a multinational federation several times the size of the EU might be, if you were lucky, leavened with decorative mosaic panels on revolutionary, scientific, heroic and historical themes; and often, in the southern republics of the USSR, the need for shading led to some more sculptural, op-art effects with loggias. Variations didn't go much further.

Automating the Ideal Communist City

Mostly, this is a story of mind-boggling homogeneity: areas the size of small towns made up of the exact same prefabricated module. The intention appears to have been automation of both design and construction, and aesthetics was a matter of optional applied façades. These were arranged in coherent districts, which at best attempted to combine social facilities and open space. The architect and writer Kuba Snopek describes them thus:

> The building block of Soviet society was the *Mikrorayon* (or "micro-district"), a standardised housing unit that has been replicated all over Moscow since the 1950s. Simple prefab residential buildings, free plan, schools and kindergartens are an integral part of both the programme and its composition. In the heart of each neighbourhood is a public building, most often a cinema or a club. At first glance, a *Mikrorayon* is a typical modernist neighbourhood, commonplace

> in the West. Yet there are things that differentiate the *Mikrorayon* from its French or Dutch counterparts: the degree of uniformity, the repetitiveness of the structures and the enormous scale.[12]

Buildings themselves were taken from standard catalogues, mere "ready-made objects distributed in space".[13] These districts were already being criticised within a few years, and there is much implicit criticism in a similar volume to *Life in the Twenty-First Century*, the collaborative *The Ideal Communist City*, put together at Moscow State University at the end of the Fifties and published a few years later.

Whereas the prefabrication programme can be seen as a sort of ultimate Fordist city, with mass production brought out of the car factories and into the planning of the city itself, the authors of *The Ideal Communist City* were trying to work out what to do next. Partly, the problem is aesthetics:

South-west Moscow, around Moscow State University

> Functionalism never defined the role of single buildings in total urban space. This space, rolling over many miles, loses all traditional points of reference and cannot be perceived as a whole, appearing rather as an unending and accidental continuity of spatial events, incoherent and lacking expressive significance.[14]

This matters, because "the development of an urban environment made up of standardised residential units is of paramount importance for the building programme of Communism". These must be planned in a way that makes them adaptable and more like "a living organism".[15] An illustration closely resembling the design of Novye Cheryomuskhi is captioned: "A great number of standard forms are incorporated in contemporary building, but the spatial solutions arrived at differ very little. The result is a depressing uniformity".[16]

The problem with this is, the new society that is being created by Soviet socialism and the "scientific-technical revolution" is going to be complex and differentiated, and defined not by the repetition and industrial labour of the car factory – that problem will be increasingly solved by automation, given that under Communism, "man's role [...] is to program and control the labour of machines in a fully automated system of production".[17] This is becoming a reality, something shown in the production process of the micro-districts themselves – one illustration in the book shows gantry cranes on rails constructing almost an entire suburb without visible human input. For the authors of *The Ideal Communist City*, this poses questions for the design of the new districts themselves:

> In the coming years, with the reduction of the work day to five or six hours and the parallel reduction of other chores, leisure time will consist of about six to seven hours per day. If we further decrease the work day to a period of not less than four hours and assume a minimum system of daily services, leisure in the next decade may increase to an average of eight to nine hours a day, not counting

> holiday or the extended annual vacation. The increase in leisure time in coming years will present a social problem of extraordinary significance: how to make use of this free time in a manner consistent with the Communist ideal, that is, how to use it in the interests of each and all.[18]

The micro-district in this context is inadequate, because it's too simple, straightforward and standardised – instead, the authors advocate what they call the "New Unit of Settlement", a sort of changeable, mutable version of the Garden City, with pedestrian priority:

> Pedestrian walks are cut under the buildings, and in the shadow of the bearing walls along the walks there are bodies of water. The whole includes stairs, ramps, porticoes, show windows, cafes, and open-air amphitheatres. All this produces a lively sequence of architectural and spatial impressions, a rich variety of colours, forms and light. The individual regains the pedestrian street with its human scale, something that has been missing since the middle ages.[19]

It is on these more ambitious measures that the programme can be considered a failure. The nuclear family, the eight-hour working day, the repetitive production line – none of them were eliminated. In fact, as Lynne Attwood finds in her analysis of gender relations in Soviet housing, the new developments often replicated them. While "one third of the population were re-housed in the course of six years, between 1957 and 1963,"[20] "Soviet planners had a distinct tendency to standardise, and the general perception was that two or three different apartment designs would accommodate all types of family", that is, "the average family", which "apparently consisted of a married couple with two dependent children".[21] This became "the main focus of the housing programme", for much of its duration. "If apartment design was over-standardised, there was little standardisation in distribution".[22] Some municipal allocation took place, but mostly the new housing was distributed via workplaces, on the basis of work, length of time in job, and need. This meant that often flats were in the name of male workers, making divorce difficult and obtaining housing hard for single women and single mothers. Nonetheless: industrialised housing made up 75% of all stock by 1991, and was kept at minimal rents – between 3 and 5% of a resident's total income, so that by Perestroika, "Market Socialist" economists were worried that "people had come to expect to have their accommodation provided by the state virtually free of charge",[23] something which stood in the way of their attempt to introduce the concept of prices reflecting value into the system. Rather than an experiment, this became normality; the equivalent of a mock-Tudor semi or a Victorian terrace is a flat in a four- to ten-storey block. This is where the overwhelming majority of Muscovites live, not in the Tsarist-Stalinist palaces within the inner city, nor the hipster enclaves of Chistye Prudy or Gorky Park.

But first, the half-constructed grand boulevards had to be completed. Vast Neoclassical apartment blocks line the main roads into Novye Cheryomushki. However, here the money ran out for the more flamboyant features – the decorative pilasters stop half-way up, or are outlined in brick; the grand archways lead to scuzzy courtyards. As soon as these were inhabitable, grandiose pride and formal order would be replaced with utility. The contrast between the Stalinist boulevards and the first parts of the new Cheryomushki is striking. Around Akademicheskaya Metro station, the blocks are lower and simpler, and the in-between spaces are full of fountains and benches rather than afterthoughts behind the grand façades. Novye Cheryomushki also featured an abundance of public space and public buildings; health centres, crèches, schools, cinemas, libraries, theatres, clubs. Initially, each *Mikrorayon* was planned with all of this included, all to equally standard designs. Little on this scale had been attempted anywhere, and visitors flocked to see it. Shostakovich composed an operetta titled after the district, satirising Muscovites' desperate desire to move there; it was adapted into a colour film in

Stripped Classical

It went on fire

1963. Built in the year of Sputnik, it seemed to suggest the Soviet way of doing things – an egalitarian, centrally planned, mass production economy – was getting results. A certain nostalgia for these days pervades it – the photographs here are from a visit on May Day, when residents were enjoying the day off and the public billboards were stuffed with Soviet-nostalgic paraphernalia or posters for the upcoming Victory Day. That sort of bombast was incongruous with the easy, sociable space.

Each *Mikrorayon* was meant to have a factory, an institute or both, in order to be self-contained to some degree; the risk that they would become dormitory suburbs was realised early on, and here, at least, it was partially prevented. Around the Novye Cheryomushki Metro station are several research institutes, moved or founded here in the 1960s. Cheryomushki was not just a "sleeping district", as they call them here, but a hub of the USSR's scientific-military-industrial complex. The centrepiece was the Institute of Scientific Information on Social Sciences Library, the Soviet equivalent of the Library of Congress, reached from the street by a concrete bridge over a (long-since drained) lake. Adjacent is the tower of the Central Economic Mathematical Institute, one of the drivers of the Soviet central planning system, a glass grid by architect Leonid Pavlov with a colourful Möbius strip sculpture set into the middle floors. This building is itself a useful index of the failure of the attempt to realise a fully automated, computerised Communism in the 1960s. Intended largely as a computer centre, its bespoke, luxurious, non-standardised design was so complicated for the Soviet building industry to produce that the building was effectively obsolete when it was finished in 1978 (twelve years after construction began) given the rapid shrinking of the size of computers.[24] It became an image (and a rather impressive one) of computerised socialism rather than an actuality.

However, in recent years, the shift in the urban economy from production to speculation has invaded this carefully arranged space and smashed up its order, with a dozen or so thirty-storey towers with pitched roofs crashing into the open space around, creating a looming, claustrophobic feel; the sense that planning has been abandoned here and it's everyone for themselves. Moscow's suburbs have faced extreme levels of "infill" development, with immense towers shoved into the parks and gardens of the *Mikrorayons*, throwing flats into darkness and obliterating the communal amenities. One tower is even crammed into the small square between the tower and the Institute of Scientific Information on Social Sciences Library, blocking out its light. The latter suffered a catastrophic fire in January 2015, described by the head of the Academy of Sciences as the academic equivalent of the Chernobyl disaster. Over a million priceless volumes were damaged. The fire was ascribed to an electrical fault, but given the intensity of development around it, it wouldn't take a conspiracy theorist to suspect foul play. You could easily imagine the original attempts at making this something more than a suburb being erased in a decade or two, as it is turned into a commuter district like any other.

Standardising Non-Conformity – Belyayevo

Novye Cheryomushki's pioneering status makes it a little different from the Soviet norm. That begins a couple of stops south on the Metro, at the *Mikrorayon* of Belyayevo, developed from the 1960s onwards. This is, in design terms at least, a quintessential "sleeping district'. From here on in, the original notion of self-contained districts with their own identity was watered down as a numbers game took over. The "winning" square panels of Cheryomushki are extended into long slabs, tall towers and squat maisonettes, unrelieved by any variation or individuality whatsoever, without an obvious centre, and with relatively sparse social facilities compared with its predecessor. The recent infill is depressing – malls, and more speculative behemoths crammed into the open space. In fairness, some improvements to the poor construction have been made – Styrofoam and a layer of render to insulate the panels, which are rickety in their unrenovated form, with mortar leaking from the crudely connected joints.

Living cubicles

Off the main road, where they survive, the green spaces are Belyayevo's saving grace, enclosing schools, ponds and park benches. Belyayevo has become a minor cause célèbre after the Moscow-based Polish architect Kuba Snopek, as part of a project at the Strelka school, submitted it to UNESCO as a potential entry on the World Heritage list. This was, he argued, partly because of the design of the communal spaces, one of the few places where architects could actually do anything much with the standard volumes they were expected to use in housing.

> Although designing houses was taken away from (architects), they were still able to design great spaces between buildings, urban planning solutions, comfortable streets and paths [...] designers were also able to create interesting urban situations with surprising composition, rhythm and urban openings. Although this aesthetic was of a totally different nature to an archetypal city, using grand objects and vast patches of green, blue and white instead of streets, squares and perimeter blocks, it definitely had its own value.[25]

So in the case of Belyayevo, the preserved orchard and the lakes and the layouts of the buildings are intended to offset the unnerving effects of mass production. Belyayevo is, accordingly, a place where it would be great to be six – loads of free open space and playgrounds to play in – and very probably a boring place to be sixteen, like most suburbs. It is the green spaces which made the area desirable once, and they are most at risk from development.

Either way, Belyayevo implies a city which is homogenous, based on the nuclear family, with a small series of housing types designed to provide for a population with, so the planners assumed, statistically predictable needs. Today this has been thrown into chaos by the decline of the built fabric and the new instability of the population, as flats are rented, sold and subdivided. However, the other reason for Snopek's attempt to get Belyayevo on the World Heritage list was an appeal to the fact that most of the "Moscow Conceptualists", artists and thinkers like Boris Groys, Dmitri Prigov and Ilya Kabakov, lived and worked here in the 1970s. The Conceptualists' famous 1974 "Bulldozer Exhibition", broken up by police, took place in one of Belyayevo's empty green spaces. Snopek argues this subversive activity was implicit in the area's "uncontrolled common space, ready to become exhibition space or whatever else". The mundanity of the area "conceals complicated and nuanced stories". This is an important point – the lives being lived in such a district can be as multivalent as the architecture is one-dimensional, and in that sense, the hope of the authors of *The Ideal Communist City* had that leisure time could thrive in new standardised housing was fulfilled, although in a more critical way than they would have expected.

The idea of listing the district, though, is akin to one of the Conceptualists' knowing jokes – to argue that the true "hipster" district of Moscow, the real "arts incubator", was a mundane concrete suburb. This is still part of the capital, with all its draws, its centre reachable easily from the Metro, and much of what made it such a hothouse for art and experimentation was its connection to the scientific, technical and ideological institutions nearby, from the institutes in Novye Cheryomushki to various art schools and the Patrice Lumumba University that trained cadres in the newly decolonised countries, something that made the Moscow southwest unusually multicultural. In that sense, the area is interesting precisely because much about it was not at all standard.

Standardising Individuality – Chertanovo

There are certain aspects to Soviet practice that always invited the monolithic aspects of the *Mikrorayon*, particularly the limits of the command economy. One of the famous – if inadvertent – results of Khrushchev's 1954 decrees on Industrialised Building and "Against Architectural Excesses" was that an international style truly took hold in a way that those who coined that term couldn't have imagined

– precisely the same style, aesthetic and often constructional approach for a transcontinental territory that stretches from the borders of Scandinavia to the edge of Afghanistan to a sea border with Japan. From the mid-1960s onwards, architects and Communist thinkers actively tried to solve this problem. Some initial attempts were made to reintroduce the 1920s idea of collective housing, which would dissolve the nuclear family and create districts with individual units for sleep and study but with communal spaces for eating and leisure, but the first communal house built since the early Thirties – the House for the New Everyday Life, not far from Novye Cheryomushki – was turned just before the building's completion into a student dormitory.[26] On the other hand, the construction systems became more extensive – it was now normal to prefabricate entire rooms, not just panels – and new systems also offered the possibility of elaborate skylines and visual drama. More flexible modules were developed, such as the

The House for the New Everyday Life

BKR-2, developed in Krasnodar, which in theory offered architects and clients the possibility of creating any façade they wanted on top of the structural module. "The lack of structural function of exterior wall elements allowed for the creation of façades of any texture, rhythm or scale", points out Dimitrij Zadorin. However, the Soviet economy preferred simple, "factory-ready" modules such as the massively used 1-464 series, which needed little post-production on site, making the jobs of construction institutes and local governments easier. Because of this,

> practically every ambitious project based on BKR-2 never left the drawing board. What were launched into production instead were residential blocks of nine and twelve storeys. One after another, the filled new developments [...] making them barely identifiable blood brothers of the cheerless panel outskirts in other cities.[27]

An entire "third generation" of what Philipp Meuser calls "Tetris" blocks was launched in the USSR, and most of them faced the problem that "any alteration to the product range was stressful"[28] for the specialised house-factories which produced most Soviet housing.

So while there are thousands of Belyayevos, there is only one Severnoye Chertanovo. It's further south, reached via a recent, fiddly Metro interchange that usefully attempts to connect up the *Mikrorayons* rather than link them solely to the centre. You can tell something is different as soon as you get off the Metro; while the stations in Belyayevo and Cheryomushki are as standardised as the housing, Chertanovskaya station is a return to the strange, opulent dreamworld created under Moscow during the Stalin era. Architect Nina Alyoshina's hall is a moodily-lit expressionist cathedral, speaking of arrival at somewhere special, not of departure to the centre. Outside, apartment blocks spread around a large lake. Half of these are standardised in the Belyayevo mould, but the other half are mid-rise buildings arching around artificial hills and valleys, connected by

Arriving in Chertanovo

glazed skyways. Looking closely you can see that they're also made of standardised panels, but arranged in such a way to give variety to the buildings; it's the first of the *Mikrorayons* where you can really speak of "architecture" (credited to a team of architects headed by Mikhail Posokhin, Abram Shapiro and engineer L. Dubek) rather than just engineering. The *Mikrorayon's* centre consists of a square in front of the Metro with two shabby buildings, a rotunda with a bar looking out over the water, and a long, low block (now used as a supermarket) facing the lake. They're bleak, but bustling; their bleakness comes from their chaotic subdivision and mess of adverts, not from their dereliction or neglect.

When writing about the district for the *Guardian*, I spoke to photographer Yuri Palmin, who has lived in Chertanovo for eighteen years, first in what he calls the "bad", standardised blocks, and then in the more prestigious, bespoke blocks opposite, which still have a more stable population than is the suburban norm. He pointed out to

Prefabricating complexity

me that the area doesn't only look unlike the other *Mikrorayons*, but has a totally different layout. Rather than the interchangeable units for nuclear families, there are "forty-two different kinds of single and double level flats, with winter gardens in the ground floors" within these long complexes. This was a late attempt under Brezhnev to show that "developed socialism" could have room for different kinds of families and lives, "a sign of hope, a training ground and a lab". That is, they come closer than most to the promises of futurology such as *Life in the Twenty-First Century* or *The Ideal Communist City*. After the question of solving an urgent problem, one of basic need – getting the population out of overcrowded, subdivided communal flats and into purpose-built apartments with their own front doors, not to mention heating and sanitation – the planned economy could finally move from "quantity" to "quality". Except that transition never happened on a large scale, and the standardised blocks were rolled out to the edges of Moscow right until the end of the Eighties.

The mistake often made is to assume that standardisation ended upon the capitalist "shock therapy" applied to the planned economy in the early 1990s. The new blocks built into the interstices of the *Mikrorayons* are still industrialised and still pieced together from concrete panels, albeit with silly decorative roofs to give a shallow impression of individuality. Even the Orthodox church built near the lake in the late 1990s is standardised in its thin, tacky application of old Russian details. What has changed is two things – space, with communal areas considered parcels of land ripe for development; and speculation, with a vibrant property market in the capital generating fortunes for a few and insecurity for most. Dominating Chertanovo today is a forty-storey monolith, called "Avenue 77". According to Palmin it limits light for many Severnoye Chertanovo residents for much more than "a few hours in summer". It tries to break up its enormous grid of standardised flats via a Koolhaas-like "iconic" shape, but nobody could be seriously fooled; this is form following speculation, an image of public space and equality being crushed by avarice. It is fair to suspect that this is the sort of place that will result from the Khruschevka demolition programme. If in the centre, public space has been recreated, with some success, in the suburbs, the same period – 2010-2017, roughly speaking – resulted in the continued, uninterrupted evisceration of public goods. There is no evidence at all that this will change. How have they managed to get away with it?

Critics from both the left and right argued that the monumental uniformity of housing was the greatest possible indictment of the Soviet system: a rigid plan that assumed everyone wanted the same thing, while giving them a mass-produced product that few really desired, but had to accept for want of anything better. The assumption was that the free market would result in variety, liveliness and complexity. What has actually happened is a property boom that has taken over the biggest cities, and a grim decline everywhere else. Blocks became bigger, longer and much more careless of public

Building as profit graph

space, but were still built via the methods that the newly privatised construction companies had learnt well in the good old days.[29] As Bee Flowers pointed out in 2006:

> Within the monolithic construction sector remarkably little has changed. The sector has no internal stimuli for change, and in the absence of alternatives there are no effective market pressures. Moreover, now that the vast majority of Russians live in system-built housing blocks, these have come to define the urban experience – the expectation of things being any other way has died'.[30]

Outside of central Moscow, this is still the case. The ideals of Novye Cheryomushki are dead as much more than fond or ironic nostalgia, but its methods and techniques remain, and now manage to make some people very wealthy. What the Soviet prefabrication programme promised, and failed to deliver, was at best something more than simply lots more housing. Instead, it suggested that mass production could actually create a society that was both communal and differentiated, industrialised and green and placid. The end of the USSR finished much hope of the first of these, and the infill of green spaces and the Khrushchevka demolition programme are currently obliterating the second. Whether mass housing could achieve greater things in more propitious circumstances, and in a society, with less dominance of patriarchy, bureaucracy and Fordist labour, is another question entirely.

A WEEK IN THE KREMLIN

NIZHNY NOVGOROD, Gorky

For a couple of weeks in the spring of 2014, I got to stay in the Kremlin. I informed many people I knew of this situation, hoping I would receive post addressed to me in said citadel, but nobody bothered to do so. The Kremlin in question was not, obviously, in Moscow, but in Nizhny Novgorod, a large industrial city which was known for several decades as Gorky, after its most famous son, Maxim. This was only the nom de plume of Alexei Peshkov, whose memoirs about a working-class childhood in the city make clear the reason why he chose to rename himself; *Gorky* means *Bitter*. The city's new/old name was replaced in 1990 with the original, translatable as Lower Newtown, to differentiate it from Veliky Novgorod, Great Newtown, a much more famous and well-preserved historic city, once centre of a republican city-state. Lower Newtown is the last really big city going directly east from Moscow to the Urals, and the fifth largest city in the Russian Federation. It is, on any of today's definitions of "Europe", within the continent, though some earlier definitions that drew that shifting border along the Volga would have it just in Asia, with the city centre on a ridge at the confluence of the Volga and the river Oka. It is also unadulteratedly Russian; not an enlightened, ruthlessly planned "window on the world" like St Petersburg, not a megalopolitan multicultural city like Moscow, not a basically

Soviet foundation like the Federation's third and fourth largest cities, Novosibirsk and Yekaterinburg – and unlike other "Russian" cities in this book, it has never been in any other country. "Russia is not Europe" might be a standard declaration of Central European liberals, and if that is so, we should be able to find out here what some of those non-European features are.

The very use in English of the Russian word "Kremlin" is exoticising – in function and plan, there's not a great deal here that should stop you using phrases like "Castle" or "Citadel", because that's all a Kremlin is. There is one in every historic Russian city, like there is one in most British historic cities – a walled city of stone to defend a town against attacks by foreign armies and raiders, or to enforce a conquest. The Nizhny Novgorod Kremlin was begun in the fourteenth century, and what is there now is an early-sixteenth-century design by the Italian architect Pietro Francesco, when the walled city had to be reinforced during a war with the Tatar Khanate of nearby Kazan.

So far, so straightforward for late-medieval Europe, right down to the hiring of an Italian for complex matters such as architecture and planning. The Moscow Kremlin's (also Italian-designed) towers are, however, notoriously exotic in their shape, something often ascribed to the influence of the Tatars; the Nizhny Novgorod Kremlin is a bit more squat and lumbering, but there is also something in the design here that you wouldn't find in Western Europe. The Kremlin bridges the divide between Nizhny Novgorod's strongly defined "Upper" and "Lower" towns, with its redbrick walls mounting a steep incline. Some of the towers that mark its gates, particularly the heavy, decorative Demetrius Gate, are free fantasies, part military, part Florentine, part Islamic, topped by a triangular copper peak – but this is actually auto-exoticisation. They look as alluring as they do because they were reconstructed in the late nineteenth century in the "neo-Russian" style; the Demetrius Gate, for example, was remodelled to become an art museum. Within these walls, little more survives from pre-revolutionary Russia than the small, seventeenth-century

Demetrius Gate

Kremlin walls leading to the Lower Town

Cathedral of St Michael the Archangel. Unlike the Moscow Kremlin, which was meticulously preserved – the revolutionary Commissar of Enlightenment, Anatoly Lunacharsky, threatened to resign when he heard that parts of the Kremlin had been damaged in the fighting in the city in Moscow 1917 – the Nizhny Novgorod Kremlin is a citadel of the medieval Grand Duchy of Moscow, enclosing an administrative centre of the Union of Soviet Socialist Republics, inherited, but not significantly added to, by the oligarchic, statist capitalism of the Russian Federation.

Despite its historic significance, Nizhny Novgorod was never on the Soviet tourist itinerary, never on the tours of the "Golden Ring" of Muscovite citadels organised by Intourist, never with a Progress Publishers Guidebook translated into the major world languages. That's largely because it became an industrial city in the late nineteenth century, and became even more of one in the USSR, with the motor manufacturing industry concentrated here – the Soviet Detroit, or more appositely, Turin. It became a "closed city" under Stalin due to the amount of military engineering here. Sakharov was famously exiled to Gorky from Moscow. Being exiled to Gorky sounded terrifying to non-Russian ears, but in terms of relative distance, it's roughly the equivalent of being sent to Coventry. All this may be one reason why the Soviets were so careless with this Kremlin – no tourists were meant to be here anyway, and preserving it all for the people of Gorky was hardly a priority. There were tourist cities and there were industrial cities, and only the great metropolises like Leningrad, Moscow and Kyiv were allowed to be both. Well into the Russian interior, Gorky was a place foreigners weren't even allowed into unless they had special dispensation. A certain paranoia evidently lingers. The English editor of the notably Russia-friendly website *The Calvert Journal* was deported from Nizhny Novgorod in 2016; he was there for the same reason I was, lecturing at Arsenal, an art gallery built into the Kremlin's old arms store, with guest rooms to sleep in above. It was a memorable place to stay. One night, kept awake by cars screeching to a halt outside the Kremlin wall and chants of "ROSS-I-YA! ROSS-I-YA!" – this during the dirty war with Ukraine over Donbas – it was a relief to find that the reason for the patriotic celebration was simply victory in the ice hockey championship.

First to go, when the Kremlin was redeveloped by the Bolsheviks, was the nineteenth-century Transfiguration Cathedral, replaced by the House of the Soviets, a Constructivist local government HQ, completed in 1931. It is a rare pleasure to find a building of the Soviet avant-garde within such a citadel of ancient Russian power, their rationalist, technocratic Year Zero forcefully asserted on the ruins of backwards, superstitious, autocratic Muscovy. It is mounted on a ridge, sheltered by pine trees, a grey-rendered concrete building, using one of the abstract pin-wheel plans that the Constructivists favoured. A ribbon-windowed, curved volume marks the entrance, hauled up on thin pilotis borrowed from Le Corbusier. In its clarity and confidence, it is as radical as any European or American building

The House of the Soviets in the Kremlin

of the time. Few of the later additions to the Kremlin are as exciting – lumpy official architecture of the 1950s and 1970s dominates.

There is also an excellent Art Museum in the Kremlin, with a first-rate collection of the abstract painting that immediately preceded and for a while, succeeded the October Revolution, with major work by Malevich, Popova and others; so sure are the people who work here that nobody would want to visit this room that, when we did so, we found one staff member had spread herself out on the floor, painting flowers and bunnies. Hostility to modernism, which stamped its concrete and glass on the Transfiguration Cathedral's golden domes, is obviously still the norm. The gallery markets itself on its collection of work by the turn-of-the-century painter Boris Kustodiev, and a room full of his ripe, colourful paintings of merchants and their zaftig wives

Eternal Flame of the Thaw

in pretty, exotic cityscapes is the museum's main attraction. However, at the other end of the Kremlin, the Great Patriotic War memorial's eternal flame features interesting etched figures in the "severe style" of the Khrushchev era, expressive and modern. Gorky was far from the front, but was still bombed by the Luftwaffe; the Kremlin suffered major damage. From the war memorial, you have a magnificent view of two rivers: the Oka, which has industry and housing clinging to its banks, and the Volga, which has been left untouched, with marsh and steppe visible as far as the eye can see.

The Upper Town is a regular Russian-Soviet city. The pedestrianised Bolshaya Pokrovskaya street features good examples of twentieth-century architecture from most eras; some art nouveau, some Stalinist classicism, some very mild Constructivism, and the

The Puppet Theatre

State Bank, whose tented roof and cantilevered steps are again in the neo-Russian style, from the nation-building era when everywhere in Europe had to accentuate its local vernacular, after centuries of international classicism (it is also politically promiscuous, with the Tsarist eagle on the main gable, and a gold globe with the hammer and sickle on top of the tower). The late-Soviet era experimented in a similar vein – the Academic Puppet Theatre features a 1980s entrance façade slotted across the side wall of an earlier classical palazzo, with a spiky roof and a relief sculpture of pipers and puppets under an

Old Russia

abstracted old Russian skyline; next to it, the all-glass, international modernist Technical Museum is capped by a colourful mosaic of folksy cockerels, suns and lions. More official structures, such as the red sandstone classicism of the local KGB – now FSB, with no major change in function – or the early 1930s "Postconstructivism" of the post office, where classical details fill in the modernist lines, are drab by comparison with these goofy, enjoyable games with the local style.

Walk a little further into the side streets, and you'll find – as in Chișinău – that you're still in a town of tiny, one-storey wooden houses. Given that they're less drastically dilapidated and mostly cared for as a historic townscape, they're somewhat less distressing. One is well-kept as one of several Maxim Gorky House Museums, several are falling apart rather elegantly, one contains a sex shop, its sign rudely placed alongside the exposed logs of the structure. This sudden fall into seediness is especially noticeable given that Bolshaya Pokrovskaya itself is an affluent, modern street of sushi bars, department stores and cafes, with only the preserved façade of the Sverdlov family shop left as a nod to the past – and that's because of the family's favourite son, Iakov, the Bolshevik leader who ordered the killing of the Tsar and his family in 1918. At the end of the pedestrianised street is a green square with a giant statue of Gorky, sculpted by Vera Mukhina – tall, gaunt and defiant – and the only Metro station in the older part of the city, on the east side of the Oka. It had just been opened when I visited – until then, the Gorky Metro built in the 1980s and abandoned in the 1990s only served the industrial, western side.

The recommended means of getting to the Lower Town is not via the Metro – it isn't covered at all – but via the Chkalov Steps which lead from the Kremlin to the Volga. These are one of the sights of the city, built between 1943 and 1949, partly by German prisoners of war, and at enormous expense even for the time. They begin with a statue of the titular Chkalov, local boy and transatlantic aviator, then descend in three curved, sweeping flights, with each level marked by obelisks and benches, for those exhausted by the climb. It is three times the height of the Potemkin Steps in Odessa, which must make it one of the tallest public stairways in Europe. At the end, you can see nothing but the steppe on the other side, but turn left, and you're in the pretty, well-preserved Lower Town. Some of what it has – such as the River Station – is typical Soviet fare, but the streets are delicate and classical, like a miniature St Petersburg. There is a hipster bar which serves fresh fish and whose staff seemed very pleased to encounter foreigners. The churches are what really makes the Lower Town memorable, and so completely unlike anything west of Brest.

There are two in particular that showcase Russian architecture in all its strangeness and exoticism – the Assumption Church, with five gold onion domes, and the fabulous Stroganov Church, founded by local merchants at the end of the seventeenth century. This was in a style often called "Naryshkin Baroque", but it doesn't resemble the faithful Italian-style Baroque of, say, Poland in the same period.

The Chkalov Steps

Russian Baroque

Russian architects plundered Baroque's rich details and added them to the clusters of onion domes that defined Russian sacred architecture. The twisted, whipped domes themselves, on the Stroganov Church, are amazing confections, faceted, multicoloured and fruity, with the highest dome inset with gold nuggets. The provenance of these romantic skylines – ushered in with St Basil's Cathedral in Moscow – is speculative, with claims that the idea came from Tatar mosques; no matter how much Russian architecture was designed by Italian architects, it looks distinctly, inescapably "other". Whether this joyful architectural originality denotes a substantially different civilisation to that of its Western neighbours is deeply questionable – a serf in Poland and a serf in Russia was a serf either way, whether their masters' architects directly copied Italian designs for their churches, or came up with their own style. Already, when the Stroganov Church was built, Peter the Great was on his way back from Deptford to found a city on the Baltic modelled on Amsterdam. The persistence of this more piquant style is sign of backwardness and insularity or of confidence, of refusing to copy and replicate, depending on your view.

When you cross the bridge to the other side of the city, the side with a Metro and factories and the main railway station, and turn back to look at the skyline, you'll get a shock. As expected, there's all those polychromatic bulbs and onions below and the Kremlin above, straight from a Kustodiev painting – but on the highest ridge, a single, standardised square tower of flats has been placed, as some sort of deliberate insult to townscape. The main monuments, when you've crossed the bridge, are another "neo-Russian" complex of the late nineteenth century, the sprawling Nizhny Novgorod Trade Fair; a huge square with a concrete hotel and a colossal Lenin monument, one of at least half a dozen in the city; a yellow neo-Russian church; and the Moscow railway station, connected to the Moskovskaya Metro station. Below is a clone of the Moscow Metro, with a classical hall and trains taking a leisurely journey out to Avtozavod, the district where Gorky's industrial might is, or was, concentrated.[1]

Constructivist corner

Directly in front of the station is the last sight we'll see in the city, Revolution Square. Here, unlike in most of the Upper and Lower Town, you can examine some architecture of contemporary Russian capitalism. McDonalds is housed in a 1990s Postmodernist building, erected especially. Nizhny Novgorod had a respected "school" of Postmodernist architects, and their approach here involves a slightly lumbering approach to form, borrowed from the bulges and curves of the "neo-Russian" idiom, but with little non-structural devices and features pulled away from the building and emphasised, an "advertising-architecture" – the golden arches are mounted on a little plinth, ceremonially. As commercial architecture, it is more lively than either the lumbering classicism of the Soviet GUM department store or the Norman Foster-style glass blandness of the Republic

Postmodernist corner

shopping mall, on the other side of this extremely mis-named square. The McDonalds tries to complete a small "traditional" shopping street, ending in the dynamic corners of another Constructivist building, housing a bingo hall, but the effect is futile, as the street is sliced in half by a flyover. The dilapidated high-rise headquarters of the Metro, opposite, seem like a lot of office space to run a single line; the car is king round here, Motorcity USSR. Within the station, you can be dazzled by a mosaic of war and revolution, filling every inch of each of its walls. In the roof is an outsized chandelier and a suspended ceiling, and these, I'm told, were the sole contribution to the city's public infrastructure of one-time governor, the liberal playboy and later, assassination victim Boris Nemtsov. In a straight line east from here, the next big city is Kazan, and you are in the Republic of Tatarstan.

Railway Station, showcasing chandelier

The Kazan Kremlin

THE ARCHITECTURE OF SOVEREIGNTY

KAZAN, Qazan

English-language news sources owned by the Russian government are not notably sympathetic to the practice of Islam, or to Muslims in general. In terms of the warnings against the Islamification of Europe, the dangers of multiculturalism to Western civilisation, and against the welcoming of refugees from North Africa or the Levant into the continent, the likes of *Sputnik* and *RT* have presented a fairly unified front with the outlets of other aggressively hard-right governments, from Hungary to Poland to the United States. Racism, and racist attacks, aimed against Muslims from the Caucasus or Central Asia are a serious and growing problem. All this makes it hard to know exactly what to make of something like the Kol Sharif Mosque in Kazan. This, the largest mosque in Europe outside Istanbul, was opened in 2005 for the city's thousandth anniversary – a date which long precedes the invasion and sacking of the city by Ivan the Terrible in 1552, and its yoking subsequently to the Russian Empire. It commands the Kazan Kremlin, standing as the largest and most powerful building in a relatively fast-growing city, one that has been recently, if rather meaninglessly, described as the Russian Federation's "third capital". No cities with large Muslim minorities in Britain or France or Sweden have anything on the scale of the Kol Sharif. One quickly discovers in walking around Kazan that this is only the most obvious example of a peculiar experiment in architectural multiculturalism, comparable to the Soviet *Korenizatsiya* (roughly, "indigenisation") efforts of the 1920s and 1930s, where a culture was to be developed that was "national in form, socialist in content". "Islamic in form, Putinite in content", you could call much of contemporary Kazan, were it not for the fact that this limited cultural devolution is increasingly being circumscribed. The blue dome and minarets come into view across the Volga as the eastbound train pulls into Kazan's main station, over a fairly standard post-Soviet panorama of mass-produced speculative towers and cheap business parks. Navigating with a map, as I did, you might make the mistake of trying to get to the Kremlin along the river. This is unwise, though it takes you past a modernist hotel, clad in shiny stuff but with its propagandistic-ethnographic graffito work

Ethnically Coded Agriculture

restored (workers on the port and in the factories, Russian peasant girl with wheat, Tatar peasant girl with grapes), to give you a view, in amongst the car parks and pedestrian-hostile highways, of leisure buildings both Soviet – a levitating saucer of a Circus – and post-Soviet, a bizarre mirrorglass pyramid, the latter overlooking a muddy canal. The Kremlin is on a ridge above these, its walls whitewashed, with blunt, conical towers, designed by architects from distant Pskov. The minatory, ethereal Spasskaya Tower forms the main entrance for tourists. Outside of this is a memorial to Russian and Tatar fighters in the Red Army, with inscriptions in Russian, and in Tatar in both Arabic and Cyrillic scripts. Both of these scripts were rejected in Soviet Tatarstan in the first twenty years after the revolution, in favour of Latinisation, a measure that was revived in the 1990s, only to be ruled

Spasskaya Tower

Soyembike Tower

illegal by the government of the Russian Federation.[1] Inside are the Soyembike Tower, the most distinctive structure in the Kremlin, a tiered, leaning redbrick spike used in the twentieth century as the model for the Kazan railway station in Moscow the classical buildings that make up the Presidential Palace, the Annunciation Cathedral of 1562, whose clustered simple and beautiful blue and gold domes belie a busy and dull Victorian interior, an exhibition centre housing a show on Mikhail Kalashnikov and the guns he designed (smiling, he holds up an AK47 in the poster), and of course the mosque. The sparkling, polished newness of Kol Sharif, designed in 2001 by a firm with the marvellously post-Soviet name Tadinvestgrazhdanproyekt, makes it immediately incongruous with the historical buildings, but it gets round this by creating around it a distinct, enclosed urban space, with a public square of decorated tiles and a colonnaded arcade around it.

There was a mosque on this site before Ivan the Terrible destroyed the city and slaughtered its inhabitants, when Kazan was the capital of

Contemplating the model mosque

a powerful Khanate, a successor state to the Golden Horde, but little is known about its design other than the fact it had eight minarets. Kol Sharif has six, four of them tall, two smaller, around a full, bulb-like dome. The Library and Imam's Office alongside has a shell-like dome that makes clear a derivation from pop architecture of the Sixties nearly as much as Turkic mosque design – Mimar Sinan and Eero Saarinen, together at last. Inside, this Sunni mosque is relaxed, with worshippers and tourists in roughly equal number, a gift shop and theologically questionable mosaics of old, pre-Russian Kazan. An illuminated model of the mosque stands in the centre of the prayer hall, as if it were the real focus of worship. Evidently, this place meant a great deal – enough to risk the ire of UNESCO and Russian nationalists to get it built.

The Republic of Tatarstan – the geographical designation of which Kazan is the capital – was never a Union Republic (SSR) in the Soviet Union, but an Autonomous Republic (ASSR), a lesser designation in terms of the enforcement of the native language and culture in the education system; until recently, Tatars and Russians were of roughly equal demographic weight here. Under Gorbachev, the Tatar ASSR pressed for Union status (which would without doubt have resulted in Independence when the USSR collapsed), and from 1990 declared "Sovereignty", with the agreement of Yeltsin – roughly equivalent in practice to devolution in the British or Spanish sense. That in turn has been severely circumscribed since 2000, with the Republic commanded again to give the majority of the tax receipts from its oil and its industry to Moscow. Tatar, although used in bilingual announcements on the Metro and on the odd road sign, is still considered an endangered language, and at the time of writing, the law that made Tatar lessons compulsory in schools has just been rescinded, causing a crisis in the Republic.

Soviet nationality policy, early theorists of which included Tatar socialists like Mullanur Vakhitov (killed by the White Armies in 1918) and Mirsaid Sultan-Galiev (killed by Stalin in 1940), initially stood strongly against Russification, but had a static conception of "nations" that was curiously reifying, linking nationhood firmly to language and cultural practices in a very nineteenth-century, liberal fashion. The only difference was, the nations were not meant to form nation states. Whereas Union Republics had the right to secede – one which they availed themselves of in 1991 – Autonomous Republics like Tatarstan (and of course Chechnya) did not. By the end of the 1930s, the policies of the early Soviet "Affirmative Action Empire", as the historian Terry Martin described it, had been watered down, and by the 1980s Kazan was widely considered to be just another large Russian provincial city. The "Sovereignty movement" of the 1990s was aimed at changing that, and the mosque was its largest monument, achieved when it had already been largely politically neutered.

Walking around central Kazan, you can see the difference between

The Palace of Agriculture

Sovereignity Baroque

being the capital of a Union and an Autonomous Republic, in that the somewhat kitsch ethnic gestures used by Soviet architects in, say, Tbilisi, Chişinău or Almaty are wholly absent. What you find instead is Soviet design of a straightforward kind, both in its classical Stalinist and modernist Brezhnevite variants, with very little local variation. Because of this, the Republic's government has been building itself the grandiose governmental buildings it has hitherto lacked, and it has done so in the common style of post-socialist dictatorships, that is, in a style that could roughly be described as Postmodernist, if that didn't suggest degrees of irony and playfulness absent in these wild, hieratic hulks. Just outside of the Kremlin you'll find the Palace of Agriculture, designed in 2008 by Leonid Gornik. It's a work of demented aggression and historical syncretism, a crescent of masonry cladding capped with domes and dragons, giant order columns and a stylised four-storey high "tree" at the entrance. Around it is a scrubby park, a small mosque and some similarly encrusted office blocks, it forms a public space facing the Kazanka River. It's horrible architecture, half-understood classical components shoved together randomly, but the scale and confidence are impressive in their unnerving way, like the boom architecture of early-twentieth-century America, only executed in mirrorglass and fibreglass rather than granite and marble, and with the symbolic lions and pointed arches about establishing continuity with imagined Tatar ancestors rather than American skyscrapers's attempts to link themselves to Italy or Greece.

As in similar projects of its kind in other post-socialist cities like Skopje (or, to a degree, Moscow), these mock-historical essays are about creating new histories, frequently through overwriting the old ones. In Lenin Square, the surviving statue of Vladimir Ilyich – who had family connections here – stands in front of a neo-Stalinist governmental block bearing Tatarstan's lion emblem, which can be seen, when you go round the corner to see its backside, to be a Soviet office block, barely touched. Opposite that is a small park, and the city's old Lenin Museum, a fine modern building designed by Anatoly

Polyansky in 1987, in the shape of stylised red granite flags fluttering. It has long been reconsecrated as a Museum of Tatarstan, but it was closed and under renovation when I visited in spring 2017. In front of it, middle-aged men enjoy a morning beer in an overdesigned square that the building works have turned into a quiet cul de sac. Walking in the other direction, away from the river, you'll see unexpected little remnants of what must once have been a pretty little city, wooden houses and flats with great cantilvered bay windows; plaques reveal that Rachmaninov and Lenin lived in some of these. This is crushed soon enough with an avalanche of kitsch hotels, offices and shops in an eternal late-1980s of multicoloured stone and mirrorglass; a heroic statue of Mullanur Vakhitov gestures pointlessly at it all.

This road will lead you to the city's busiest junction, where the pedestrianised Bauman Street meets the wide, arterial Tatarstan Street. Close by, past some horrendous new malls, is Lake Kaban,

Sovereign Lenin

The former Lenin Museum

Fossil Fuel Baroque

commanding which is the most impressive post-Kremlin building in the city, the Tatar State Academic Theatre, designed by Gorlyshkov, Korneev and Agishev, opened in 1986. This is a late-modernist public building of real quality and, extremely unusually for the USSR's construction industry, impressive attention to detail, with the fine concrete work of its public terraces extending right down to the embankment – and that's continued by a rare subtle new building, a very faintly hipsterish wooden cafe. On the main street are standardised Soviet blocks, and some symmetrical neoclassical flats, evidently part of an unfinished Stalinist grand plan, and a hideous Neoclassical university building that manages to ignore everything else around it. Yet the pretty Nurulla Mosque, built in the 1840s in a style that tries to combine Islamic precedent and the classicism of the Catherine the Great era, denotes that you're entering somewhere more interesting – an area of attractive, narrow streets and Russified

Brutalism and Pigeons

minarets. This is the "Old Tatar Settlement", outside which Tatars were not allowed to live until the late nineteenth century, and where the city's historic mosques are concentrated. This place still feels distinct, though more for its wooden houses and relatively "authentic" architecture than for its ethnic specificity.

Bauman Street itself is one of those pedestrianised streets most large Russian cities have, modelled on the Eighties renewal of the Moscow Arbat, that have comprehensively drained themselves of any perceptible atmosphere via over-restoration and kitsch street furniture; there are interesting buildings nonetheless, such as a 1930s Printing House by the unfortunately homophonic Constructivist architect Semen Pen. Continuing the two-three storey scale of the street, it breaks with its decorative aesthetic through Corbusian ribbon windows and pilotis, with an open ground floor and a curved concrete stair-tower. Just off here is a side street leading to

Nurulla mosque

the Museum of Socialist Everyday Life. A private venture, it claims, deeply questionably, to be the only museum of its kind, and has very attentive English-speaking staff. It is stuffed with Soviet stuff, the sort you could find anywhere from Latvia to Krygyzstan, nothing distinctively "Tatar". Old cigarette packets and Vodka bottles, Stalin, Brezhnev, Gagarin, Cheburashka, Viktor Tsoi, Dean Reed, Lenin Lenin Lenin. Like most of these places, what it really is, is a museum of the popular culture of the 1970s and 1980s, and political change has led this to be labelled "socialist". Foreign visitors are encouraged to write messages on the walls: "Retro fun for Australian curling team".

At each end of Bauman Street is a Metro station, and it's in the Metro that you can see the architecture of "sovereignty" at its most complete and impressive. The Kazan Metro's first stations were planned in 1997 and opened in 2005 as part of the city's Millennium celebrations, and it has the honour of being the only Metro system in Russia to be entirely post-Soviet; in fact, the only one in any former Soviet Republic to be built from scratch after 1991. You wouldn't know, but for subtle differences in the iconography – the generous dimensions, the lush, glittering materials, and the switching off of half the lights in underused stations, are all exceptionally Soviet. Some of the stations – especially Tukay Square, named after the "national poet" – are decorated with mosaics and murals from local mythology, all of it figurative, but all of it distinctively "Tatar" in terms of the costumes, the script and the world that is being evoked – though curiously there are no stations in the places where Tatars actually lived between the sixteenth and twentieth century. It tells its tales about a culture the city has spent much of its history consciously suppressing. In some of the more recent stations, this imagined land is being supplemented with less rhetorical, more futuristic architecture, the same as anywhere else.

Tukay Square station leads into an underground mall, an exhibition of children's drawings taken from Tukay's stories, and a clothes shop called "Sale". The initial unfamiliarity of this city may be deceptive. Kazan's ecumenical, multicultural architecture and planning coexists

The Constructivist Printing House

The Real Socialist Lifeworld

with all the usual things about Russian cities – crass commercialism, poor public spaces, kitsch, adverts, and a vast gap between rich and poor. It fits neither the narrative of Christian-defenders-of-the-West that the Russian government sells abroad, nor the image of hardline, ruthlessly misogynist, homophobic and violent Islamism enforced by the government of Russia's other powerful Muslim republic, Chechnya. The point of *Korenizatsiya,* and of *Sovereignity* after it, was always that superstructural – "cultural" concessions could always be made so long as the political and economic base stayed the same. Then, that was a sign of a faith in the popular appeal of socialism; now, it suggests a confidence in the longevity of a quite different system. But the ruling on compulsory Tatar teaching suggests that even this circumscribed devolution is too much for Russian nationalists. If it is worth going to war to protect the (largely imaginary) infringement of the rights of Russian speakers in Ukraine, they couldn't possibly have to share official speech with others in the heart of Russia itself.

The Metro the Khanate never got the chance to build

CONSTRUCTIVIST CAPITAL

YEKATERINBURG, Sverdlovsk

At the centre of Yekaterinburg, the "capital of the Urals", is an embanked expanse of water, usually translated into English as the "City Pond", though "Lake" captures its scale rather better.

The City Pond

It's the heart of this industrial metropolis, an unusually compact city by Russian standards. Yekaterinburg, founded in the eighteenth century as part of the Russian colonisation of the Urals, lacks any classical or axial grandiosity. It has instead a rough juxtaposition of styles thrown together unpretentiously in a manner that will be familiar to an English observer. In being so far from the front in the war, it avoided the Stalinist grand plans imposed post-1945 on comparable historical cities further west, a paradox where the less destroyed a city was, the less coherent its planning and architecture. There are towering redbrick mills from the years immediately before 1917; there are classical palazzos; there is a high-rise Central Business District; and there is something called the Boris Yeltsin Centre, which we will come to. An unfinished TV tower[1], just an untopped shaft, and a shiny golden-domed church, look out over the scene. On a warm day in May, this is one of the loveliest urban spaces in urban Russia, an exemplary public space, calm and lively. In the last year, this "pond" has been the subject of popular protest, one where architectural style and public space have led to the contestation and debate that isn't meant to happen in contemporary Russia.[2] Architecturally, the most interesting part of the pond is the peninsula occupied by the Dynamo Stadium and the smooth streamlines of the Dynamo Club, an attractive Constructivist ensemble set among trees. This is the stylistic antipode of the current proposal from the city's oligarchs and authorities (as always, the funders and the enforcers are impossible to extricate from each other), for a new church to be built on an artificial island in the heart of the pond. The project would destroy most of what is worthwhile about the space – its placidity, openness and architectural heterogeneity, where nothing dominates. The sponsors' choice, stylistically, is Moscow's St Basil's, the pre-Petrine style otherwise absent everywhere in the city – as if to stamp a traditional Russian identity upon a deeply modern place. Many of those involved in the "defence of the Pond" have been involved with a parallel project, to rebrand Yekaterinburg as a capital of Constructivism. To choose this city as a place to commemorate the most strongly modern, revolutionary period of the Soviet Union would once have been very controversial. Overlooking the pond is an aggressively revanchist reaction to the Soviet past, pointedly stamped on the city best known outside Russia for being the place where Tsar Nicholas II and his family were killed, in the basement of a merchant's palazzo, at the start of the Civil War, as the White Armies approached the Red city. The Church of All Saints Resplendent in the Russian Land stands on its place – the house was demolished in the 1970s by the order of the region's governor, one Boris Nikolayevich Yeltsin. The city named after Catherine I was renamed Sverdlovsk in 1924, after Iakov Sverdlov, a prominent Bolshevik who died young in 1919, and who had a role – the extent of which is disputed – in the execution of the Romanovs. In a typical post-1991 rhetorical compromise, the city was renamed Yekaterinburg, but the region continues to be known as Sverdlovsk Oblast. The resurgent Orthodox Church canonised the Romanovs in 2000, and this church is their monument – a tacky Neoclassical-Byzantine melange that is, nonetheless, positively restrained in comparison with the St Basil's mooted for the lake. Elsewhere, the city of Sverdlov and the city of Yeltsin can be found in roughly equal evidence – a Constructivist industrial settlement, full of experiments in Communist living, later becoming the power base of the politician who dismantled the socialist system.

Already an industrial town, Sverdlovsk had its big bang between 1928 and 1932, during Stalin's first Five Year Plan, which entailed a massive expansion of Urals industry, exploiting the mineral deposits in the area. New towns like Magnitogorsk and existing centres like Chelyabinsk expanded around the mountains which are the alleged geographical border between Asia and Europe. Yekaterinburg is just over the border in Asia, commemorated by various monuments around the railway station. In architectural terms you can't spot much of this – it is less "Oriental" in skyline than cities to its west like Kazan, or even Moscow. There are a few peculiar little experiments which try to make something of its geographical importance – the Sevastyanov

House, built in 1866, is the city's most interesting pre-revolutionary building, its bright colours, pointed arches and florid swags a piquant mix of Russian Baroque and Turkic Orientalism. Otherwise, this is a modern city, and unsentimental about it. The identity the city received in the first Five Year Plan defines it still.

Most Constructivist buildings in the USSR were built during the First Five Year Plan, and Sverdlovsk was no exception – the main distinction here is the sheer quantity, and the state of preservation, with dramatic office blocks like the Dom Kontor even retaining their original signage. The city was transformed through two things – first, what was referred to as the "Big Sverdlovsk" Plan, which turned the city centre into a showcase for avant-garde housing and office complexes, and the development of a new town on the outskirts, Uralmash, which still has a distinct feel, and is considered by locals to be a place apart. Big Sverdlovsk is strung out across the two parallel main streets

We are in Asia

– Malysheva, and Lenina, with a tramline running east-west along a tree-lined esplanade. Given that the Constructivist notion of the "social condenser" entailed an abolition of strict zoning and the overlapping and overlaying of different functions and different groups of people, the first thing that may surprise is that Constructivist Sverdlovsk is effectively a series of segregated, often gated, communities, built for particular professions. Since the 1950s this has loosened up somewhat, but they are still referred to by their original names. The Builders' Village, for the building workers. Justice Village, for lawyers and the legal profession; a village for Uraloblsovnarkhoz, the administration of state farms; a district for Government Workers; and the most famous of them, the Chekists' Village, for employees of the secret police and their families, designed by Ivan Antonov and Venjamin Sokolov in 1929.

These vary in coherence, completeness, quality, and in the degree to which they're still distinct and gated. The Chekists' Village has

Lenin Street, Big Sverdlovsk

Hotel Iset

long since had its fences removed, although the gateposts still stand. It is entered through Lenina past two monumental buildings – one, the Hotel Iset, is currently derelict, a ten-storey curved block with plate-glass shops on the ground floor (one of them a canteen named, in notable ironic-avant-garde manner, Fabrika-Kuchnia – Factory Kitchen); connected by a walkway, which has grown a restaurant beneath it, one of those opportunistic, parasitic constructions Russian cities specialise in, is the Chekists' Club, now a Museum of Archaeology. These, together, supposedly have the ground-plan of the hammer and sickle, but if you ask nicely, staff of the Archaeology Museum will let you see their exquisite staircase, a spiral in wood leading to an abstracted five-pointed star at the top.

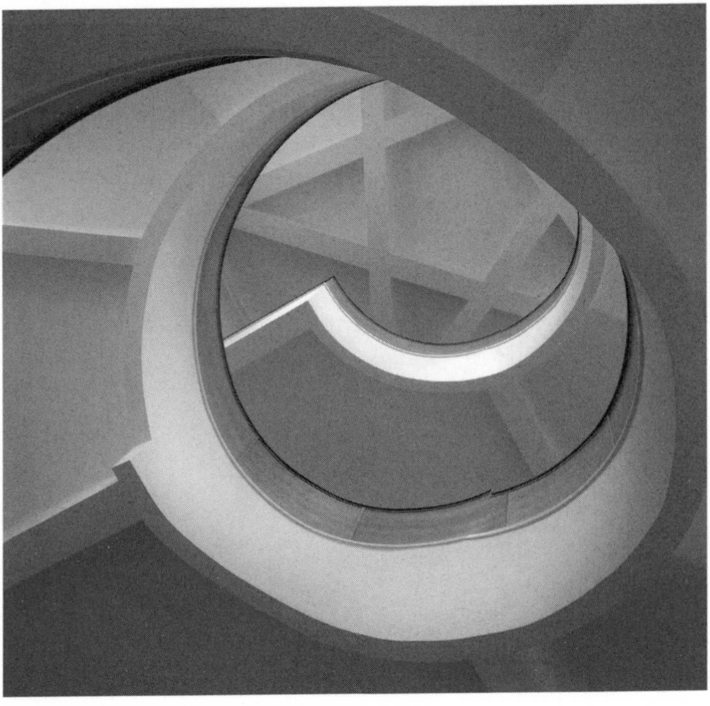

The star staircase of the Secret Police Club

Inside the complex, tree-lined pedestrian streets define elegant, if severely dilapidated tenements that you could imagine in Glasgow or Brooklyn, with grand bay windows, rendered in a weathered soft red. The interiors – I was lucky enough to be invited for a drink in one of the flats – are not huge, but are well-designed and full of light. This impressive showcase in socialist living was, and it should not be forgotten, grace and favour for the enforcers of the early Stalinist system, then engaged in, among other things, going round the Union confiscating grain from starving peasants and condemning Kulaks and Trotskyists to concentration camps. One of the designers on the project was "repressed" by the Chekists himself. Under Khrushchev, the Village was opened up to non-Chekists, and is not owned or used by the FSB – though they do operate a clinic here, and urban myths abound of secret passageways and dungeons.

Bay windows for the Chekists

Just on the other side of Lenina, the Builders' Village is less impressive, though still decent, with white-walled blocks of flats, the same clinics, gardens and schools. It feels just a little edgier, with more street drinking, although the simpler construction means it doesn't look quite as shockingly distressed as the Chekists' Village. Facing the street is the Builders' Club, designed by Iakov Kornfeld, which is much more strictly modernist than the secret policemen got opposite, an asymmetrical, lightweight composition of separated cubic and curved volume which could have fit easily in MOMA's exhibition on The International Style, held at the time of its completion. This is pure interwar modern architecture, as carefully considered and abstracted as anything being built at the time in Berlin or Paris.

The administration of collective farms, on the other hand, received something truly avant-garde for their complex of flats and dormitories

Builders Club

on Malysheva. Designed by Moisei Ginzburg, it is a forgotten cousin of his Narkomfin building in Moscow, a "transitional" collective house including flats with and without kitchens, linked by walkways and a small park to communal facilities. It uses the same dimensions, developed by Ginzburg and other members of the Constructivist OSA Group for STROIKOM, set by the Russian republic's building commission as standard types, and abandoned almost immediately after. It is still gated, and many of its original features – the open ground floor held up on pilotis, a roof garden – have been removed, although apparently many interiors survive. It shares the Narkomfin's laconic, unfussy proportions and its functions of housing young bureaucrats and training them to be good Communists through spatial encouragement, but aside from its provincial location, its fate lacks the Narkomfin's high tragedy. Rather than rotting to picturesque pieces, it is merely nibbled around the edges by the kipple of Russian

Ginzburg and badly drawn Gagarin

capitalism. The last of these Villages, for Government Employees, was home for many years to the man who restored capitalism, Boris Yeltsin. Its courtyard flats are centred around a high-rise, like the Hotel Iset, but the Constructivist proportions are masked by decorative details introduced at the end of construction, which ironically make it look even more like the middle-class urban housing of Victorian Scotland or turn-of-the-century America.

Scholar of Constructivism Mikhail Ilchenko, who was raised in Uralmash, has described the approach taken by enthusiasts and campaigners for avant-garde architecture in the city, aiming to raise it both in terms of public consciousness and in the esteem of the government bodies tasked with preserving it, as being a reminder of the original utopian blueprint. He argues that rather than making it part of heritage culture or concentrating on raising support from the international modernism and preservation club, local activists and

Bureaucrats' village

fans have produced works – posters, pamphlets, booklets – which lay stress not on real built fabric, or on the buildings' current state, but on the original drawings and photographs taken soon after construction, where you can see just how beautiful and confident they were before history started to run its claws all over their pretty faces. Not the actual USSR people remember, but what it once dreamed of becoming. I'm sceptical of this as social history, but as activism, it's a very smart approach, stressing not the mundane reality of lived-in and familiar places, but something unfamiliar – dreams of collective living and unrealised societies, futuristic buildings whose materials will never wear, placed in abstract empty space. This activist effort to resurrect the untainted Communist-Constructivist dream must be hardest to achieve in Uralmash itself.

A fair few miles from the centre in an otherwise tightly defined city, Uralmash was effectively cut off until the city's short, infrequent Metro was built in the 1970s (like many late-Soviet Metros, its beauty

Machine Builders Metro Station

– with some stunners, like the twisted, organic-sci-fi light-tubes and chrome sculptural reliefs of Maschinostroiteley station – is in inverse correlation to its utility). Its centre is a vast square that any urbanist or planner today would regard as an example of how not to design a square, and they would not be wrong – a vast and useless desert around some rather fascinating buildings. These range from the Constructivist lines of the House of Culture, the faded pomp of the derelict, early Stalinist-classical Hotel Madrid, designed during the Spanish Civil War by German emigre and Bauhaus student Bela Scheffler, who was murdered in 1942, and the administrative offices of the Uralmash (Ural Machine-Building Plant) itself, guarded by uniformed men who will not let you photograph the sparkling mosaic on one side of this stark modernist building, caught exactly between avant-garde dream and Fordist reality.

The monument is the White Tower, a startling work of architecture that dominates the new town. Its function, a water

The Hotel Madrid

The White Tower

tower, is straightforward, but Moisei Reischer's design is utterly extraordinary, a circular panopticon on stilts, looking out across the city and the forests around. Its alien nature is compromised a little by the malls and car showrooms around, but when you look at it dead-on towards the forest, you can see it as originally seen, as Ilchenko and the Constructivist activists would like it to be seen – a pioneer, in virgin territory, fearless. It is run today by volunteers, who show films and exhibitions in the circular overlook room, and have only minimal help from the city or the government. This is one of the great things in twentieth-century Russia, but the residential Uralmash around it doesn't inspire the same awe.[3] Its blocks of flats, some of them Constructivist in shape and Stalinist in ornamental detail, others drab *Khruschevki*, are flattered by a wild density of trees, untamed and twisting all over the pocket parks and drained fountains. The early blocks, with their spacious flats, were popular with organised crime

In the Jungle of Uralmash

kingpins in the 1990s, and the huge balcony extensions are one sign of their presence – many flats inside were knocked-through, making two flats into one, fit for the Uralmash gangmaster.

The first housing for Uralmash workers, built at the end of the Twenties, has not been so favoured – traditional houses made of logs, which are in the process of being knocked down while this piece is written. Similarly, round the back of the Palace of Culture are dilapidated streets of miniature classical blocks of flats, similar to those in Sillamäe and Minsk, which are slated for demolition – something that is, according to Ilchenko, largely supported by residents, who have become tired of the gradual crumbling and collapse of these buildings. The typical ultra-high-density towers that are emerging at Uralmash's edges make clear that more will be lost by their destruction than a few sad blocks with pediments – the intimate scale and green space will disappear with them. Ilchenko, despite being from the area,

Uralmash Palace of Culture

The first Uralmash

was reprimanded by residents for taking photos here, which may owe something to the fact that the derelict cinema opposite has become an "urbex" destination, with young Yekaterinburgers coming here to hang out, make mildly subversive street art and so forth. "Do you know what it's like to live in somewhere like this?", he was asked, as if only a poverty tourist could find anything of interest here. It's a familiar story – the choice is living in and/or frolicking in the crumbling ruins of a failed utopia, or a mean, cheap modernity sustained by gas receipts.

The post-Soviet descent of Uralmash and Yekaterinburg into violence and chaos, via warring consortia of managers from the "Red bourgeoisie" and formerly marginalised working-class gangsters, the ancestors of today's smoother administrators and oligarchs, can be enjoyed, if you're so inclined, at the city's notorious "mafia cemeteries". Here, shellsuits and Nineties cars are preserved forever on headstones of granite and marble. Sverdlovsk Oblast's chief administrator Boris Yeltsin cannot have imagined that these groups would come to be the social base of his policies when he came to prominence here in the 1970s. His ambitions for the city can be seen in the short, one-line Metro, the unfinished TV Tower that was intended to be visible all over the city, and the high-rise office block he commissioned to run the city and district from at the end of the 1970s. Its thin mullions of stone are modernist-Gothic, like a cheaper Sovietised World Trade Centre. It is now joined by a half-empty series of hotels, luxury flats and offices, shoved into the open spaces around wooden houses, some preserved for historical significance – including one that has competing plaques immortalising both the Red and White Armies. This "CBD" is lit up with pulses of neon at night to give it a sense of activity it lacks by day. In front of this is the Boris Yeltsin Presidential Centre.

Designed by the American architects Ralph Appelbaum Associates – why try and emulate when you can import, a lesson Yeltsin applied to the Russian economy, with catastrophic results – the Yeltsin Centre is a decent enough public building. Curved volumes with multiple entrances, a cafe, some shops, a clear path to the embankment and an amusing neo-Soviet statue of Yeltsin, set in high relief into some sort of stone spatula. The talks programme, library and art gallery do in fact fulfil the aim of the project, which is, I'm told in confidence, to create an anti-Putin museum without actually doing so, proceeding by implication through openly praising things such as representative democracy, freedom of press and freedom of assembly, for which the Russian government has little respect.

The main museum is however the most nakedly, grossly propagandistic space I have seen anywhere in post-Soviet Russia. It's very well presented, its narrative carried through with some aplomb. From the dramatic, skilful opening 3D animated film depicting the struggle for democracy and liberty from the middle ages to 1991, to the films of the 1996 election campaign (some sort of Soviet EMF with a mullet, rap at you that the election will decide "who's really

Yeltsin Spatula

cool and who's a real loser"), to an apotheosis of Boris under a giant glass dome, celebrating the Constutution he forced through in 1993, it is state of the art. Aside from the question of presenting democracy as a personal gift, the problem is that the still hugely controversial questions that laid the foundations of today's "managed democracy" – the deepest economic depression any country has ever suffered in peacetime, the invasion and levelling of Chechnya, the bombardment of parliament in 1993, the rigged presidential elections of 1996 – are either batted away or blamed on the Communists, with the same disinterested dismissal with which Soviet war museums treated the Molotov-Ribbentrop Pact.

However, in presenting Yeltsin as the founder of the far from free or democratic Russian state, it tells an unintended truth, one that Russian liberals are often loathe to admit. The most telling story of all is that of the first president himself, and is told inadvertently, in the footage. Here Yeltsin ages quickly, from the eloquent, brave and quick-witted operator of the late Eighties – seen in holographic form delivering his epochal 1987 speech to the Politburo, the first time anyone at the top had rebelled so openly since Trotsky – into the hapless, drunken, slurring slug he was by 1996. I wonder what Yeltsin would have thought about the fact that just outside, on that lovely riverside embankment, people are trying to apply those 1980s ideas about civil society and public protest to the preservation of the monuments of the Communist idea he did his utmost to crush into dirt.

Hologram Yeltsin

Part Four:

THE EASTERN PERIPHERY

BRAND GEORGIA

KUTAISI, Kutais

Around a hundred years ago, enlightened Western visitors queued up to visit and praise the small West Asian republic of Georgia. As described in Eric Lee's recent book *The Experiment – Georgia's Forgotten Revolution, 1918-1921*, this was the end result of a series of uprisings in Kutaisi province from 1902 onwards, which became known as the "Gurian Republic" and was specifically hailed as a great peaceful experiment by none other than Leo Tolstoy.[1] Peculiarly, the result of this event – eventually crushed in the aftermath of the failure of the 1905 Revolution – was that politics in this then rural country became dominated by the Menshevik wing of the Russian Social Democratic Labour Party, which elsewhere considered itself the representative of the advanced urban proletariat. In the Constituent Assembly elections of late 1917, where the Mensheviks were humiliated everywhere else, they won Georgia by a landslide. Intent, unsurprisingly, on maintaining their power in the country, they formed first a Transcaucasian Federation with Armenia and Azerbaijan, then quickly declared independence, under the military protection first of Germany, then of the British Empire, both of whom were keen that oil keep coming through the Georgian railways from Baku in Azerbaijan to the Georgian port of Batumi. In that time, the Mensheviks held elections, which they won again by a landslide, instituted an impressive and successful land reform, and encouraged trade unions and co-operatives, hence avoiding the bloody "War Communism" imposed on the peasantry to Georgia's north. Criticised, including by other Mensheviks, for the deals with Britain and France, the Georgian leader Noe Zhordania proclaimed that while the Bolsheviks would lead Georgia eastwards, occupation by these two openly counter-revolutionary imperial powers would lead them instead to Europe.[2] This was crushed when Georgian Bolsheviks such as Josef Stalin and Sergo Ordzhonikidze launched an invasion in 1921. Independent Georgia, wholly dominated by the political right, considers the (unabashedly socialist) republic of 1918-21 its legal precursor. In the late 1980s, the Georgian Soviet Republic descended into ethnic conflict with its autonomous provinces of Abkhazia and South Ossetia (which had a legal status within Soviet Georgia roughly similar to that of Tatarstan or Chechnya within Soviet Russia), which intersected with economic collapse to create an economic and social disaster. The 1990s are generally considered lost years. Since the "Rose Revolution" of 2003 that, in response a contested but probably rigged election, overthrew the remnants of the Gorbachev Politburo who were then governing the country and brought to power "pro-Western reformers", Georgia has again been on what is called a *European Course*. Unlike Azerbaijan, or Kazakhstan, or Belarus, or the Russian Federation, the press is uncensored if of course oligarchically owned, public assembly is reasonably free, and elections are not rigged. The war with Russia over the unrecognised breakaway republic in South Ossetia in 2008 meant that it broke with the Soviet legacy in a similarly demonstrative way to Ukraine, a few years earlier. Among the monuments it demolished was a Red Army memorial, a huge edifice in an organic-expressionist style, in the city of Kutaisi; one minister justified this act by the necessity to save younger generations from having their taste warped by hideous Soviet architecture.[3] In its place was built an enormous new parliament, designed to bring power in Georgia a little closer to the breakaway Russian-backed Republic of Abkhazia. Designed by the Japanese architect Mamoru Kawaguchi, it's a huge glass globule in the structure-as-decoration style pioneered by Santiago Calatrava. If it was just a bit more worn and made of better materials, it could feature in one of the Amazing Soviet Architecture photobooks. It's surrounded by fields, beamed down from a much richer and more extravagant place. A little fragment of Europe, that doesn't resemble anything I know of in Europe.

It was, like most of the post-Rose Revolution architecture, a personal project of Mikheil Saakashvili, the Georgian politician who is currently an opposition leader in Ukraine, but is banned from returning to Georgia because of allegations of corruption; the building is currently disused, as the parliament returned to Tbilisi after he lost power. Saakashvili was, however, paid a rare honour a couple of years ago. He is to my knowledge, the only living world leader, with the possible exception of Barack Obama, to be specifically mentioned and credited on the cover of an architectural magazine for his work. That cover, of *Mark* magazine, with the headline "BRAND *NEW* GEORGIA – SAAKASHVILI REBUILDS A COUNTRY" was actually displayed as a poster in front of the old parliament in Tbilisi during the 2012 elections; the honour didn't help Saakashvili's political career, as he lost power in a landslide defeat. Articles on Georgia's architectural policy have tended to stress his personal choice of architects for large projects, the fact that he keeps abreast of the architectural and design press. In the hiatus between the end of his political life in Georgia and its commencement in Ukraine, he lived the life of a hipster in Brooklyn – hipsters, he insisted, were a great example of civil society. He might be the only politician in the post-Soviet space who would even think of reading a book like this. Aside from the promise to "tackle corruption" as he apparently did in Georgia, and his having defended the country against a brief Russian invasion, his appeal in Ukraine partly stems from his grand building projects, seen as a successful rebranding project. Kutaisi offers a glimpse of what neoliberal governance with a selection of design magazines by your side looks like.

One reason why Saakashvili is often specifically credited with a beneficial architectural influence is that, unlike many similar figures, he was actually elected – coming to power in 2004 in the aftermath of a revolt against voting fraud. That difference is why you don't see cover stories on the "Architecture of Nursultan Nazarbayev", or the "Architecture of Sheikh Khalifa bin Zayed Al Nahyan", although they may be equally instrumental. Unlike nearby Azerbaijan's hereditary dictator and Zaha Hadid fan Irham Aliyev, Saakashvili doesn't come across as a KGB man's spoiled son, but as the kind of politician liberal locals and Westerners love, fluent in multiple languages, educated in the US, savvy, quick-witted. Although democratically elected and democratically defeated, there's a reason why he's in Ukraine and not in Georgia. He is wanted on multiple criminal charges related to his tenure in office. His government was heavily criticised by the UN Commission on Human Rights for appalling prison conditions and for violently suppressing protests. Economically, Georgia grew, but from a disastrously low level – at the reckoning of World Bank

Relational aesthetics airport seating

economist Branko Milanović, the country would need at least two decades at current rates to reach the economic level it had achieved in the late Eighties.[4] It's one of the most unequal countries in an already highly "Brazilified" region. The only unquestioned success Saakashvili is credited with is a drastic reduction of corruption – which, in a region beset by bribes and petty hierarchies, matters. But, on to the architecture.

Probably the best way to see "Saakashvili's Georgia" is to fly to Kutaisi. The airport here, opened in 2012, was designed by the Dutch firm UN Studio, and is a good indication as to the Saakashvili style. The control tower is an organic, sensual design in white concrete, and inside, a smooth white and red interior features spreading sofas to lie on rather than the usual grim rows of benches, a surprising but clever borrowing of the seating arrangements of contemporary art galleries. As you enter, leaflets informing you of customs and visas feature Jurgen Mayer H's customs posts on the border with Turkey, making clear that the architecture is the brand is Georgia. Then, they

Belle Epoque

give you, the Wizzair passenger, a free bottle of wine that features a text quietly imploring you to invest. The wine is good, and so is the building – bright, optimistic, informal, and slightly pretentious. When the bus drops you off in Kutaisi itself, though, you'll find that outside a central grid of renovated streets around a 1950s Stalinist Baroque square, the money quickly ran out. Streets are potholed, crumbling or barely even there, and most buildings are ad hoc one- or two-storey creations, with their electrical wiring spilling out all over the street. You never have to look far to find how the other half lives here – it's usually on the other side of the road.

So after walking down the slurry and tarmac to the city centre of Kutaisi, you'll come to an impeccable little turn-of-the-century-cum-Stalinist-Fifties town, devoid of the design magazine courting gestures of the airport and the parliament. Rather than a place that desperately wants to be somewhere else, this feels like what it is – a Russian imperial town in Asia, built on the back of a turn-of-the-century industrial boom. The buildings – banks, the Hotel Orient, a great little archaeological museum (Georgian history is long, complex, and rich), a Stalinist drama theatre in the "Oriental" version of the Moscow style – are seldom extraordinary, but make a very pleasant townscape, decorative, street-centred, undemonstrative. It isn't perfect – the theatre square has a clever little fountain of stylised horses on some sort of terrace, but it's a roundabout that is tricky to cross in order to actually enjoy the space – but it's amiable townscape.

At night, the shops are lit in red neon, which highlights the whips and curls of Georgian script. Food is as outrageously good as it is obscenely cheap, both of which are indications that you are very definitely not in Russia. Then there are two wonderfully fruity art nouveau buildings that speak vividly of their time – not of the social revolution then raging in the countryside around, but of a provincial urban bourgeoisie committed to the enjoyment of modernity. That is, two cinemas – the Radium, of 1911, a gabled structure that now hosts a seedy-looking nightclub, and the Mon Plaisir, which you reach first

1910s townscape

1950s townscape

through an open colonnade, and then enter through a gateway like a gaping jaw, more funfair ghost train entrance than cinema. Nearby is a monument to Vladimir Mayakovsky, the great Communist-futurist, who grew up nearby, and went to college here. He is portrayed in the sculpture as a precocious and pugnacious student.

This recently restored centre, with its clean streets, new cobbles and cafes full of people speaking Polish, leads to Kutaisi Market, which is a descent into, again, messy streets, full of people selling whatever Chinese tat they can alongside fresh and first-class produce, pockmarked by amusing but somewhat relentless anti-Putin graffiti in Ukrainian. This place, in turn, is a reflection of what Kutaisi is, in the present – a former industrial town with a fast-declining population, few jobs, few prospects, bar its current strange status as a gateway to Georgia for international hipsters and the curious, owed to its placing on the global cheap airline network. Wandering around

24 24

My pleasure

Georgian-Ukrainian Alliance

Kutaisi Market

this market can be a little unnerving, but the actual market building is incredible. A tiny, gabled sandstone structure, one side of it has been treated as a monumental relief sculpture. Dozens of faces in low relief – apparently of locals – look out above a succession of figures from Georgian history and mythology, from Great Patriotic War propaganda, and a typical Soviet nuclear family. Where it meets the ground, it becomes a collection of strange bits and bobs, the sorts of things you might find for sale here. Sandstone bric a brac, amphoras and bowls and tubs. Then an archway takes you into the market itself.

If you go in the other direction away from the market, you come to the River Rioni. On its banks, "authentic" Georgian architecture, with pretty wooden galleries and cantilevered balconies, mixes imperceptibly with the current Euro-shanty style, spilling its way down a steep hill. At the top, as is typical in the South Caucasus, is the church – the eleventh-century Bagrati Cathedral, in the Georgian church style – Greek cross plans, influenced by the Byzantines, but with a sense of circularity that is all their own, with conical domes. A ruin since the seventeenth century, the church's reconstruction to something approximating its original state was another of Saakashvili's projects – something that led to its UNESCO World Heritage Status being removed. As so often, the idea of what will make a peripheral place more like the rich "centre" and the centre's own ideas of good taste and historic preservation, do not necessarily coincide. Georgia has plenty of ruins; most of them lived in rather than visited by tourists. It doesn't want to be a ruined exotic backwater, where it wants to be, of course, is Europe – nowhere else is quite so intent on resisting geography. This is the continuity between the neoliberal Georgia of today and the Marxist Republic which it traces its lineage from, but what Europe *means* has shifted somewhat. For the one-time Brooklyn hipster Saakashvili, Europe really meant America – low taxes, the freest of free markets, privatisation, paradise if you could afford it. For the Mensheviks, it was a European social democracy, based upon trade union power, co-operatives, and a version of "scientific socialism" very different to the apocalyptic transformation envisaged by their erstwhile Bolshevik comrades. As a historical goal, both are equally distant here.

Kutaisi railway station is on an elevated position, and gives a dreamlike view of mountains, a bronze king on a horse, dilapidated prefabricated housing estates, and two turreted Stalinist apartment blocks, the beginning of some long-forgotten magistrale The station is a cheap box, reminiscent of the sort of temporary market buildings you get growing up around 1960s shopping centres, made of components you could pick up in Wilko for a fiver each. From there, slow trains take you through glorious scenery and grinding poverty – at each stop, there's people waiting to sell you their stuff – to the real capital.

AN EXHIBITION OF ACHIEVEMENTS

TBILISI, Tiflis

Books on Soviet Georgia – "the Italy of the Caucasus", with its great food, hospitality, archaeology, architecture, landscape and laid-back attitude to graft – liked to claim that it has 360 days of sunshine a year. The week I spent in the Georgian capital in January 2015 just happened to be on the exact seven days that the weather was overcast, damp and clammy, without the crisp, clear (if easily lethal) quality of the winters in Georgia's overbearing northern neighbour. My experience of the city was perhaps irrevocably affected by this; a city literally cast in an unflattering light. Tbilisi is an exciting city, full of daring and precipitous townscape, heroic infrastructure, and a brusque yanking together of the ancient and futuristic. It is energetic – "vibrant", to use the estate agent euphemism, with real street life, great bookshops and bookstalls, street art, cafes, and this being Georgia, amazing food; in short, it boasts all the fruity things that Minsk will never have, and had them in the Soviet Union, too, though no doubt to a lesser extent. An enormous gap between the rich and poor is a nearly totally ubiquitous feature of the former Soviet Union, whether you're in affluent Tallinn, middling Yekaterinburg or impoverished Chișinău. But I have never seen anywhere where the gap was so enormous and at such close proximity as in Tbilisi. At times, the city is genuinely shocking – a modern surface that suddenly and frequently opens a portal into hell. This seldom gets mentioned in descriptions of the city, which I can only put down to the effect of the sunshine. A series of starchitect baubles have been placed atop an unnerving self-build dystopia which had been built on top of a functional Soviet city which had been built around a romantic Asian city of galleried houses piled on top of each other up a mountain. That is all unique, but the way that the effects of social and economic collapse and glassy architecture magazine megaprojects overlay and intensify each other is something that could happen to anywhere. In Tbilisi, Western Europeans might think they're seeing something exotic and untamed and local, but it's likely that what they're actually seeing is the near future of their own cities, what will happen to them when planning dies, when wars become endless, when migrants are left to fend for themselves, but with the affluent carving out their own spaces in the same fabric. Tbilisi railway station, rebuilt in the 1980s, is a partially renovated example

Outside Tbilisi Station

of the late-Soviet-futurist genre, a cantilevered cruiser-like curved concrete volume on top of a low entrance pavilion, which has recently had a shopping mall placed into it. In that volume on top you can also find a small hotel. Staying in it is quite the experience, as the windows of the cheaper rooms look out not onto the street outside, but into the mall itself, with its multiple levels of dubious Chinese goods and questionable cures. Outside here is a quite normal large Soviet city of wide streets and mixed use retail/apartment buildings with Neoclassical dressing; there are a lot of broken bilingual neon signs in Georgian and Russian on the buildings, which date the shops to before 1991.

A sprawling market spreads itself out here all the way to the boulevard of David Aghmashenebeli Street; when you reach the junction with it, the market descends into the colonnades of one of the Stalinist street blocks, and people stand behind desks with random choppings of animals bleeding into the wood – a red lamb chop here, a severed sheep's head there. Flies flit around them. But then, as you turn onto the grand boulevard, very suddenly everything changes. By which I mean, everything. The streets are properly paved, the buildings are clean, the shops are international, the vistas are clear. You have walked around three yards between these two places. It's like teleporting.

David Aghmashenebeli Street has a clutch of art nouveau buildings and eclectic-style hotels and theatres, similar in their florid style to those in Kutaisi, but bigger, and commanding much larger public spaces. They have been so heavily restored, with their metalwork buffed and the masonry painted more often than cleaned, that it feels almost as extreme in its wealth and cleanliness as the teeming market just round the corner does in its poverty. By McDonalds, it expands out into the lavish Stalinist Marjanishvili Square, enclosed by two huge, identical flanking blocks of hotel rooms, shops and high-end offices and retail, with decorative towers, airy open galleries and spacious colonnades on the ground floor. It makes very clear that a gap between those at the top and those at the bottom is by no means a recent, neoliberal invention in this city.

After the square, the scale is closer to Kutaisi, with little apartment buildings in the various styles available to the late-nineteenth-century bourgeois architect in the Russo-Persian-Ottoman borderlands, alternately Neoclassical, Baroque, Turkish or some combination of these. Inserted into that street are two very indicative monuments; one block which is a direct copy of the Old England department store in Brussels, a florid black wrought-iron block whose projecting bay almost resembles the cantilevered wooden terraces and balconies you see on the older, eclectic buildings; the other unusual block is the former House of Political Education, a standard modernist box which has been enlivened by a multicoloured smalti mosaic in orange, blue and green, an abstract jungle of geometric foliage. Astonishingly, it was designed in the 1970s by Zurab Tsereteli, now best known for his ridiculous monumental sculptures in Neoclassical-Disney style, such as the Peter the Great statue on the Moskva river that we have

Stalinist planning, modern living

already encountered. There are other early works by the artist in the city, and they show a deeply unexpected shift in official art from free, light, colourful abstraction under Brezhnev to pompous, figurative monumentalism under neoliberal capitalism.

And then... it stops again. The houses are beaten up and bent, the paint is flaking off, the balconies are dangling, the pavements are broken. It makes no sense whatsoever. A piece of graffiti reads "BON JOVI". A cafe in the only restored building (again, so heavily that it looks unreal) calls itself "EURO MAIDAN". We're back in the Street of Crocodiles. And then, suddenly, as you cross the bridge over the River Kura, you spot a massive new building, a series of glass blocks with wilting, petal-like roofs kept up by spindly concrete columns, something that has given rise to the nickname "the Mushrooms". This is a large Public Service Centre, to the design of the Italian starchitect Massimiliano Fuksas. Architecturally, the shift is, again,

Tsereteli, the early years

nosebleedingly sudden – poverty into Euro-Muscovite wealth into poverty again into something faintly resembling contemporary Maastricht. It also reveals something unexpected about Saakashvili's architectural programme – the Euromimicry which continues after his departure. The Public Service Halls, of which several were built across Georgia, are civic centres, combining under one roof libraries, courts, advice centres, as part of the effort to show a public face of government that isn't corrupt, slow-moving, obstructive, intimidating, Soviet.

Many places in the post-Soviet space could seriously do with such a project. For all his neoliberal market-knows-best politics – which included harsh labour laws, the dismantlement of what little social safety net survived from the USSR, flat taxes which benefit the wealthy, and privatisation of public services – Saakashvili's projects were, without exception, state-driven. This is mostly because, with a major exception that we will come to, oligarchic capital is not so much a presence in a country that mostly lacks the abundance of resources that has allowed a parallel First World infrastructure to emerge for the extremely rich in Russia. Saakashvili, just like the dictators around him, recognised that the state can act where business can't, here. So the civic centre in Tbilisi by Fuksas serves some sort of useful purpose underneath the biomimicry of its fussy engineering. I can't comment on its functional success, but as a building this riverside complex is a reasonably convincing approximation of an Award-Winning Contemporary Building, based on computer-aided engineering allowing a series of long glass volumes overlapping each other to be sheltered only by what appears to the eye to be thin concrete supports propping up flopping roofs, like teflon jellyfish.

On this side of the river is Rustaveli Avenue, the other main flat street in a city which is otherwise defined by extreme topography; it was laid out specifically as the colonial city centre in the nineteenth century, and was originally known as Golovin Avenue, after the local Tsarist commander-in-chief. For Georgi Chakhava, the designer of Tbilisi's most interesting twentieth-century building, this place is a mistake, an example of "Steppe Urbanism"[1], wide and straight and level, in a city whose historic centre, as we'll soon see, is defined by galleried houses stepping across precipitous slopes. What Chakhava describes as the properties of the steppe are of course the properties of mainstream European urbanism, and it is not a value judgement, or an assent to Russia's clearly colonial approach to Georgia over the last two hundred years, to point out that until the last few years, "Europe" has come to Georgia almost solely via Russia. Either way, Rustaveli does what it is meant to do very well, standing as the exemplary governmental street of a capital city with the appropriate confidence and grandeur, and because of the city's complex history, it achieves this without homogeneity, but rather a series of exciting experiments in style, none of which dominate the others. It begins at Freedom Square, where one of those Biblical figures on a gilded column that for some reason are considered symbolic of freedom in

Public service spectacle

the post-Soviet space (this one by, of course, Zurab Tsereteli) stands in front of the polychrome brickwork of the City Hall – which was built as the office of the Viceroy of the Caucasus in the Russian colonial period. The buildings around include a luxury mall, a bank that was once robbed by the Young Stalin, and a hole where a 1960s glass building was. The hole has exposed something unexpected at the back of a grand classical apartment block: every available surface has been covered with balcony extensions, one atop the other, to the point where there is a second layer of building atop the original. The effect is a stage set where at one corner someone has violently torn down the curtain.

The rest of Rustaveli is as "normal" as Tbilisi gets, with only some disquieting moments. There is an opera house in a late-nineteenth-century Orientalist style, there is a Stalinist cinema that could be anywhere from Kaunas to Bishkek; there is the former Marx-Engels Institute, a design by Alexey Shchusev that was saved by a preservation

Rustaveli Avenue rear end

campaign only to be – in current plans – transformed into the entrance to a thirty-storey speculative tower – and there is the old parliament, marked by a giant order portico of thin stripped classical columns; in front of that is a moving memorial to those killed in the 9 April 1989 protests, a Georgian nationalist demonstration that was attacked by Soviet troops, who killed one woman, causing a stampede that killed nineteen more people. The memorial evokes the crush, through a square of arms pressed together; it is an unusually subtle and disturbing image for the usually more sentimental "victims of Communism" genre – until you spot that there's a stylised angel just behind it. Opposite is an excellent National Museum and a poor Museum of Communism, which somehow manages to discuss the Sovietisation of Georgia while seldom ever mentioning the name of Josef Stalin (he is still distressingly popular round these parts). At the end of Rustaveli you can find one of the city's few 1920s buildings, a printing house which is a basic asymmetric Constructivist block with pointed arches

Constructivist Orientalism

to the windows to indicate that you're in the Orient. The National Museum has much more interesting contributions from the 1920s Georgian avant-garde, with a small but significant selection of reliefs and paintings by little-known artists. The gaps between buildings offer a view of the hilltop TV tower, a spindly spike on stilts, and a Stalinist viewing gallery, much photographed in the 1930s as an image of Soviet luxury.

At the end of Rustaveli, the scale leaps up into three huge buildings: one is the most interesting of Tbilisi's Art Nouveau structures, arranged around stone swags and silver domes; and in the same warm yellow stone is the grandest of the city's Stalinist buildings, the Academy of Sciences, which rises to a towering spike, once capped by a Red Star, and though that was removed, there's no mistaking the period. Like many Stalinist buildings it shows a complete mastery of disparate forms (a little Orientalism, a little classicism,

The Academy of Sciences

a Gothick-Moorish silhouette) and a dominating sense of scale. Next door is Rustaveli Metro Station, its façade decorated with scenes from Georgia's epic poem, composed in the twelfth century by the eponymous Shota Rustaveli, *The Knight in Panther's Skin.* Opposite this piece of medieval-modernist Georgian infrastructural folk art, is a Radisson Hotel with a supermarket selling seemingly only German goods. The Radisson was once the Hotel Intourist, and as Georgia collapsed into ethnic warfare in the 1990s, it effectively became a refugee camp, a vertical shanty town. Its erasure and replacement with a proper Western hotel was one of Saakashvili's first projects; it also involved demolishing the speaker's platform below, a bizarre structure of concrete arches known locally as "Andropov's Ears". The mission was accomplished, insofar as the Radisson really does look like any other Radisson anywhere else in the world (specifically, to my eyes at any rate, the one in Bristol).

Medieval Metro

Rustaveli was always intended to be a European façade, a normal capital city street, and in adding his own effort of clearance and tidying Saakashvili was continuing an old project. It is in the side streets around that you can get a taster of the "real Old Tbilisi", before its Russification/Europeanisation/Sovietisation (delete according to preference). These low-rise galleried houses and flats are fascinating and intense in their decorative excess and overwhelming neglect, with the tresses of the long-haired maidens obligatory on Art Nouveau buildings drooping and dissolving into the slop of the plaster; with the damp and petrol fumes in the air, the place feels literally poisoned. In good weather, of course, such as the city has most of the year, these tightly packed alleys would offer shade rather than claustrophobia. And if some houses look, with obvious cracks in the middle and tottering sides, like they're falling down, that's because they are. An earthquake in 2002 had particularly severe effects on the Old Town, and efforts to clean it up and repair the buildings were best described as "incomplete "in 2015.

However much it isn't for the faint-hearted, the Old Town is absolutely fascinating, and an essay in how to build cities in extremely unsympathetic topographical conditions, a series of loops going up the steep hill, caked in graffiti stencils (one that appears often is the sad face of Saakashvili, with the legend "where now?'), with access to the buildings as often from wooden stairwells and decks as from straightforward doors on the street. Holes in the wall dispense (usefully captioned in English as well as Georgian and Russian) "GEORGIAN BREAD", which is very good. Old Tbilisi seems to have been left almost completely untouched by the Soviet Union; this is as complete an 18th and 19th century streetscape in its own way as St Petersburg, just with despotic planning replaced by benign anarchy. The public buildings are, of course, mainly religious – a brick synagogue, in good condition, a florid Iranian mosque (with a bathhouse nearby) and half a dozen churches, stony and conical. Walk up the spirals and you'll come to a fortress and to Mother Georgia,

Exotica

The Lisbon of the Caucasus

the only real Soviet contribution to the ensemble, in the Giant Female Warrior genre otherwise seen in Kyiv, Volgograd and Yerevan. Clad in titanium, she holds a sword and a teacup, to show that she is as welcoming as she is vigilant.

You could imagine this wonderful, if appallingly dilapidated, townscape gradually tidying itself up into a sort of Caucasian Lisbon, retaining its faded grandeur but smartening into a top Creative Class destination. That's obviously what the city's authorities want; as we've seen, Saakashvili regards hipster districts of New York to be a model for post-Soviet "civil society". However, the means of going about it are typically blunt. Several streets just by the river have been completely rebuilt into Disney versions of the Old Town, still obviously with the same architectural features of dangling wooden galleries and cantilevered bays, but with all of the patina, the texture, removed, often along with the residents, who own their properties as a result

Mother is watching

of post-Soviet "instant privatisation" of housing. At the centre of the Disney Tbilisi is a statue of the great film director Sergei Parajanov, an Armenian born and raised in the city. This Old Town, mostly until comparatively recently inhabited by Armenians along with Jews and Georgians, is the sort of ethnographic space that he charted in his major films, each of which created a colourful, eroticised and abstracted portrait of particular folk cultures, of the sort that Soviet ethnographers catalogued, reified and celebrated – Ukrainian Hutsuls in *Shadows of Forgotten Ancestors*, medieval Armenia in *The Colour of Pomegranates*, the Persian culture of Azerbaijan in *Ashik Kerib*. Late in life, Parajanov, who was jailed for several years under Brezhnev for his bisexuality, spoke sadly of the ethnic conflict that engulfed the Caucasus, and of how "only a Stalin" could unite it. Here in the statue, he leaps out of a wall to grinningly greet tourists in a mini-Caucasian theme park.

Here's Parajanov!

That's the past – what of the future? Cross the river again, through a glass bridge by the otherwise fairly obscure but big-in-Georgia architect Michele de Lucchi, whose sanitary towel-evoking form has led to it being nicknamed "the *Always* Bridge" (they're good at derisive names for buildings in Tbilisi), and you come to the recently constructed Rike Park, a public space that shows the ambition, schizophrenia and horror vacui of "Project Georgia" maybe better than anywhere else. It is surrounded by a gorge, onto which are some typically dilapidated Old Tbilisi houses and two crowning structures, which suggest a profound shift in taste as "Project Georgia" progressed. The earliest, again by De Lucchi, is a totally typical post-Soviet governmental building that could be in Azerbaijan, Uzbekistan, Tajikistan, Kazakhstan, an illiterate combination of fibreglass Roman

Sanitary Tbilisi

columns and a glass dome, in the usual attempt to combine the image of the White House and Norman Foster's Reichstag, an image of power that is banal and tediously authoritarian, set, here, in such a position that it can survey the surrounding city. It's also not even used for its intended purpose – after Saakashvili was voted out, the new government decided to move back to the city centre. Next to it, though, is something else. A set of bent squares of raw concrete, this is a private house similar to, but not apparently actually designed by, the work of Jurgen Mayer H, the German firm who have so impressively branded the "Project". Below these is the park.

Rike Park is not a very restful park. It contains a theatre and art gallery in two intestinal glass tubes, again by Fuksas, a statue of a grand piano, a bronze statue of Ronald Reagan, and a set of giant

Bad Taste Palace

Star politician, star architect

Tbilisi is exciting

chess pieces. There is evidently some symbolism here but it's hard to work out what exactly it is, or who the pawns are. A cable car will take you back to the Old Town, giving a panorama of that extraordinary hilltown; just outside it, you'll see a sprawling private house, with a flying saucer, a 2000s Britain-style swooping roof, some steel and a lot of green glass. This is the overdesigned lair of Saakashvili's nemesis, Bidzina Ivanishvili, an oligarch who made billions in the usual para-legal manner in post-Soviet Russia (not, tellingly, in Georgia) and who essentially runs the governing party. Who are of course called "Georgian Dream". Just like in the old days, you don't expect a change at the top to involve a change in ethics.

One puzzling side-effect of the architectural attention paid to Georgia, as it rebranded itself with the aid of *Dezeen* and *ArchDaily*, was people noticing – assisted, importantly, by an active local branch of the international modernist preservation group Docomomo – the extraordinary architecture that was built here in the late-Soviet era. Most of all, two buildings are now almost famous: the expressionist cathedral that is the Palace of Weddings, and the tumbling Constructivist skyscraper of Georgi Chakhava's Ministry of Highways, which now finally gets its due both via a restoration to house the Bank of Georgia and through appearing on thousands of Tumblrs, Instagram accounts and Pinterest boards. The building is as remarkable in person as it is on a smartphone, and might even be more so. Made up of two vertical, and what can probably best be described as five "horizontal towers", it clings to a gorge fronting the river; both from above, where the horizontal blocks plunge vertiginously into the air, and from below, where it becomes a modernised image of the precipitous cantilevered pile-up of the old town, it is a profoundly physical piece of architecture. It is however a pain in the arse to get to, without a pedestrian approach from the ground, and with the elevated part in a messy suburb. Walk around it, as you will have to in order to eventually find a place to safely cross the road (the Ministry of Highways was evidently not talking to a Ministry of Pedestrians), past two yellow parasols that were presumably once part of a bus stop, and there's another, lesser known awesome building, the Georgian Radio Headquarters (now "Radio Fortuna"), which also responds to the sharp topography by forming itself into overlapping upper and lower sections; but this one is more obviously in a "national" style, with Babylonian-Soviet sculptural reliefs, and raising its long upper volume on almost classical columns. Further on is a national heroic monument of some kind, with gorgeously carved but sadly to me illegible Georgian letters and a man fighting a lion, bulging, organic and macho, it sums up the Georgian Soviet-National style well. Then, you can cross the road.

Little of the Awesome Ruined Soviet Architecture of Tbilisi can be found in the city centre. You can reach one cluster of it via the

Around the Ministry of Highways

excellent Metro, to Isani station, whose billowing concrete shell roof is not dissmilar to, but significantly more elegant than, those of Fuksas' Public Service Hall. It has been all but destroyed by poor quality restoration. This is modernist Tbilisi, and the first thing you notice is the extreme balcony surgery. What brought this into being was an accounting fiddle with the Five Year Plans under Gorbachev, where the local planners intended to use the already existing habit of self-building extensions and cantilevering buildings over each other to achieve the Republic's housing targets purely through residents building their own housing onto their existing state-provided prefabricated flats.[2] That this comes from plan, and not accident, is visible in the steel frames that cling to the 1960s flats, into which the new extensions are inserted – relatively high-tech, as self-building goes (of course,

Ancient Brutalism

even then it's a deeply unwise thing to do in a country prone to earthquakes, which have sent these extensions toppling). What you can see in all the suburbs of Tbilisi, however, is the result of the refugee crisis caused here by the 1990s wars in the breakaway "republics" of Abkhazia and South Ossetia, both of which ethnically cleansed their Georgian population at the climax of the conflict. The image of Soviet modernity – the provision of mass-produced housing, practically for free – became an image of state collapse or of individual "resilient" endeavour, or both. These have only been cleansed from the Hotel Intourist, so in every suburb of Tbilisi they are the first thing you see when you look at any building.

One street of them leads to the Exhibition of Economic Achievements, laid out in 1961. As we have seen in Moscow (there is another, very similar, in Kyiv), these were a Soviet typology that was somewhere between Trade Fair, Expo and Propaganda Theme Park,

Balcony surgery

where the amazing things about the planned economy would be showcased to dazzled visitors. The degree to which Soviet Georgia ever built the smooth Fordist economy depicted here is moot; Georgia did well out of the post-Stalin USSR, with a high standard of living, and higher than average levels of consumption and car ownership (along with the usual Soviet state provision) that belied a relatively low level of industrial development and economic growth, a disparity usually explained by Georgia's centrality to the Soviet "second economy" of private plots, graft and deal-making.[3]

Unreal as it is, the society imagined and depicted here is attractive. Unlike the Ukrainian and Russian examples, the Exhibition of Economic Achievements of the Georgian Soviet Socialist Republic is not Neoclassical or Baroque, and is devoid of marble or gilding. It is a showcase instead of Soviet modernism, here deployed to similar ends of propaganda narratives and optimistic gateways. The entrance

We are planning

to the complex is through a thin concrete arch, beautifully engineered, and through that, Japanese gardens around ponds are fringed with low glass blocks, decorated with reliefs and mosaics themed around the Soviet economy. On a polychrome smalti mosaic are cogs, satellites, rockets, blueprints, held up by confident and faceless men and women; on a green stone relief, curvaceous peasants milk cows, play pipes, pick pomegranates and harvest crops. It is not dissimilar to Parajanov's ethnographic world, except here combined with an image of the noble past passing unstoppably to the Communist future. Can it honestly be said that these images of a conflict-free and pristine socialist path are significantly different from those of Georgia's European path? Not really, although without doubt the socialist version was much more fairly distributed. Both also utilise a flashy modern architecture of vaulting engineering and structural dramatics, both are state-

Atom, cog, plane

sponsored, and both are largely a matter of enclaves. Both of them also rested on repression.

Walking back to the Metro station, you come to an unfinished tower, into which people have already inserted their flats, a building that is a squat before it has ever had the chance to be anything else. The housing pressure on the capital is clearly immense, even twenty years after the end of the wars over Abkhazia and Ossetia, and the state clearly doesn't intend to do much about it. Just opposite, the police station seems to be watching this unconcerned. The one typology which never featured in all the glossy photo stories on the New Georgia is the police stations, which is curious given that they were probably much more crucial to Saakashvili's successes than the galleries, civic centres and glossy airports. Big, green glass buildings (for "transparency", though you can't see inside) in a cheap, wipe-clean

Squatting a work in progress

idiom that recalls British PFI architecture, there are more of them in Tbilisi than I've ever seen in any capital city, on corners, overlooking the crumbling apartment buildings and chaotic street markets and the tiny little enclaves of "Western" hotels and shops. This massive beefing up of state power had the desired effect, in that corruption did indeed go down – unlike the level of arrests, with zero tolerance policies leading to an increasingly huge prison population. The regeneration of New York, the inspiration, relied as much on an aggressive police force and a massive rise in incarceration rates as it did on sourdough bakeries and boutique art galleries. Here, Georgia has followed the model faithfully. It was the stick, not the carrot, which worked for Saakashvili until his eventual defeat, and to design the stick, there is no need to commission interesting European architects.

A very big police station

FROM THE PURGES TO PARADISE

SEVAN WRITERS' RESORT, Sevanavank

There are a lot of accounts by famous writers of Lake Sevan, in the centre of Armenia. In his 1933 *Journey to Armenia*, Osip Mandelstam writes of how he "spent a month enjoying the lake water that stood at a height of two thousand feet above sea level", and the monastery that overlooked it, "literally paved with the fiery red slabs of nameless graves"[1]; Nadezhda Mandelstam remembered in her memoirs testing new Zeiss binoculars on the landscape around, whose bright primary colours created a "naïve painting" effect.[2] Three decades later, Vassily Grossman described the landscape as a "rough stone dish, black and blue and the colour of rust" within which the lake was "deep blue, and almost boundless".[3] Simone de Beauvoir, who visited with Sartre, wrote in 1972 of "a pinkish, chaotic desert with a bright blue lake in the middle of it".[4] What all these writers were doing here was visiting the Sevan Writers' Resort, built in the early 1930s by the Writers' Union of the Armenian Soviet Socialist Republic. What none of them wrote about, however, was the story of the building itself (just a "hotel", for de Beauvoir), a tragic saga encompassing the Soviet avant-garde, Stalinist repressions, the optimism of the Thaw, and the slow decline of the post-Soviet years. With the resort having recently held a group exhibition about its history, and about to face a full restoration, that story might become better known. The site where the Writers' Resort stands was originally an island in the lake, which became a peninsula when the lake's level was lowered for irrigation works in the Thirties. On the top of the peninsula's steep hill is a ninth-century monastery, whose conical churches were made from the same harsh red and brown rocks as the landscape around. But the craggy aesthetic of the monastery didn't influence the architects Gevorg Kochar and Mikael Mazmanyan when they were commissioned to design a Writers' Resort here in 1932. In the mid-1920s, Kochar and Mazmanyan had been involved with the Constructivist group Standard, an Armenian equivalent to groups like LEF in Russia and New Generation in Ukraine; their ideas were opposed to those who tried to create a "national school" in Armenian Soviet architecture. The image on the first issue of *Standard*, a montage of Lenin atop some cranks and cogs, gives a good idea of where they were coming from.[5] Subsequently founding

The mountains around Lake Sevan

an Organisation of Proletarian Architects of Armenia, they argued for ignoring the stylistic elements of historic architecture in favour of engaging with climate and topography. So their Writers Resort is laconic, rationalist, and calm – four storeys, built into the lower part of the peninsula, with curved balconies and a glazed stair-tower to offer as much sight of the lake as possible. In 1937, not very long after the resort hosted its first guests, Kochar and Mazmanyan were arrested and deported to the Arctic Circle, about as far from Lake Sevan as it's possible to imagine. They would spend fifteen years in Norilsk until they were "rehabilitated" after the death of Stalin. It's here that the story has an extremely unusual second act. In the early Sixties, after his return to Armenia, Kochar was commissioned to design a new cafe wing to the resort he'd co-designed thirty years earlier. The result is astonishing. While in the 1920s and 1930s, Soviet avant-garde architects dreamt of using new technology to create almost weightless,

The 1930s Writers' Resort

The 1960s Writers' Resort

precipitous structures of concrete and glass, what they built was the simpler, boxy modernism you can see in the 1932 resort. In 1963, Kochar got to actually build an avant-garde dream project. A long curved glass volume is cantilevered right out above the rocks overlooking the lake, so far that you could park trucks underneath it, with the whole construction balanced on one thick concrete leg. It's a genuinely spectacular vindication of the ideas about a local modernism that Kochar and Mazmanyan had advanced in the Twenties: completely integrated into its site, a sentry nestled above the rocks, allowing cafe customers panoramic views of the lake and the mountains. It doesn't genuflect to the monastery or the historic architecture around, preferring instead a futurist aesthetic suited to a country that was sending people into space. Since the Sixties – and especially in the last few years – the building has become an oft-photographed emblem of the modernism of the Khrushchev Thaw, here given particular poignancy because of the fact that it was the creation of one of Stalin's victims, coming back to complete the unfinished business of the 1920s.

The terrace of the 1930s Resort

The Writers' Resort, still owned by the Writers' Union of Armenia, is dilapidated, and is now ringed by caravans, huts and some dodgy looking new hotels, and a market in front of the steps leading up to the monastery. But it still takes guests, and the cafe serves trout fished from the lake, described by Simone de Beauvoir as "delicious", which seemed to me an understatement. In late 2017, the resort had an exhibition about itself in its two buildings, part of The Mount Analogue, a multi-part series of installations across Armenian towns and cities. In Sevan, "DéjàVu Standart", curated by the architectural historian and writer Ruben Arevshatyan, combines historical exhibits about the Armenian avant-garde, with reproductions of issues of Standard and drawings and models of utopian projects of the Twenties, 1960s family photos and Sartre and de Beauvoir publicity shots. A series of films on modernism, utopia and socialism by the likes of Gerard

Futurist paradise

Byrne and Igor Grubic played in the public spaces of the two buildings. It felt like a rare successful Soviet utopian project; the resort is not luxurious or opulent, but sitting on the curved terraces of the 1932 building, precisely calculated to parallel the sudden swoop of the cafe, with the red and green of the bushes on the shore, the snow-capped black crags in the near distance and the sun sparkling on the water, it is some kind of paradise.

But what now? The surroundings are messy, but the landscape could hardly be ruined no matter how hard developers tried. People still holiday here, mainly from within Armenia itself, and the caravans are as oddly fitting as the new hotel buildings are typically post-Soviet gimcrack. The resort clearly needs repair and renovation, and the current plans are ambitious. A grant as part of the Getty Foundation's "Keeping it Modern" programme has funded an investigation into the building's fabric by architects from Helsinki's Alvar Aalto Foundation. The resulting proposals by the Armenian designers Urbanlab envisage this as a pilot project to show what is possible in the renovation of Soviet modernist buildings, in a context where they are either mutilated in clumsy "Euro-renovations" or demolished in favour of approximations of medieval churches. According to architect Sarhat Petrosyan, reminding me that "Armenia is a very poor country", the results will need to be "self-sustaining", so that the renovation can pay for itself, and the building not fall again into neglect and dilapidation. There will be a conference centre and a high-end restaurant; after all, this was never a building for everybody, and writers will still get a 50% discount. But at the time of writing, at the turn of 2018, you'll find something entirely unique: a cheap hostel in a mountain lake, a modern art gallery, and a living museum of Soviet tragedy and achievement unlike any other.

Air Cathedral

MYSTERIOUS CITIES OF PINK AND GOLD

YEREVAN, Erevan, Erebuni

The first sights of Yerevan do not suggest a city planned or built with a great deal of care and consideration. Zvartnots Airport is named after a ruined, circular-planned cathedral nearby, and consists of two parts: a totally standard contemporary airport, and the disused original terminal, built in 1975 to the designs of Levon Cherkezyan, Spartak Khachikyan, Zhorzh Shekhlyan and Artur Tarkhanyan. Its circular form was allegedly inspired by Zvartnots Cathedral, but it doubled as a space station in the Polish-Soviet children's epic *Pan Kleks*. A circus of concrete and aluminium surrounds a central control tower, which is a little too commanding to be just keeping an eye on the Aeroflot flights to Moscow. From this derelict building you can already infer two very important things about Armenian modern architecture – an appeal to the glorious past, combined with a flamboyant futurism; and along with that, a tendency to neglect, with unique things passed over for standardised products. The road from the airport, meanwhile, gives a completely false sense of what sort of a city (central) Yerevan is. Dusty, small houses and dozens of neon-lit improvised kiosks and gas stations, and behind them, the nondescript fortress of the largest US embassy in the world outside of Baghdad – the largest, when it was built in 2005. It's not here, as it might be in the Baltic, to keep an eye on Russia, but because of Armenia's position on the borders of Iran and

Turkey, and a short distance from Iraq and Syria; this geography doesn't otherwise benefit Armenia much, given that the borders with Turkey and Azerbaijan are firmly closed, with trains allowed through Georgia and *marshrutki* passing from the Armenian-controlled Nagorno-Karabakh Republic (officially in Azerbaijan) into Iran. And then, quite abruptly, you're in an absolutely exemplary, planned, and impeccably "European" city. Yerevan offers the spectacle of a city that is extremely ancient (it was founded as Erebuni in the eighth century BCE – some fortress ruins are preserved in the suburbs), but where almost everything you can see was built between the 1920s and 1980s. It also offers the spectacle of a Soviet city where the notion of a "national form" was deployed consistently by "national" architects from the very beginning, practically within days of Soviet power being established; modernism, even in the Soviet era, has always been an exception. Some explanation of this can be found in the horrific events that immediately preceded its incorporation into the Soviet Union. In the nineteenth century, Armenia was divided between the Ottoman and Russian Empires; the assumption that Christian Armenians would sympathise with the Russians was the logic of the first genocide of the twentieth century, the extermination in 1915 of over a million Western Armenians by the Young Turk government. Refugees streamed into Yerevan – a small city which became briefly the capital of an independent republic in the aftermath of 1917, though in those years it was constantly under threat of disappearance through wars with Turkey, Georgia and Azerbaijan. The Bolsheviks, who had a large proportion of Armenian activists, eventually retook eastern Armenia in 1920, with the Red Army marching in without firing a shot.[1] Within a couple of years, the Bolshevik government of Soviet Armenia commissioned Alexander Tamanyan – an exile from revolutionary Petersburg, and now one of the "bourgeois specialists" whose expertise the Reds found useful – to design a town plan for its capital.

The resulting plan is an icon of the city.[2] You can find it on logos, as a relief in cafes, as an object of branding. It is not a twentieth-century plan in any way, more of a last flowering of the nineteenth: with its green Ringstrasse, and its radial spokes terminating in a vast opera house, it was more like the Hapsburg Empire reborn in the Soviet Caucasus. And as with a Hapsburg city, the result is exceptionally pleasant, logical and easy to understand. There is a rhetorical aspect to it, too. Many of the main streets lead up to slopes, from where you can get jaw-dropping views of Mount Ararat, the double-peaked mountain where Noah's Ark ended up, its snowy top roaring up out of the clouds. Mount Ararat is, however, just over the border, in Turkey. It featured nonetheless on Soviet Armenia's coat of arms. The plan seems to have been deliberately executed to create a longing for the lost Western parts of Armenia, and for the hundreds of thousands who were massacred there. It's either town planning as memorial, or town planning as irredentism, depending on what side of Ararat you're on.

There are two main squares in Tamanyan's plan – Lenin (now Republic) Square and Opera Square, the former largely laid out in the

Relief of the Tamanyan Plan in the Nova Hotel

Twenties, the latter in the Thirties. Lenin Square is a elongated circus, flanked by opulent classical buildings built between the Twenties and Seventies by Tamanyan and his students, which aim to be deliberately timeless. The House of Government, the main hotel, and the National Museum, all feature the gorgeous stonework that defines the city, in pink tufa, yellow sandstone and grey basalt; every building has colonnades, paired columns, deeply inset archways and abundant ornamentation, based on an at least partly imaginary idea of ancient Armenian architecture; friezes of ancient warriors and workers and peasants represent the "Soviet" contribution. All this rhetoric – "national in form, socialist in content", as the Stalinist cliché went – is common to socialist realist architecture all over the union, but there are two major differences in the Armenian version. The first is the richness of the craftsmanship. In Ukraine, Belarus, Kazakhstan, this would be tiles or stucco on top of concrete or breezeblock, but

Soviet Armenia's coat of arms, with Ararat in the centre

Republic Square, gold

Republic Square, pink

here, what you can see is beautifully cut, rich ashlar, warm in colour, which ages handsomely, however little it is renovated. The second is the fact that much of this actually *precedes* the shift in the early 1930s to a pompous Neoclassicism. As much as he was one of the last great beaux-arts architect-planners, Alexander Tamanyan was perhaps one of the first Stalinist architects, hitting early on that comparison of nationalist imagery, monumental symmetry and heroic "the people's right to colonnades" populism.

His Opera Square is less ripe and unusual. The building (by Tamanyan himself, of 1933) is fairly conventional, a big, heavy Opera House much like the one in Minsk, with one design feature that speaks of its time – a processional route through the building, under huge open colonnades, intended for public parades. This factoring in of public assembly proved influential – the Opera Square has been the focal point for demonstrations ever since it was built, whether centrally organised or oppositional. The city government has responded to this

Opera Square

by trying to fill the space with cafes and funfair attractions, but it still had a central role, among others, in the "Electric Yerevan" protests of 2015.[3] From here, open-top tourbuses, with the ambiguous promise "Yerevan, Feel the Warmness", can take you around Tamanyan's city.

What you will see placed on the hills are the major monuments of the planned Neoclassical city: the Ararat Cognac Factory, designed by Rafael Israelyan in 1938, in a lurid, almost orange stone; the Mother Armenia statue, replacing one of Stalin in the Sixties; and the major presence on the horizon of Mashtots Avenue, built as "Stalin Avenue" – the Matenadaran, a museum and archive dedicated to the display and keeping of illuminated manuscripts, from Armenian churches and monasteries that stretch from the Armenian republic, historically Armenian lands in Asia Minor, and the huge diaspora that reaches from the USA to Poland to the Middle East. The Matenadaran was designed by Mark Grigoryan in 1945, and completed twelve years later, by which time it was out of fashion, surely one of the most

Manuscript monolith

"superfluous" and "excessive" of Stalinist schemes. Regardless, it is an unforgettable building. Hewn from grey-white basalt, and rising from a monumental plinth at the top of the hill, it is heavy and square in its form, given a sense of height and dominance through carved niches and archways; carved out of the same basalt, as if emerging out of the building, are hieratic, ancient Mesopotamian-style statues of great Armenian scholars. Attempts to simulate the ancient are of course ubiquitous in eclectic and historicist architecture, but this has the kind of despotic power and seamless craftsmanship that could convince you it really has been here forever. In the interior, the spaces (if not the exhibits) are more prosaic, in a normal Stalin-classical vein, and a large picture window gives you the view out towards Ararat. These ceremonial spaces of Stalinist Yerevan give the place the air of some sort of Biblical epic, a Cecil B. Demille approach to quasi-ancient scenography. In fact, what it most reminded me of was the 1980s French cartoon *The Mysterious Cities of Gold*, whose Mesoamerican-Postmodernist cities of ziggurats, sculpted lions and birds could plausibly have been inspired by the city, were there any evidence of its creators paying it a visit.

Unusually for a big city on the USSR's periphery, it is hard to imagine what a successful bourgeois independent government would have done differently to this. It's also notable that, like in a bourgeois Mediterranean or Levantine city of the same date (but unlike an average Soviet city of the same), all the interest, wealth and grandeur is in the centre, and there are "informal settlements" as well as worn and unrenovated prefab slabs and towers on the outskirts. However, unlike in Tbilisi, informality has not quite taken over the centre. Tamanyan's city, and the ancient-Stalinist architectural style he pioneered, has not been given much in the way of ungainly balcony extensions inserted into its grand loggias, and the pink tufa is largely uninterrupted by plastic and plasterboard. At least, that's the impression you could form by just walking around the streets themselves. Pass inside the courtyards – marked by cute street art murals of cityscapes – and the situation is completely different. Here, informality and planning failure are as inescapable and unstoppable as they are in the Georgian capital. A second layer of balconies, some of them, in the Georgian manner, an entire flat deep, has been attached; new towers, everything from blocks of flats to office towers to hipster hotels, have been inserted into these public spaces. A tangle of services and power lines stretch above the asphalt, and the individual gas metres are attached via convoluted pipes to the bottoms of the buildings. Because of this, it's clear that has happened isn't actually a continuity of planning culture at all, just the creation of a city plan so strong that thirty years of neglect couldn't seriously affect it.

The traces of the genuinely ancient city are also to be found behind the main streets: rather than being made prominent in Tamanyan's plan (unusually for a neoclassicist), they often appear like afterthoughts and surprises. One of these surprises has recently been uncovered from

Second layers in a city centre courtyard

its former place in a courtyard, and Tamanyan's presumably deliberate downplaying of the "real" ancient Armenian city has been redressed. When the plan was being executed in the 1930s, the city's authorities demolished an eighteenth-century basilica, which they considered to be of little worth. But in the process of destruction, they found that what they thought was an altar, was actually the tiny, red and yellow thirteenth-century Katoghike Church; this they decided to preserve, as it was of genuine "historical significance" in a way that apparently the later church was not. It's fascinating for how similar it is to a Byzantine church in its plan and frescoes, and how unlike, in the way that the façade has been covered with Biblical verses in Armenian script, and even with drawings and sketches, so that it can be "read" from the outside. It's also an easy place to see the sources for the Graeco-Persian ornament etched into the façades of the city's twentieth-century buildings. Originally, the Katoghike Church was just in another Stalinist courtyard; but recently, the buildings around it were demolished and the much bigger St Anna Church in a similar style was built around it in 2015, framing, or rather dominating, the miniscule chapel. The new church is much better crafted than you would have any right to expect of a new church in the post-Soviet space – compared, for instance, with the Gateshead Metro Centre materials of the Cathedral of Christ the Saviour, it's not so bad, and proves that surprisingly, good building standards have continued in at least one former Soviet republic. But as townscape, it's sad and literal, and gives an unfortunately comic "little and large" effect.

The other historic building in a courtyard is Yerevan Mosque, built in the 1760s; until as recently as the late nineteenth century, the city had a Muslim majority. The mosque was the Museum of the City of Yerevan under the Soviets, but has since the 1990s been a mosque again, thanks in part to a restoration paid for by the southern neighbour, Iran. It's opposite the Central Market, another dramatic building in the Matenadaran's Babylonian-Stalinist manner, with golden gates, ornamented with wheat, berries and other abundant things; cross

Little and Large

Orient

the road, and the mosque is reached through a decorated gate, and with a lovely, quiet green square between that and the mosque itself. It is a mosque in the Persian style found across Central Asia, rather than in the Ottoman style of the Balkans and Western Asia. The brick construction and geometric tiles of the gateway-like façade are topped by a gorgeous and highly mammarial blue dome, inset with yellow tiles shaped into what look like, but clearly are not, masks.

With a simulated ancient city of such grandeur and intensity, any kind of modern architecture has found it hard to make much of an appeal. The architect and historian Karen Balyan talks about the "two deaths of Armenian modernism"; the first happened when the avant-garde "proletarian" architects of the Twenties and early Thirties lost their positions when the Opera House was built and happened to chime with the new, hierarchical and historicist ideas being insisted upon in Moscow. Yerevan's savvier proletarian architects,

Orientalism

like Karo Alabyan, followed suit, and became major figures in Soviet architecture, designing prestige projects like Moscow's Red Army Theatre, and heading – and purging – the Union of Architects. Tellingly, despite the city being built up largely in the Twenties and Thirties, there are few interwar modernist buildings in Yerevan, none of them rivalling the originality and prominence of those in Moscow, Kharkiv, Yekaterinburg or even nearby Baku; the most interesting is probably the NKVD headquarters, laconic modernism with emphasised circular stairwells, clad in heavy, rusticated tufa. The "second death" took place in the 1970s, and was preceded by a much more extensive flowering of modernism, inserted into the Tamanyan plan between 1956 and the mid-Seventies.

The first part of the project is actually now invisible, and consisted of the replanning of Abovyan Street, a major Stalin-era artery, with pools, sculptures, benches and other attractive public spaces in a

Haut en Bas

lightweight mid-century-modern manner. A few of the sculptures survive, but otherwise this exists only in pictures. These public spaces were intended to link up with the green Ringstrasse of Tamanyan's plan, and some major new buildings were placed into the green space itself – the Komitas Chamber Theatre designed by Stepan Kyurkchyan in 1968, the same architect's Yeritasardakan Metro station, designed in 1972 and opened in 1981, and the House of Chess Players, designed by Zhanna Mesheryakova in 1967. These are part of a green ring which is very extensively used, though not cared for particularly by the city authorities – not only cafes but also a KFC has been opened in the middle of the parkland.[4]

Along with other scattered modernist complexes – such as the powerful but small-scale Brutalist Puppet Theatre, with its shutter-marked concrete and polka-dot high-rises above, designed by Margarita Hayrapetyan in 1968 – these show the scope that Armenian

Public Space

architects were capable of in that era, even when moving away from the emulations of the ancients on the tops of the hills. There is still much obvious inspiration from historic architecture, only in a much more subtle way – the carved chessmen on the otherwise unornamented stone flanks of the House of Chess, or the concrete hall of the Komitas Theatre, which has the lofty, contemplative proportions of an Armenian chapel. Other effects are entirely inventions of the architects themselves. The protruding cylinder of Yeritasardakan station is actually a lightwell for the deep escalators below, so that you emerge right out of the depths into sunlight.

Modernist buildings that have occupied island sites have fared less well. The largest is the Rossiya Cinema, designed by the team of Spartak Khachiyan, Hrachik Poghosyan and Artur Tarkhanyan and built from 1968-75. Its two auditoriums are scooped up into two concrete wings. It has been disused for some years. In a telling anecdote

The Puppet Theatre

indicating the way in which owners think about their buildings, and how small a city this is, the Armenian-Ukrainian-British-Finnish participants in an architectural conference encountered the owner of the Rossiya Cinema in a bar, while the conference was going on. He showed off the kitsch he was going to replace the ugly Soviet building with, and they showed him, as means to convince, pictures of the similarly "ugly" South Bank in London and implored him to reconsider; he was apparently close to being convinced – London, after all! Opposite, is an image of where the Armenian national tradition in architecture ended up. Begun as the Soviet Union collapsed and finished in 1997 to the designs of Stepan Kurkchyan, the Gregory the Illuminator Cathedral is a repro ancient church, the cathedral Tamanyan's socialist city never had, modernised slightly through a cubistic approach to form, but otherwise "looking like a church" enough to satisfy the brief.

Rossiya Cinema, potential London South Bank

How architecture in Yerevan went from the confident Brutalism of the Puppet Theatre or the Rossiya Cinema to this sort of traditionalist bet-hedging is best described via the triumphant return of the national style in the 1970s – Balyan's "second death" of Armenian modernism. Most of the buildings that resulted from this in the first instance are wonderful, and they mark a triumphant return to fantasy, scenography, ornament and patriotic tale-telling. The building that, for Balyan, finished off Armenian modernism for the second time was the National Museum, designed in the Seventies on Lenin/Republic Square. Integrated seamlessly into Tamanyan's ensemble, these seven storeys of Armenian church frescoes, bad Russian paintings and decent Soviet ones are most notable for the paintings of Martiros Saryan, whose visions of the Armenian landscape look fauvist-inspired, but actually represent quite accurately its unusually bright colours. Another example can be found just adjacent, at the Republic Square Metro station, designed by Jim Torosyan. Steps take you down to a lotus-shaped square around a fountain; tufa canopies above are shaped into abstracted little horses, with a mystic crypt beneath. A reminder of the city's actual geographic location (and the extent of the Armenian diaspora) can be found in this sunken square – "Damascus", a street of Syrian shops opened to cater for the Syrian Armenians that have fled here in recent years.

A small-scale example of this fantastical style can be seen in the Khnko Aper Children's Library, designed in 1980 by Levon Ghulumyan and Rouzan Alaverdyan. Its presence on the street, in two angular blocks with a staircase up the middle, is straightforward enough, but inside, you're deep in the fairytale world of ancient socialist Yerevan, with the wooden front doors carved like Assyrian tablets, and a mindbending mural in the main reading room filled with a highly *Mysterious Cities of Gold* depiction of Armenian history from the eighth century BCE to the 1980s. Atomic power, tower blocks, very late-Soviet facial hair and coiffures are the eventual terminus of a world of pagan temples, Sphinxes, goddesses and tunics.

Republic Square, above

Republic Square, below

Doors into the Children's Library

Using similar imagery, although to a much more extreme end, is the Cascade, begun in 1975 and left unfinished at the USSR's collapse, by the architects Sargis Gurzadyan, Aslan Mkhitaryan and Jim Torosyan. This travertine-clad stairway, a sort of steroidal, Biblical Odessa Steps that doesn't lead to the sea, is one of the emblems of the city, the only other twentieth-century structure that competes with the Tamanyan plan in Yerevan's image of itself. Fountains and sculptures at each level aim to represent, in an abstract form, different eras of Armenian history, which was intended to end, right at the top, with a representation of Communism, which presumably would have been built by the time the Cascade was finished. This part of it is bare concrete with rusting reinforcement sticking out, the symbolism of which doesn't escape anyone here. There is a monument to Tamanyan at the foot of the Cascade, and like his plan, this is public space of such quality and imagination that nothing could destroy it.

Historical Materialism

The "Soviet Armenia" part of the Cascade may never have been built, but there has been major building activity in the last ten years, as the country gradually recovered from the war and economic collapse of the 1990s. It has presented itself not as the repudiation, but as the "completion" of Tamanyan's plan (an interpretation of it that architectural historians in Yerevan find deeply dubious). The Northern Avenue leads from the opera through what was, until 2007, the only surviving district of "old Yerevan" left in the centre. Unsurprisingly, given how little survives from before the 1920s, this was bitterly opposed, not least by the residents, who were offered – at first – token amounts for their homes. A campaign emerged out of this, one of several "right to the city" movements that have taken hold in Yerevan in the last decade – another was focussed on the proposed demolition of an open-air 1960s cinema to make way for another reconstructed church. Eventually, the state-business conglomerate behind the venue offered enough to residents to induce them to back down, and a few

The Cascade

Civil Society

houses were saved, here and there, by being integrated into the new buildings. The avenue's architecture is in a reduced, dense version of that of the 1920s and 1970s – not entirely unskilled, with some residual command of materials, corners and vistas. The kicker is in the salvaged houses, where two-storey red-stone villas are encased in ten-storey Postmodernist constructions, which makes them look ridiculous. Pointing to one of these, the architect Sarhat Petrosyan, who had been involved in the campaign, ruefully comments: "that was the first great victory of Yerevan civil society".[5] Much worse is Vazgen Sargsyan Street, a "neo-Stalinist" (in Ruben Arevshatyan's words) collection of obnoxious domineering office blocks and hotels, lining one of Tamanyan's green strips, on either side of a monument to the Bolshevik leader Stepan Shahumyan. It's one of the few parts of

Old Bolshevik and Neo-Stalinism

central Yerevan that is not a pleasure to walk down. In both, though, the dominance of Tamanyan's ideas is still unchallenged, even in this attenuated, somewhat lumpen interpretation.

Yerevan has the distinction of having the only Soviet-built Metro where the surface entrances, often formed into sculptural open public spaces, are more interesting than the underground halls, which are mostly quite reduced versions of the usual marble-clad subterranean cathedrals. One of them is full of adverts for Debenhams. The fact that this compact city has a Metro at all comes, according to Ruben Arevshatyan, from the creative lobbying of Moscow by the Armenian Communist bureaucracy – insisting that despite the city's small size, they had so much congestion that they needed a Metro, Yerevan's authorities arranged traffic jams to impress the visiting Ministry of Transport. Mostly, at least in terms of architecture and city planning, Moscow seems to have been treated as if it was not there, unless it came to getting funding for something. The Metro's nomenclature shows the ecumenical, or schizophrenic attitude to Soviet history, so different from the absolutes insisted on elsewhere; the network was renamed in 1999 after Karen Demirchyan, the chair of the Armenian Communist Party when it was built, and one of its major stations was renamed in 1992 after Garegin Ndzheh, a nationalist leader and sometime Nazi collaborator, who allegedly pleaded with Stalin while in prison to be allowed to serve Soviet Armenia, because he'd been so impressed with their rebuilding of Yerevan. It serves the Central Railway Station, a typical, if attractively restored Stalinist station with a spire and a barrel vault, whose domes are currently reimagined into an artwork of overlapping multicoloured arcs, in an installation by Felice Varini. It's very nice, but the station itself is half-empty, unsurprisingly given that it only serves stations in Armenia and Georgia. Flyposted adverts everywhere implore you to travel to Russia (where many Armenians travel for work) in tiny vans.

Also renamed after Karen Demirchyan – who was killed, along with much of the then-government, in a shooting at the Armenian

Abstract Baroque

Parliament in 1999 – is an enormous sports and concert centre, up on Tsitsernakaberd hill, overlooking the city and Mount Ararat. From the tufa classical streets below, you reach it by another cascade, a series of monumental steps and pools framing the bird-like profile of this vast complex, originally opened in 1983. It throws different monumental and modernist ideas at the wall, with enthusiastic abandon – Eero Saarinen's TWA terminal is an obvious presence, but along with further cascades going up the roof, and another ancients-and-Soviets sculptural frieze. This is the less famous of the two monuments on the hill: the other is much more important. After demonstrations calling for a memorial to the dead of 1915, Moscow acquiesced – despite the obvious antagonism it caused in relations with Turkey, which then as now denies the genocide – a competition was held, and the memorial complex was opened in 1967.

Sports cascade

The winners, Sashur Kalashyan and Artur Tarkhanyan, proposed a set of black granite stelae, leaning inwards to create an enclosed circle around an eternal flame, and a short distance away from this a spiked obelisk was created, visible at various points around the city. It is a powerful work, even without the requiems that the complex's management insist are piped through to be heard inside the granite circle. Its abstraction is rare in Soviet monumental architecture, except for a few other projects of the Sixties, where the insistence on striving bodies and obvious narratives was briefly challenged. Perhaps because of this abstraction, people have tried to impose meaning onto it, such as that the number of stelae represent ancient Armenian provinces, that the steps downwards were to represent the experiences of the victims, and so forth. According to Karen Balyan, who has written a

The Memorial to the Armenian Genocide

book on the complex, all these symbolic interpretations are mythical – the architects intended it to be abstract, nothing more, speaking only of itself, as a space of contemplation, remembrance and thought. In that, it is exceptionally modern still. The view from here towards Ararat, past the straggle of suburbs, retail parks and the US embassy, is overwhelming, particularly given the knowledge that it is not, nor is ever again likely again to be, a part of Armenia; and that it's on that side of the unpassable border that the Ottoman Armenians were massacred and driven into the desert to starve. Walking back to the bus from the memorial, still on the hill, my phone has its own commentary. The message chime goes, and the message reads: "Welcome to Turkey. Calls cost..."

Retail parks and Ararat

International

National

THE GREEN FRIENDS OF MANKIND

ALMATY, Alma-Ata, Verniy

The Almaty Hotel, in the centre of the former capital and largest city of Kazakhstan, was designed in 1963 by a team led by the architect Nikolay Ripinsky. Clad in blue tiles and curving seductively away from the city's rigid grid plan, it's the sort of chic mid-century modernism you'd expect to see in Miami or Havana. Only the polychrome mosaic of frolicking folk in folk costume gives it away as a distinctively "Soviet Sixties" product. A few months ago, this hotel held a round table on the preservation of modern architecture in Almaty, organised by the Garage Museum in Moscow.[1] Beginning with quite sober papers defining and charting the architectural developments in the former capital across the twentieth century, it had some very harsh words about the renovation of another building by the architect of the hotel: the Palace of the Republic, or as it was originally called and as everyone still calls it, the Lenin Palace. Photographs show a precisely calculated brutalist pavilion, disciplined and ordered, with a magical interior of coloured glass, suddenly covered over with mirrorglass and fake classical columns. Then, the architect who redesigned the palace stood up to defend himself. At this point, there was a furore, as he made excuses for what had happened. First, he pointed out that he had proposed seven different plans, beginning with a simple restoration, to the building's owners, only for them to choose the most destructive of the original fabric; clearly reluctantly, he justified the change with the comparison "in Soviet times we wore grey clothes, and now we wear colourful clothes". The speaker, Elizabeth Malinovskaya of Almaty's ARK gallery, was not impressed. "I do not have words for the emotions I feel when I look at the current façade". I tried to follow the argument through a translator, but it soon got out of hand, with claims about the drinking habits of the original architect and counter-claims about who really designed it in the first place. This heated, public argument about the preservation of the city's modern buildings seemed to stand for an entire complex of opinions about the city's history and its future. Not the least irony in the events was that this was a smaller adjunct to a larger conference and exhibition at the 2017 Expo in Astana, the planned capital that has supplanted Almaty as Kazakhstan's administrative centre. The exhibition, centred around photographs by Yuri Palmin and quasi-architectural wooden models of these "utopian skeletons" by the Kazakh ZIP Arts Group, argued

Colourful clothes

that the shift to Astana meant that unlike in other Central Asian capitals like Tashkent or Ashgabat, the Soviet city was untouched, with few buildings demolished or destroyed, and relatively little new construction. This contrasted with the ferocious argument at the Hotel Almaty, and with how many people in the city describe their buildings and the spaces around them, often with a sense of loss of an international "garden city".

Remembering the Gorod-Sad

The most obvious quality of Almaty – especially compared with Astana – is its extraordinary integration of landscape, urbanism and vegetation. It sits at the foot of the Tian Shan mountain range, where it meets the interminable Kazakh steppe, near the border with China. The greenery on the city's grid-planned streets is intense, and it grows onto the buildings, with creepers nearly covering limestone-clad brutalist apartment complexes, with cafes on their ground floors

Modernist Garden City

spilling onto the two-level pavements, with fast-flowing irrigation canals rushing alongside raised pedestrian levels, usually audible bubbling away when you sit outside and drink your tea. It is the greenest city I have ever seen. Although you gradually notice the poor quality of much of the built fabric, the effect remains of an exceptionally well-planned city – especially when you've experienced Astana, where the vast distances and lack of tree cover or pedestrian shelter make it feel like one city's unwinnable war against its own climate. But that's not geographical luck on Almaty's part. Beautiful as its mountains are, it is a highly inhospitable place to build a city, with extremely hot summers and extremely cold winters, and frequent earthquakes. The difference is that its builders – in an era before air conditioning and mass car ownership – recognised this, and planned accordingly

According to the scholar Caroline Erin Elkin, the Almaty "garden city" is a "meme"[2], which has informed the way the place has been discussed ever since the 1930s, when it was first built up as the capital of the Kazakh Soviet Socialist Republic. One official guidebook of the 1960s wrote of how "the green outfit is the pride of Alma-Ata, legally called a garden city. Greenery and flowers decorate the city, creating the conditions for cultural recreation, developing aesthetic tastes and love for the green friend of mankind".[3] The curator Yuliya Sorokina describes it today as the "Ghost of a Garden City"; a "fairy-tale landscape" of "lilacs, jasmine, uryuks and apple trees"[4], maintained by a specially set up local body, Zelenostroy, which is gradually being whittled down by unsympathetic businesses and an indifferent government.

Almaty is old by the standards of Astana, but very young compared with ancient Silk Road cities like Taraz or Turkistan, in Kazakhstan itself, or Tashkent, Bukhara or Samarkand outside it. The city that exists today was founded by Russian colonists as a citadel, Verniy, and then gradually built up as a local centre, largely through the work of the engineer Andrei Zenkov, whose earthquake-proof lightweight wooden structures were the first responses to the city's aggressive geology. Zenkov designed the city's major pre-Soviet monument, the 1911 Ascension Cathedral, a kind of funfair version of St Basil's, made only out of wood, without metal bolts.

The Soviet city, renamed "Alma-Ata" in 1921 (apparently a mangled version of the Kazakh for "the place with apple trees", *Almaty*) was initially a place where people were dumped, as much as where they came to create a new capital. Generations of dissidents, "formalists", or the merely unlucky were exiled here between the late Twenties and the mid-Thirties – among the earliest was Leon Trotsky in 1927, for whom Alma-Ata was his last address in the USSR before being deported to Turkey. Stalin deported entire nations here, such as Koreans and Volga Germans – most of the latter have left for the suburbs of Berlin, but there are still 30,000 Koreans in the city.

The Ascension Cathedral

Many of the accounts of the city come from these prisoners and exiles, most famously in the long-term Gulag inmate Yury Dombrovsky's novel *The Keeper of Antiquities*, published in *Novy Mir* in 1964, which describes the affairs of an archaeologist relocated to Alma-Ata in the 1930s to run the History Museum in the Ascension Cathedral. Exiled to "that curious city, so unlike any other city in the world"[5], his protagonist rhapsodises about Zenkov's daringly engineered wooden buildings, whose "barbaric ornamentation [...] perfectly expresses the spirit of the old town of Verny, as Zenkov built it: its youthfulness, its total lack of roots in the past, its naïveté, its independence and finally its bold determination never to fall flat on its face".[6] The other strain in the novel is the archaeologist's baffled impatience with local politicians' attempts to find a longer pedigree for Alma-Ata, insisting that this was a important ancient city, possibly even a Roman city, based on misunderstood excavations; indifferent to these nation-building efforts, the "keeper" prefers to research the nomads of the steppe and the buildings of the Russian colonists. At the end of the book, the cathedral is to be replaced with "a sort of shiny prismatic cube of glass and steel. The profusion of windows gave the building a multi-faceted look that reminded me of an insect's eye. There were arches at each end and the roof was crowned by a tower and a flag".[7]

This of course didn't happen – the church survives, and became a church again after 1991. But the description recalls a modern building that *was* built, the House of Government of the Kazakh Soviet Socialist Republic, designed by Moisei Ginzburg in 1928. Derived from research on Uzbekistan (actually a long way away, culturally and geographically), it resembles Le Corbusier's attempts at making a modernist "casbah" in North Africa, tightly packed cubic volumes with plenty of shelter and roof gardens. It is currently barely recognisable, and painted a queasy blue. Later 1930s buildings, like the Abay Opera House, with its mock-Islamic detailing on a boxy frame, aim to be "national in form, socialist in content". Deported here in 1941, the leftist Polish writer Alexander Wat recalled that "the Soviet buildings (are) the worst, pseudo-mosque style – the Opera House and so on" (it was co-designed by the chameleonic Alexey Shchusev, never an architect to tell his client something he didn't want to hear). "But you don't pay attention to that, mostly because of the marvellous trees, Alma-Ata's poplars", which are "truly evangelical, more beautiful than King Solomon's trees. Sunlit jewels".[8]

Wat found to his surprise that the city was full of filmmakers, artists and poets, who had been sent here en masse at the start of the war, far from the front – practically the entire Soviet film industry was in Alma-Ata. Yuliya Sorokina tells me that it's this combination of artists and prisoners (frequently, both) that defined the sort of place the Soviet capital became. "We had here all of the USSR's intelligentsia during the Second World War, and through Stalin's concentration camps. These people taught our teachers, they taught us." She argues that as a result of this a multinational culture was created, where

The Opera House and so on

"even in Soviet times, people here were global in a way. They found a way to read forbidden books and wear modern, fashionable clothes; they heard jazz and rock and roll, and learned foreign languages – my father put me into English school in 1975."

The Modernist Garden City

The two names I heard most in conjunction with the Soviet garden city were Nikolay Ripinsky, architect of the Hotel Almaty and the Lenin Palace, and Dinmukhamed Kunayev, the head of the Communist Party of Kazakhstan from 1964 to 1986. Kunayev, according to the researcher and campaigner Anel Moldakhmetova of Archcode Almaty, was able "because of his close connections and good relationship with the centre – Moscow", to "increase the budget for architecture development in Almaty and improve the quality of construction and construction materials." There is little in the way of standardisation in the city's modern architecture, with façades in the local limestone rather than mass-produced tile and concrete. Kunayev's 1986 dismissal

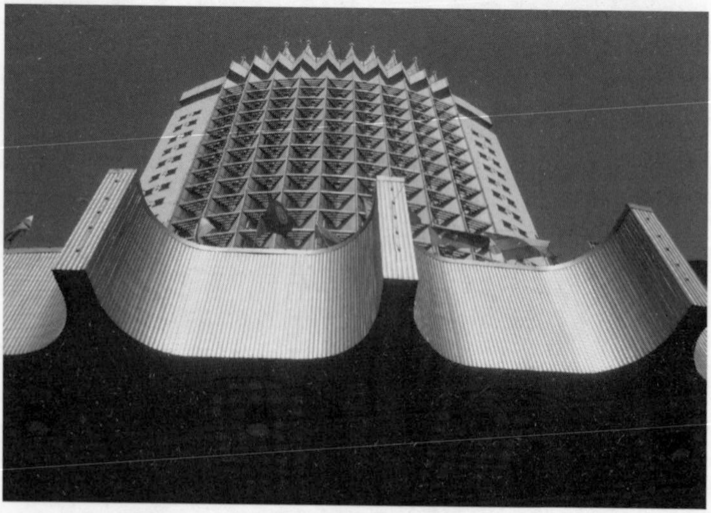

Hotel Kazakhstan

by Gorbachev on grounds of corruption and replacement, foolishly, with the Russian Gennady Kolbin, led to protests that ended in violence in 1986, now seen as the start of Kazakh statehood. Among Kunayev's proteges was the hard-working apparatchik Nursultan Nazarbayev, who succeeded Kolbin in 1989 and has never left power since. If Kunayev was a typical Soviet bureaucrat, able to pull strings for his people and for the edification of "his" republic, then Ripinsky was at the other end of the scale, a victim, then a beneficiary of the system. A student of the Constructivist Vesnin brothers in Moscow, he was deported to Kazakhstan in 1949. After Stalin's death he was made head of the state construction body Kazgorstroyproyekt, becoming the most important figure in the city's planning and architecture, teaching a generation of Kazakh architects, and developing a distinct "school" of modern architecture, internationalist with delicate local touches.

The low, long Lenin Palace and the city's first high-rise, the Hotel Kazakhstan (the latter of which still features on Kazakh banknotes as an icon of Almaty) were intended as vertical and horizontal

The Revolution in Kazakh

complements to each other. Alongside them is the Cinema Arman, a simple late 1960s box with bulging relief sculptures carved for the fiftieth anniversary of the revolution in 1967. On the same street is the "Three Knights" residential complex, an aggressive brutalist composition of three interlinked towers, softened and worn by the residents' insertion of new balconies and additions. Another cluster can be found around the Azueov Theatre Metro station, where an early 1970s "Wedding Palace" and Circus, both designed as rotundas decorated with concrete sun-screens, flank the surging design of the theatre. It is all overlooked by a silvery TV tower, placed on the Kok-Tebe mountain above the city. It's this city that played host to the World Health Organisation's conference, held at the Lenin Palace in 1978, that issued the Alma-Ata Declaration, committing governments worldwide to "health for all", free and accessible, by the year 2000; this colonial citadel turned multicultural metropolis, on a scale both epic and humane, must have seemed like the ideal place for this – eventually utopian – declaration.

The Circus

Kok-Tebe TV Tower

Later Soviet architecture, after Ripinsky, goes much further into a Communist-Islamic-Postmodernist "national style". Early 1980s buildings like Vladimir Kim and Tolegen Abildayev's Palace of Pioneers, and A.V. Khan, M. Ospanov, E.V. Chechelov and K. Tulebayev's Arasan Baths combine domes and towers in the manner described by the architectural historian Boris Chukhovich as the "made in Moscow national style", although several of the architects were local. Dreamlike, full of nostalgic and orientalist motifs – golden domes, minarets, great marbled baths, ceremonial stairs – these buildings are intensely atmospheric, but may have more to do with a Russian, imaginary idea of the "east" than the international and highly Soviet city Alma-Ata actually was. The centre of "Kunayev's City" is Republic Square, originally Brezhnev Square (he had for a time been the local viceroy), a series of towers and office blocks

Minarets of the Pioneers

The Arsan Baths

Inside the Soviet Nationalist Postmodernist Bathhouse

The former Brezhnev Square

The leader

placed symmetrically at the point where a steep slope runs from the mountains to the garden city below. It is an authoritarian space, much more so than anything else in Almaty, but an extremely impressive one: vast, commanding and coherent, and with sweeping views of the mountains around. A sculptural monument in the centre tells the current "national story", with nomads gradually becoming citizens becoming violently repressed protestors in 1986, then to be watched over by the kindly eye of Nursultan Nazarbayev. Glass domes, just like those in Moscow, Kyiv and Minsk, show the typical way of fitting shopping malls into grand Soviet squares.

Efforts to preserve this city have not been particularly successful. The Hotel Zhetsyu, a simple and elegant modernist building, was, Anel Moldakhmetova tells me, "set on fire soon after our article on its historical value was published in the mass media". It is currently gutted, stripped to its concrete frame, revealing the red-

Domes of Brezhnev Square

painted slogan "Builder! Prepare for the 40th Anniversary of the Kazakh SSR!", that is, 1965.

I asked the photographer Yuri Palmin, who had documented the city's Soviet architecture for the Garage exhibition, whether or not there was any nostalgia in his lovingly-detailed depiction of the city Kunayev and Ripinsky built. "There never was, and I hope never will be, any nostalgic element in my work with the architecture of Soviet Modernism", he replies. "I'm 51 now and was born and raised in the period of most obvious stagnation of the Soviet bureaucratic regime when its cynicism and hypocrisy were impossible to hide under the thin film of (mostly imported) modernity." Instead, the photographs are a matter of "relocating the time that was out of joint", showing the way that the buildings' age in a manner determined by lack of maintenance, general negligence of the urban environment, combined with initially poor construction quality. The Three Knights

An uncovered address to the builders

residential complex is the perfect example of a modernist project being dynamically inhabited throughout its history in the absence of strict codes and regulations. Rather than his work here being about showing off a perfectly preserved Soviet capital, "I am generally interested in the ways architecture survives and approaches ruination".

It may be hard to tell from the typically late-Soviet kitsch – all mahogany, figurines and doilies – of his private House Museum, but Kunayev is reckoned by local architects, artists and activists to have had a very positive influence on the city. Oddly, this doesn't extend to his bureaucratic inheritors. According to Yuliya Sorokina, "Kunayev's heritage is still valuable for the oppositional intelligentsia, but current state leaders actually hate Kunayev: I am afraid that they would like to forget everything he did. Maybe that's the reason they don't mind about barbarous reconstructions of Almaty's modernistic buildings as well." Partly this is a matter of taste: "It is not their style... they prefer Stalin's quasi-empire", and in Astana's flamboyant but cheap neo-Stalinist buildings, with their spires, Corinthian columns and triumphal arches, they've had a chance to realise it. She is scornful of the architectural aspirations of Kunayev's protege. "Nazarbayev is talented leader, but he is poorly educated in comparison to Kunayev". For her, this Father of the Nation "is a kind of primitive architect, let's say. He uses architecture as a tool for showing his power and thinks that he's glorifying his country during his epoch." At the heart of this, she tells me, is the fact that Nazarbayev, as a worker turned bureaucrat, was never fond of the city. "Almaty was and is a city of progressive intellectuals. Almaty and Astana are like two different universes. I guess Nazarbayev did not like Almaty – he felt like an alien here, and probably that was one of the reasons that he changed the capital. He wanted to build the city of his dreams and he did."

Soviet in Form, Kazakh In Content

However much it might seem to be a thing of the past for long-time residents of the city, the intelligence and elegance of the city built between the 1960s and 1980s is still very striking to the visitor. It is so not only by comparison with the ruthlessly inhospitable and riotously kitsch new capital, but seen alongside other Soviet cities of the same era that were not able to resist Moscow's pressure for standardisation and cost-cutting. Oddly enough, however, its recent buildings are distinctly post-Soviet, in a style which you can see in Moscow or Kyiv or Baku – concrete-framed residential towers inserted into the green interstices of the garden city, clad in brightly coloured "stone" and mirrorglass, with no natural ventilation, and with the roofs given a profusion of domes so as to look "local". Many of them are placed in the way of the carefully planned vistas of the Seventies – old pictures of the TV tower show it standing clean away from anything else on a green mountain, and now it is crowded in with poor quality, unplanned construction. One is tacked onto the end of the Almaty Hotel; another cluster crammed in behind the Palace of Pioneers, another lurking above the Auezdov Theatre.

Anel Moldakhmetova tells me that the work of the campaign and research group Archcode came initially from trying to create an "inventory" of the city: "We were trying to find out the roots of architectural landscape of the city and its historical and cultural value. At some point it became clear that more than 50% of architectural landscape of Almaty consists Soviet modernism." They then "created a list of 100 objects which we published in the form of an online catalogue, to start a conversation with the public about the importance and value of these buildings." So far this is proving to be a difficult task, taking into account that architects and restoration professionals often have to compromise their values to their "clients", who are "shaping architectural landscape of the city based on their personal tastes and beliefs" – something that was obvious when the hapless architect of the "restored" Lenin Palace tried to defend himself by blaming the client.

There was no public oversight over planning at the Lenin Palace, she points out:

> Construction works started before anyone could realize what was happening, the reconstruction project was never discussed with the professional expert community and there was no publicity around the case. As a result, reconstruction happened quietly and without public attention, and poor reconstruction became an object of discussion and criticism only after all the works have been done.

Archcode's attempt to publicise a more complex "identity of the city" has included issuing postcard sets of major Kunayev-era buildings, as part of trying to create "a strong professional community which shares common values related to heritage, which is not an easy task to do". That's especially because any sort of "campaigning for the Soviet historical heritage has a lot to do with rethinking history and identity of Kazakhstan after gaining independence".

This lack of interest in the recent past might seem strange, given the fact that many of Kazakhstan's current rulers were also its rulers in the 1980s. But in terms of approaches to architecture and planning, there is, she argues, little in the way of continuity between Kunayev's rule and Nazarbayev's:

> After independence many useful traditions of Soviet construction and approaches to the formation of visual style of the buildings were forgotten, and new approaches are mostly dictated by the availability of cheap imported materials from China and Turkey and interest in the maximum profit from the most minimal investment.

There is a rushing for "Western" solutions in order to make the city look less "Soviet", which have the paradoxical but common effect of making Almaty look not so much "normal" and "European" but distinctly post-Soviet, with a rejection of long-term planning and architectural education that is common across the former USSR. This is obvious in almost all the new construction in Almaty, with one curious exception: the Almaty Metro.

The Metro was begun in 1988, given that the Kazakh capital had passed the all-important 1 million mark that got you the funding for a tube network in the USSR. But the stations that exist now were designed in the 2000s, and the currently existing single line was opened in 2011. The impression that the Metro might give, that Almaty's government is investing in transport, is deceptive – the tram network was suspended in 2015, a few years after the Metro was opened, as it was no longer profitable. In most respects, this is a staggeringly Soviet project. The dimensions of the underground halls, with their extreme depth and their grand arched vaults, are straight from Kyiv, St Petersburg, Moscow or Taskhent; so too is the approach to decoration, with each station treated as an independent artwork, with chandeliers, high relief, gilding, ceramics and stained-glass. Unlike in a Soviet Metro system, there is of course no Communist imagery, aside from one station dedicated to the Baikonur Cosmodrome – though the folksy images of people doing traditional Kazakh things are very similar to those on the mosaics across the Hotel Almaty. The Auezov

Still Soviet underground

Theatre station even features mosaic panels of the 1970s buildings above. Otherwise, you wouldn't know that this wasn't actually built and opened in the 1980s. There is one exception – a 1980s Soviet architectural project wouldn't feature any artistic images of a living political leader. And yet there he is, at the end of the tiled hall of Almaly station, on a photograph placed under glass: Nazarbayev, in front of a fruit tree, waving at the commuters.

A memorial to Soviet Modernism

Join the Dark Side

A CITY OF THE FUTURE

ASTANA, Akmolinsk, Tselinograd, Aqmola

The thing not to say about the 2017 World Expo building in Astana, Kazakhstan, is that it looks like a "Death Star". Designed by Adrian Smith and Gordon Gill as a near-perfect glass sphere, with a concave spherical perforation at the top, the resemblance will not draw us further: particularly given that the website of the US journal Foreign Policy found itself briefly blocked in Kazakhstan because of an article tactfully headlined "Kazakhstan spent $5 billion on a Death Star, and it doesn't even shoot lasers". Anyway, the Death Star, you will recall, was black, whereas the Expo building is translucent and clear. Or rather it would be, if it wasn't for the large sheet of canvas draped over half of it so as to reduce glare and heat from the deeply unsympathetic climate. The theme of the building, and of the Expo more generally, was "Future Energy " – a showcase, in a post-Soviet Central Asian country made wealthy by fossil fuels, of what we're meant to do without them. It is too easy to mock the pretensions of the Expo and the capital city that is hosting it, and of a state that became wealthy on fossil fuels speculating on the post-fossil fuel future. If anywhere knows about the consequences of an all-out-war against nature and ways of adapting to it, it is Kazakhstan. Russian colonisation in the nineteenth century was followed after 1917 by an accommodation with local intellectual elites – the Jadids, the left-leaning Muslim reformers found throughout the southern and eastern provinces of the Russian Empire – and then a total assault on historic Kazakh practices, with the largely nomadic population forced into sedentary collective farms – the resultant famine in 1932-33 was, per capita, more deadly than the concurrent "Holodomor" in Ukraine.[1] Like the rest of Kazakhstan and nearby Siberia, the country was dotted with concentration camps between the 1930s and the 1950s. One of them, for the wives of political prisoners, was within the current city limits of Astana. Nothing as outright murderous would happen here again, but Soviet Kazakhstan had a record of ecological apocalypse. The Aral Sea, shared with Uzbekistan, partly became desert as the result of irrigation. The Soviet space programme launched its satellites from here, at the Baikonur Cosmodrome. The northern steppe of this huge country was host to the Semipalatinsk Test Site, where the Soviets tested their nuclear weapons for decades. From the mid-1950s, northern Kazakhstan was the focus of the Virgin Lands campaign, which aimed, and eventually failed, at exceeding American grain production in a burst of activist enthusiasm and aggressive agricultural engineering. The "capital" of this endeavour, which saw massive Russian immigration into the Kazakh Soviet Republic, was Tselinograd, "Virgin Lands City". Since 1998, Tselinograd has become the right bank of a new capital, simply called Astana ("Capital"). The monumental spaces of the left bank of the Ishim River, masterplanned by Kisho Kurokawa with the deliberate intent of reconciling the two banks, are in part a de-colonising project, which aims to de-Russify the north of Kazakhstan, where the Russian majority created by the Virgin Lands led to fears of secession, separatism and Russian-backed Civil War, of the sort that has been so destructive to Ukraine, Moldova and Georgia.[2] Kazakhstan is highly multicultural, and has been accepting of that fact, with Russian speakers never subject to the sort of stringent citizenship tests used in the Baltic, and Kazakh elites seldom going in for either the cultural chauvinism so often seen in the Caucasus or the Islamist militancy that led to the descent into war in nearby Tajikistan. Aside from the fact that the president has to be able to speak Kazakh, there are no particular national rules or regulations in Kazakhstan. The building of this mostly Kazakh capital in the heart of Russian settlement may seem like a domineering gesture from an urbanist perspective, but from the perspective of gradually making this country distinct from its former ruler, it is rather subtle.

And where better than this flat, interminable landscape, more brutally transformed in the last hundred years than anywhere else on Earth, to imagine how to re-engineer industrial society and prepare for a post-carbon future? Unfortunately, for those of us hoping that we just might make it, and that the disasters of the last few years aren't going to become the new normal, Expo 2017 provided very little in the way of hope. That central non-Death Star, placed on an axis round which the Expo site revolves, was part of a self-powered site, with the air-conditioning that made it bearable to enter generated via wind and water power, but it was still a glass ball in a city where temperatures go from -30 in January to +30 in July – a foolish and wasteful design. The idea of passively insulating a building in a climate like this is fairly utopian, so like the city in general, Smith and Gill have just ignored it.

A great deal has been written about Astana by now, usually treating it as a rather freakish place, a fantasy capital created by a benevolent (or not so benevolent) despot, a personal peccadillo, a grandiose vanity project, that it's almost a surprise to find on its much-photographed central Nurzhol Boulevard a reasonably imaginative and well-used piece of monumental planning, with a mix of uses and multiple levels. The expectation that nobody would move here proved totally inaccurate – it has actually filled up rapidly, with a population of just over a million, and it is likely to overtake Almaty in size in the next decade or so. But planning has not kept up with migration or construction. Public transport is limited to a rudimentary bus service, though hoardings everywhere promise a Chinese-built light railway sometime around now (with little sign of actual construction). The assumption seems to be, given the ferocious weather, what sort of idiot wouldn't drive? So for pedestrians, walking anywhere outside of Nurzhol and the pedestrianised riverbanks is a miserable experience, with little shelter or cover. As you'll find, the buildings don't bear close examination, and are better seen from a (usually speeding) car, especially at night, when a multicoloured neon lightshow fizzes and pops – an idea, like many of those in the Kazakh capital, of contemporary Chinese inspiration.

I walked to Nurzhol in thirty-degree heat from the Hotel Duman. The path from there to the street already encapsulates the problem – a big wide square, with plenty of flowers, but none of the changes in level or tree cover that makes the similarly hostile weather in Almaty bearable. When you reach the main road, you'll find it lined with trees, but arranged in such a way that they only offer shade if you

Triumph Astana

walk on the green strip. I decided to take a detour on the way to the boulevard via the Triumph Astana, a neo-Stalinist skyscraper built in 2006 in emulation of the Triumph Palace in Moscow, itself built in emulation of Moscow's seven Stalinist skyscrapers. On the way, enormous buildings with enormous car parks stand between the wide streets and wide roads, challenging you to walk between them – Qazaqbank, the Circus, and then a street mid-way through construction of Neoclassical tenements leads you to the palace. The skyline from a distance is impressive – of Moscow's various spired and turreted high-rises, the one it most recalls is the Ministry of Foreign Affairs, the strongest, thickest and most intimidating of the seven. The steps of the empty square lead you up to Guinness Pub and Konyak Ui, and as you look towards the peaks of the Triumph Astana, you can't help but see how cheap it all is, with crumbly-looking brick and rudimentary ornament. In his guide to the city, Philipp Meuser argues that, while being seen locally simply as "standing primarily for luxury and comfort", the Triumph Astana is also a "subconscious post-colonial attempt to come to terms with Soviet trauma".[3] Maybe. But the memory of living Kazakhs does not extend to the famine and the Gulag, but to a post-war era of ever-rising prosperity, the Kunayev period that is the subject of such nostalgia in Almaty. And when Moscow was the "centre", buildings like this were the symbols of power, so why not build one here to show that the power is here now? And, given that we're capitalist now, why not do so as a speculative housing project? As we've seen in Belarus, people use the symbols they have to hand, that mean something to *them*, rather than to imagined Western observers. And here, Stalinist Moscow means wealth and might.

These towers can be damaging to the urban fabric in Moscow itself – Moscow State University, the tallest, is surrounded with acres of emptiness, to frame its insane grandeur. Here, the Triumph Astana is reasonably hemmed in by new construction, but that doesn't make the design of the streets around any more pleasant. In fact, the main route from here to Nurzhol goes past the back end of the Chinese Embassy, and a barbed-wire fence as the "active frontage", in a particularly mean fuck-you to pedestrians. Past that, you're at one of the main spaces of the capital city – the National Theatre. This is the sort of planning that went out of fashion sometime in the 1980s in the United States, predicated on assuming that nobody would ever want to walk ever again, and that everyone having their own personal metal tin for transport was a good and sensible idea. But these dead spaces, the wide roads, token and treeless pavements and sparsely laid out pedestrian crossings, run alongside what is in theory one of the most important buildings in the country – a National Theatre is always integral to nation-building. As architecture, it is banal, a marble Caesar's Palace with a giant order of columns offering some extremely welcome shade. Opposite that, is the start of Nurzhol Boulevard – the Khan Shatyr Shopping Centre, designed by Norman Foster.

Embassy Backyard

Foster is not the only important British figure of the 1990s and 2000s to have been working here – Tony Blair and his foundation have been hard at work helping Nazarbayev improve his international image; as neoliberal politicians that rose to prominence in self-proclaimed socialist parties, they had that in common after all. Foster's work here is an interesting move away, in certain respects, from the deliberately placeless high-tech architecture with which he had made his name. High-tech works like the HSBC tower in Hong Kong, the "Gherkin" in London, or Stansted airport, were never intended to make gestures towards the history or tradition of the places where they were built – history was irrelevant, even more so, mythology. But Foster's buildings in Astana are absolutely rife with symbolism, to the point where they seem a step on from the "made-in-Moscow national style" of 1980s Almaty – national in form, transnational

Colonnades and yurt

capitalist in content. So Khan Shatyr is in the shape, in theory, of a traditional tent, a nomadic Kazakh yurt, of the sort that the majority in this country used to take round with them on their constant travels. Visibly held up by one tilted post, wrapped around by a bubble of ETFE, it is organic and romantic in its form, and totally prosaic and globalist on the inside, with a shopping mall with all the useful international chains, meaning principally that it was the only place in Kazakhstan where I couldn't enjoy the first-class local *Plov*, and had to eat Starbucks blinis instead.

Crossing the road from here is actually quite pleasant, fun, even. Whereas there has obviously been no consideration about how you walk around just a few yards from here, the route from here to the Presidential Palace has been laid out as a flowing, multi-level pedestrian route. If everywhere around is Stalinist Dallas, this central strip is post-Soviet La Défense. First, you go under, with an open underpass taking you below the headquarters of KazMunayGaz, then you're in a huge square with a Neoclassical crescent of offices around you, and the nationalised gas company behind – a flyover is in front, sailing peacefully over your head. From being outright infuriating, the cityscape has become exciting, and from being totally empty, the streets have become full, as everyone has parked their cars in order to have a day out promenading. The main building around, KazMunayGaz, consists of two Stalinist skyscrapers linked by a grand arch, and is outrageously authoritarian in its form. Obviously inspired by the architecture of the late 1930s, it is less literal (though equally cheap) than the Triumph Astana, resembling more the unbuilt Stalinist dream-city showcased in Alexander Medvedkin's film *New Moscow*. There are fountains, kiosks, public artworks, cafes and children playing, all the things that I found so distressingly missing on the half a mile walk here.

All the ideas in Astana, you soon learn, have been concentrated on this one street. Rather than being left empty, the boulevard has been crammed full of public art. Some of it is Expo specific, in the

Processional route to the Palace of Gas

Pedestrian Astana

shape of strange bulbous figures representing each of the countries participating in the event. Others are more occasional, many of them in summer 2017, like Foster's mall, riffing off the Nomadic heritage of the Kazakhs, with more yurts and tents and lightweight things of wood than you could shake a staff at. Some of these are for touching and "interacting" with, and those that are not by big important artists, as well as those that are, have signs on them reading "do not touch, stand with your feet, swing, move from place to place!" At the centre of this – at the centre, mythologically, of the new capital in general – is the Bayterek Tower. According to Phillip Meuser, it is "based upon the Kazakh folktale that the sacred bird Samruk once laid an egg (the sun) on the tree of life that was devoured by the dragon Aydakhar. Therefore, Samruk returned the following year and laid a new egg in the tree",[4] a cycle which apparently represents nomadic life on the steppe.

Pregnant with Juche Idea

Nazarbayev allegedly drew a sketch of this event, which was then converted into the tower that you can see now, something between an elongated shuttlecock and a 1960s telecommunications tower (with a lift up to the top, too, though no revolving restaurant). The symbolism is stressed by the design of the National Archives below – an egg, below the tree with the egg on top. Students of nationalism can find something quite exciting here, the formation of myths and tales into a new national identity in real time. Unlike those of European countries like Macedonia, which pull their new mythology together out of Ancient Greece and nineteenth-century nationalism, or indeed post-Soviet Ukraine, where a significant minority are intent on rooting the nation in the "Holodomor" and the Ukrainian Insurgent Army, here we have a country run by former industrial workers and Communists, whose parents would have been devout Muslims, knowingly creating a unique mythology out of a paganism

The people, the boulevard

that they couldn't possibly have ever encountered first hand. It's rather benign by comparison. Whether it's "real" history or archaeology isn't relevant, any more than it matters whether King Arthur was real or not. This stuff has a job to do.

At this point, the cluster of individually designed high-rises that has been on either side of the road, lit at night by neon and which you could imagine in Frankfurt, Canary Wharf or Shanghai, is replaced by symmetrical Neoclassical buildings, either in a coarsened version of the Stalinist vernacular or in the more peculiar golden cones that mark the transition from the business and shopping half of Nurzhol Boulevard into the governmental half. To get there, you have to walk up onto an elevated walkway, Barbican-style, and a pedway leads you through various ministries to the dispiriting Presidential Palace. This is quite similar to the one in Rike Park in Tbilisi, and on that level another reminder of the banality and universality of post-Soviet presidential

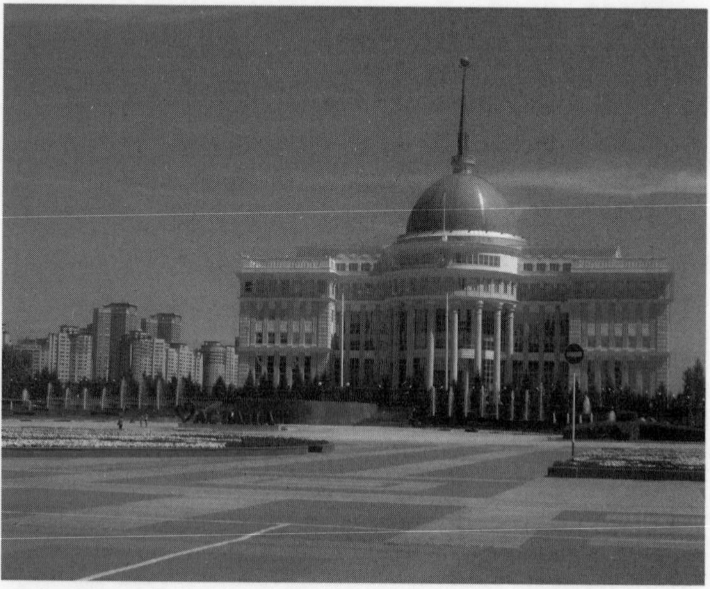

The White and Blue House

taste. You can disassemble it into components; a blue dome from a Turkistan mosque, a spire from VDNKh, and the imagery from Washington DC, a summation of Astana's aspirations. And from here, the pedestrian pathways stop and once again, the non-driver is lost. I crossed over the river past here to get to the "Pyramid of Peace and Reconciliation" but the walk was gruelling, with nothing but empty space and roads between here and the scrubby park that fences the Palace off from the people. You pass here more Foster, such as the upturned bowl of the Nazarbayev Foundation (a Presidential Library, of some sort), until you eventually come to the Pyramid of Peace and Accord.

The right angles of this pyramid are set at the opposite end of the axis to the curves of the tent. Two different poles of monumentality. It has been rather well thought out, much more so than the horrendous public spaces all around. Scorching – or, from November to March,

Norman, Nursultan and only mode of transport

freezing – emptiness, in front of a cluster of skyscraper flats with the name "Highvill"; if you went here at the wrong time, in the wrong clothes, this square could probably kill you in a couple of hours. To achieve something that seems this inhumane even in the context of the former USSR is some sort of achievement. Flanking the Pyramid and Highvill is an Ottoman-style mosque (the gift of Lebanon, in this case; there is another, near Khan Shatyr, that is a gift from Qatar) and an open classical colonnade, the National Monument, with a relief of Nazarbayev at the centre.

The symbolism everywhere in Astana – Pyramids and Yurts, Stalinist skyscrapers and minarets, Trees and Eggs – lends itself to speculation. There is a hysterical book, *Astana – Architecture, Myth and Destiny*, by Frank Albo, predicated to exploring these puzzles in the traditional conspiracy theorist manner:

Pyramid and Highvill

> Concealed in Astana are ancient secrets, symbols and mysteries that can fundamentally change our world. Masonic symbolism in Astana leads some to believe it is the command centre of freemasonry and the new world order. Architecture history of Astana reveals the city's highest purpose as harbinger of peace, stability, adaptability and security in our evolving world.[5]

It is, among other things, a way of Western observers reckoning with the strangeness of seeing nation-building happening now, rather than in the nineteenth or twentieth centuries, when the syncretic and constructed nature of it can be safely forgotten. In reality, it is all rather prosaic. The group I was in saw a young couple, just married, posing for photos here – and the landscape is photogenic, if appallingly inhospitable in every other respect. We got to see a production in the

Just married

theatre inside the Pyramid of Peace and Accord: Romeo and Juliet, in a Kazakh pop version. It's all remarkably normal.

That impression is reinforced when you cross the river into Tselinograd. By the Pyramid, the riverbank is unattractive, but near the Hotel Duman, there is a public park and a pedestrian bridge that lead across a remarkably successful illusion, where the two sides peacefully unite into one coherent image. From a distance, you wouldn't actually know the difference. In summer – doubtfully, in a -40 winter – the riverbanks are very well used, with a beach and sunbathers. Like Nurzhol, it's an island of public space in a sea of traffic, and people are using it accordingly. Wander round a little bit, after you've crossed the Ishim, and the difference is more obvious. The scale suddenly seems intimate. The smaller houses and the worn *Khrushchevki* have acquired a patina, as everything does after a while,

Megamosque

Right bank from left bank

A beach on the Steppe

and as the Left Bank will, eventually. The trees have grown, and in typical post-Soviet style, they haven't been cut or maintained, so, from a lack of any shelter or shade, there's suddenly an abundance of it, along with signs of inhabitation – the usual balcony surgery, washing lines. Even the large former Lenin Square feels relatively small-scale. Underneath the Gulf-Luzhkov cladding of the long block and the tower are the administrative buildings of 1960s modernist Tselinograd, their outline and clarity still obvious, while the 1950s Virgin Lands Hotel has been left with its simplified Stalinist-classical detail still intact. It all seems to be on a comparatively humane scale, which of course, is silly. This is a utilitarian new town, built at great speed. In most other contexts this would have seemed a schematic and harsh Monogorod. Outside of the centre of Tselinograd, there are many traces of a bleak industrial city, with unrenovated Brezhnev-era concrete panel blocks and informal commerce. But intimacy and

Lenin Square

the marks of time are exactly what the rest of the city lacks, and what Tselinograd has in abundance. Perhaps accordingly, a lot of building work seems to be happening in order to make it look more like the rest of the capital.

Nari Shelekpayev writes of the two banks of the river that "this 'innate' dichotomy must not necessarily be seen through a lens of contradiction/contrast, which so far has been the most obvious and popular approach", any more than the Left Bank should be seen as the happy outcome of "an immaculate conception by the state and a great planner, liberating the city from the original sin of its old and graceless Right Bank". He argues that "quite prosaically, the two banks complement each other, making Astana what it is now: an official city flanked by a social one where most people live". More precisely, "freshmen buy or rent apartments on the Right Bank, while the new bourgeoisie moves from the "old" to the "new" city. Moving to the

Streets of Tselinograd

Astana and Tselinograd

Left Bank thus means crossing a social Rubicon, and few can afford both working and living on the Left Bank. It is typical to see thousands of young clerks going from the Right Bank where they live to the Left Bank where they work."[6] Looking at it from an architectural perspective, however, what is noticeable is that this aspirationalism – the crossing of the river as a sign that you're getting on – has the side-effect of Tselinograd looking increasingly like Astana, with the buildings being clad and re-clad in the sort of shiny and decorative materials that adorn those on the other side, and with office blocks and new high-rises emerging in the green interstices of the Virgin Lands City. Clearly, the intention is that eventually, you will not be able to tell the difference, when the trees have grown on the Left Bank and the Soviet buildings have been replaced on the Right. But there is one big difference which will never change. You can walk in Tselinograd.

There is no getting away from the fossil fuel dominance of this city, at every level. The way that KazMunayGaz looms over Astana – it was the first construction in the new city on the Right Bank – is no accident. Ultimately, gas and petrol made this place, and they've also made it hard to imagine Astana without them. As the official guide says, "bowels of the land of Kazakhstan have considerable natural resources", listing chrome, uranium, silver, zinc, coal, gold, lead, iron ore, copper, bauxite, molybdenum, and of course oil; but "Expo 2017 enables Kazakhstan and the whole world to accelerate the transition from traditional carbon-based energetics to low carbon energy technologies and alternative sources".[7] There's no reason, of course, why hypocrisy should preclude innovation: think of Norway, made insanely wealthy by oil, placing charging points for electric cars on every main road. The Expo has few equivalents to this. Most pavilions, in fact, have taken the theme as an invitation to show off the pipelines, infrastructure and buildings of their own fossil fuel monopolies; the "energy" part of it is emphasised at the cost of much in the way of thought about the future, aside from a somewhat Soviet approach to futurism.

At the Expo, two glass streets of pavilions arc around the Glass Sphere, many are from countries that are also outposts of "the New Silk Road", a Eurasian land route from China to Europe that will purportedly see a massive programme of infrastructure and investment. They also tend, like Kazakhstan itself – where in 2011 in the city of Zhanaozen, at least 14 striking oil workers were shot dead by the army – to be highly repressive regimes. So the Pavilion of Turkmenistan displays a light-up gas pipeline alongside books by its absolute leader Gurbanguly Berdimuhamadov (Tea, a Healer and Inspiration – not for sale); Uzbekistan juxtaposes "eco-capsules" with maps of uranium and gold reserves, and Azerbaijan features an interactive oilfield you can squelch your feet on. In theory, the New Silk Road – on which Astana would be a hugely important hub – would be a very energy-efficient thing, one where hugely polluting air travel could be gradually replaced with fast trains from St Pancras to Beijing. But most places on the route, as the Expo made clear, mainly want to sell you some oil. After the Expo packs up, and the performers of Cirque de Soleil and the employees of the nuclear company KazAtomProm get to go home, the non-Death Star is being converted into a Museum of Future Energy, and it will no doubt be useful to have a permanent space where alternatives to the ideas behind this city can be discussed. Everything else here implies a future based on the ruthless exploitation of non-renewable resources, which is likely to make the climate as inhospitable in London or Tokyo as it currently is in Astana through intensifying global warming.

In his recent study of urban power, Göran Therborn calls Nazarbayev "one of the great authoritarian political entrepreneurs"[8] along with Singapore's Lee Kwan Yew, and notes the syncretic way that this national capital of the least nationalist post-Soviet Republic has been put together – a piece of the Washington Mall at Nurzhol, a big White House, a Thames-like embankment, Mosques from the Gulf, Turkish and Chinese office blocks – as a summation of everything that has been happening in capital cities for the last century, and

A healer and inspiration

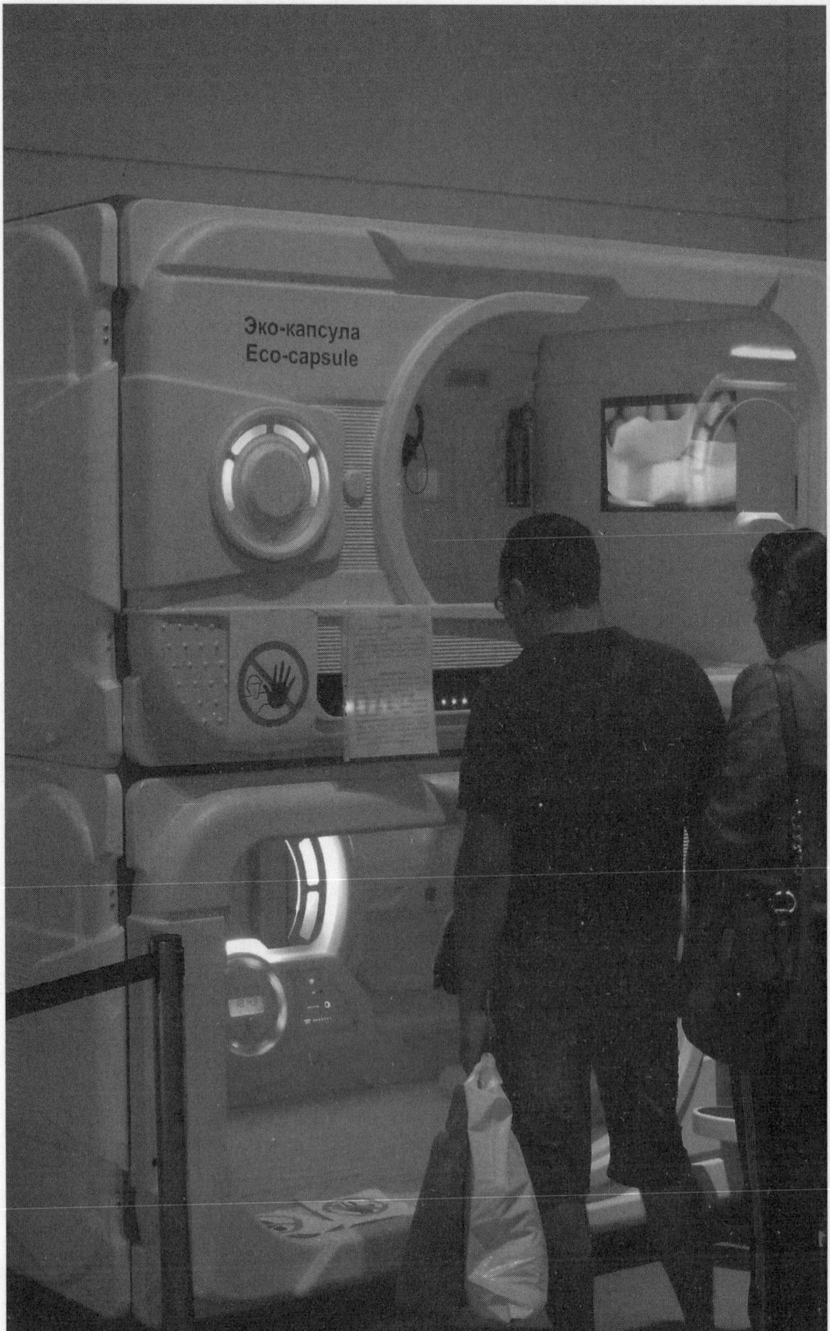

An Uzbek eco-capsule

notably "inspired by both of the superpowers of the Cold War".[9] He calls the result "the capital of the twenty-first century", but it's notable just how few new ideas there are in Astana. There are new ideas in urbanism, but you won't find them here. No public transport, no "walkable" or "liveable" districts, no recycling, no eco-industry, no "bottom-up" co-operative forms of ownership. No doubt some of that all sounds too Soviet. Instead, a Politburo partly inherited from the 1980s is setting a course for the 1980s – a slick, aggressive, car-centred metropolis of considerable neon-lit glamour and occasional grandeur, a humane nation-building project and an utterly inhumane city-building project. The Eurasian City of the Future is a twenty-first-century fusion of Stalinist Moscow, Milton Keynes, Dallas and Dubai, and a bang-up-to-date Museum of Past Energy, a steppe metropolis of in-built obsolescence.

"WHERE OUR TOMORROW IS ALREADY YESTERDAY"

BISHKEK, Frunze, Pishpek

Make Way for Queer Communism

In the 1970s, in Frunze, the capital of the Soviet Socialist Republic of Kirghizia, there existed something called the "Kollontai Commune". It passed unknown at the time but was rediscovered by researchers in Bishkek, the renamed capital of independent Kyrgyzstan, in the 2010s, through the collection of materials found in a box among the possessions of a philosophy lecturer. Taking their name from Aleksandra Kollontai, the Bolshevik leader and sexual radical whose ideas on "winged eros" and sexual emancipation were marginalised and then simply ignored from the late 1920s onwards, this small group of Communards communicated with each other through postcards of the buildings of socialist Frunze, which they distributed among themselves. The texts on the back of these postcards used quotations from the "classics of Marxism-Leninism" – Marx, Lenin, Engels's *The Origin of the Family, Private Property and The State* – to critique the persistence of the "bourgeois family" into the socialist epoch. They made posters, in which Marx and Engels propound the slogan "MAKE WAY FOR COSMIC EROS", and they wrote texts, which would go further than the "classics", arguing they'd failed to "historicise" gender relations enough – why must "love-comradeship" be between men and women, and not also men and men, and women and women? Why not consider gender itself as historically formed, and hence fluid and changeable?

Alongside this they made architectural drawings of extraordinary lightweight structures floating freely in space, evidently inspired by the "Flying City" of the 1920s architect Georgy Krutikov,[1] but again, going further than even early Soviet culture had dared. The cosmos would be the place for sexual experiment – if we can transcend gravity, we can transcend the family. The researchers, the School of Theory and Activism in Bishkek (the Russian acronym, "ShTAB", also means "headquarters"), a pan-Central-Asian collective of Kyrgyz, Tajik, Kazakh and Uzbek thinkers, artists and activists, dubbed the collection they'd found "the Frunze Queer Commune", and made a short film about it, *Queer in Space – the Kollontai Commune Archive.*[2]

At a public lecture in Moscow organised by an oligarch-backed art foundation in 2015, I saw Georgy Mamedov of ShTAB present their findings, which he saw as part of a "Utopian Bishkek" that had flourished just below the conservative surface of Brezhnev-era Central Asia. His presentation was fascinating, funny and revelatory – here, finally, was the missing piece of the jigsaw puzzle, the autonomous avant-garde, committed to a Communism I could fully believe in, working in the deep post-colonial periphery of the Soviet Union. This wasn't about sifting melancholically through the wreckage of an unlamented dead civilisation, or simply conserving twentieth-century architecture from neoliberal development – generally, the two topics of these sort of events – but was something much, much more exciting. From then on, I read absolutely everything I could from ShTAB, or all that sporadic English texts, my extremely rudimentary Russian and Google Translate could accommodate. This was a heady collection of work. There was a "Queer Communist Manifesto", which had an extremely cogent critique of the limits both of Soviet Communism and liberalism, arguing that only the synthesis of "Queer Communism" could transcend them:

> The structural connection between patriarchy and capitalism is becoming more apparent these days, amidst neoliberal reaction – the more cynical forms capitalism takes, the more aggressive the patriarchate becomes – using "family values" as a chief means of manipulation. Family – the much valorised "last fortress of love" – works as a fail-proof multifunctional machine for capitalism, providing workforce and enhancing exploitation. One of its functions is the transfer of responsibility for social security of vulnerable groups from public institutions to familial, kinship-based, or quasi-communal associations. Indeed, for this purpose strengthening of "blood ties" is essential. The second function of the resurrection of "family values" is production of loyal and apolitical citizenry – patriarchs do not stand on barricades, they have to "feed a family". Finally, the third function is to reproduce the patriarchal matrix by means of "nurture". Gender is a binding ingredient in the mortar of capitalism. Women, LGBT, childfree, single, asexual, queer – all carry stigma of unhappiness/deficiency/exoticisation under capitalism – stigma that can only be shifted to another group, but never eliminated altogether. Stigma is a constant of capitalism, the working formula of which necessarily includes biopolitical control of birth, life and death. The radical reformatting of gender order – that queer actually denotes – and other forms of togetherness apart from a model of nuclear family, are only conceivable as destigmatised practices on the Communist horizon.[3]

The USSR, committed to Fordism and Functionalism as it was, could never quite escape this logic:

> Here it is important to remember the unsuccessful experience of the Bolsheviks, who strove to "liberate women from kitchen slavery" while relying entirely on the enhanced labour productivity and development of means of production. Liberation was expected to come with an advent of new factory-kitchens and ingenious sewing machines, while humans were conceived as simple functions of dependence upon available technical means. Human bodies were defined as "means of production" – production of other bodies and commodities – and that is where "real socialism" (which saw a primary objective of emancipation of women in their increased participation in workforce) concurs with today's real capitalism, which similarly objectifies and instrumentalises a human. The fact that people produce not only other humans and commodities, but also meanings and affects has not been taken into consideration. [4]

In Bishkek itself, ShTAB ran tours of "Utopian Bishkek", produced plays and made posters and short films for leftist and LGBT political organisations, but at a distance, all I had were the texts, extraordinary things like one densely theoretical treatise on the work of the late-Soviet philosopher Evald Ilyenkov, which claimed him for Queer Communism, for his refusal to see disabled and damaged bodies as "inferior", and for his attention to how "the psychological processes which we think of as 'natural' and which emerge as it were by themselves are formed by the environment and not at all by some autonomous unfolding of a genetic programme"[5]. The theory was interspersed with "Queer City", a series of kaleidoscopic montages "showing ten sites in Bishkek related to the history of the LGBT movement in the year 2047", where the familiar Soviet cityscape has been conjoined with the new, not with the modernising blah that signifies futurism in, say, Astana, but has become instead a city as a continuous Brutalist disco. Interviews in Berlin-published books full of tedious poseurs would feature texts by ShTAB that took completely seriously the Utopian ideas about transcending the existing city, existing society and the existing family expounded in the Twenties; for ShTAB's Oksana Shatalova, the Queer Communist future would mean developing technology to eliminate "natural" childbirth, and "a feminist or rather Queer Dictatorship", where "a fundamentally different socialisation and enculturation – without the imposition of depressing male and female 'destinies' – will produce another map for the desires of the 'majority', or to be more exact, will eliminate this very concept ('majority') in relation to sex and sexuality".[6]

Because of all of this, I decided to make sure I visited "Utopian Bishkek"; and in the process of writing this book, I decided that it would end here, where I would write about these self-described Queer Communists, as a real living alternative both to the awful politics of the region – neoliberalism, nationalism, terrified liberalism or nostalgic, bigoted Stalinism – and to the purely reactive, defensive alternatives of melancholy and conservation offered by much activism. I wanted to meet the Kollontai Commune.

What I hadn't realised is that ShTAB were the Kollontai Commune. Sitting in May 2018, in a bar formed out of an old kindergarten in the courtyard behind 1970s concrete apartment blocks, Georgy Mamedov, unbidden, admitted the ruse. The Kollontai Commune never existed, except in the work of ShTAB themselves. It was a hoax. The artefacts were old postcards and posters found in the second-hand bookshops of Bishkek, which they faked into the "archive". He was particularly keen that the performance be convincing at that oligarch art conference in Moscow – and it certainly was.

But it wasn't at all intended as a joke on the art world, or on credulous leftist aesthetes, hoping to validate their politics in the Soviet experiment, though it would have been a perfectly judged one if so, but a means of filling in a gap, of inserting into Soviet history something that it ought to have but didn't. Mamedov claims that since, they've found real examples of similar texts and arguments being made, but their circumstances are a little more grim – one really existing Queer Communist they discovered wrote his manifestos in a mental asylum in Leningrad. The invention of the Kollontai Commune was, Mamedov says, part of a long-term programme on the part of ShTAB to assimilate what they could of Soviet socialism – "for us", he said, "the Soviet Union didn't 'fail'", but was instead a repository of experiences and answers, some good, some awful, to the questions that destroying capitalism would pose – and then go beyond it.

ShTAB itself had ended in the form in which I encountered it a few years earlier – Mamedov had left the group, which was reorganising itself into FEMShTAB, a specifically feminist organisation, while Mamedov was now working for Labrys, an LGBTQ campaign group in Bishkek, and was abandoning art altogether. On forming, ShTAB had, he told me, a precise plan. First they would aim to understand Soviet Central Asia – first through Utopian Bishkek, a book and a series of maps on technological, proletarian, artistic and architectural utopias whose real traces could be found in the existing city, then through publications philosophical (Queer Communism as Ethics, published by the Free Marxist Press in Moscow), historical and post-colonial (the book Concepts of the Soviet in Central Asia), and then the final part of the plan, where they would move forward into the future, in Completely Different, an anthology of Queer Communist science-fiction stories by Central Asian women.[7] Their work as artists and provocateurs was done; what came next, was politics.

From the Heavenly Mountains to the Cosmos

I had intended to come to Bishkek to write about ShTAB and the Kollontai Commune, but finding they no longer existed and had never existed, respectively, left me just with Georgy and his maps to Utopian Bishkek, and his Communist enthusiasm. What sort of a city, then, was "Utopian Bishkek"? ShTAB's version of it is derived from a real place, Soviet Frunze, in the 1920s and 1950s-1980s, a city that was founded out of a colonial enclave, created by the Russian Empire in the nineteeth century. Pishpek (the original name was Kazakh) was a fortress founded by the Khanate of Kokand, then swiftly taken over by its Russian conquerors, who built a small outpost here of one-storey houses and a little Orthodox church. "Kyrgyzstan" or Kirghizia was created by the USSR, out of the mountainous areas, set deep in the Tian Shan mountain range, populated by Kyrgyz-speaking nomads, who had rebelled against the Russian Empire in 1916, when they tried to impose conscription during the First World War. The uprising here involved Russian settlements being targeted by insurgents, a classic anti-colonial revolt that ended with a horrendously violent suppression – estimates of the dead in this small country are as much as 200,000, and many Kyrgyz rebels, nomads as they were, escaped over the mountains and through the border into China. The early USSR would celebrate this revolt as a precursor to the one a year later that founded their state, and when the imperial borders were redrawn by the Soviets, Pishpek was made capital of the new Kirghiz Republic, as opposed to the ancient city of Osh, which was populated largely

Old Pishpek

by the sedentary, literate Uzbeks. Even more than Almaty, Pishpek had no pre-colonial history. It was a blank slate. In 1926, it would be renamed Frunze, after a local boy – Mikhail Frunze, a Moldovan from a European settler family, who became a Bolshevik and a Red Army General, before dying of complications from an operation on a stomach ulcer in 1926.

The degree to which Soviet Central Asia was or wasn't "colonial" is still controversial. From the early Twenties on, the Bolsheviks, worried that segregation in Central Asia would create what Lenin called "Belfasts" out of cities like Tashkent, pressed for decolonisation within the Union, and agitation for it abroad; they were roundly mocked by the sensible social democrats of their day for thinking that "the Mullahs of Khiva" could build socialism, which naturally could only be understood by Europeans; presumably, they sneered, Kollontai's sexual revolution was modelled on "Muslim polygamy".[8] It was a Cold War commonplace that the Soviet division of Central Asia into the distinct Republics of Turkmenistan, Tajikistan, Uzbekistan, Kazakhstan and Kyrgyzstan was simple colonial divide and rule, although more recent research has stressed the input of Central Asian socialists and Muslim intellectual Jadids.

However, the fact remains that Frunze was founded as a colonial outpost, and remained majority Russian right up until 1991, although the Party and Republic was by then led largely by Kyrgyz Communists; a Kyrgyz majority emerged only in the 1990s. Reading texts about Soviet Kirghizia can pull you in each direction with every paragraph, so contradictory and complex was its development. The nomadic territory was easier to "Sovietise" than the deeply Islamic, literate and developed societies in the Persian-Timurid heartland in Uzbekistan, but the image of teacher and pupil recurs. One propaganda book intended to expound the virtues of the Republic begins with the image of a Kyrgyz nomad arriving in Frunze on horseback and there being civilised by "the great Party that has led the small, indigent Kyrgyz people, forgotten in the mountains, out of the darkness of the Middle

The Radiant Light of a Cultured Socialist Life

Ages to the radiant light of a cultured, socialist life";[9] this is colonial rhetoric, however socialist it presents itself as.

But as the Soviet Union started to fragment in 1991, and Gorbachev called a referendum to save it, Kyrgyzstan voted en masse to remain in the Union, as did the rest of Central Asia – well over 90%, on a high turnout; extremely unusual in colonial history. A recent oral history of Soviet Kyrgyzstan by the Bishkek-based American University in Central Asia gives some insight into why. Abidjan Yuldashov, a farmer from Osh, laments "during the Soviet times, we had everything. Everything was available and sufficient. People say we fed Russia. It is Russia who fed and saved us".[10] Apparent contradictions are smoothed over in the memory; a Kyrgyz teacher's comment here on any tensions between "native" culture and Soviet ideology is typical: "I am not a religious person because I graduated from a university of Marxism-Leninism, and my life has been devoted to that science. Still, I am a Muslim". Equally typical is a Kyrgyz worker's noting almost in passing that until the Second World War, many Kyrgyz were "afraid of Russians" because of their bloody suppression of the 1916 rising, not differentiating between "Soviet" Russians and Tsarist ones.[11]

After 1991, the economy of Kyrgyzstan collapsed utterly – it is one of those countries that, in Branko Milanović's analysis quoted earlier in this book, would take decades at current rates to reach the level of development they had reached in 1991. So, unsurprisingly, nostalgia for Communism is rampant. "Suddenly we realised that in the Soviet Union we had not been building Communism, we had been living Communism", recalled one participant in the oral history project. "The state had cared for us, we had been able to look to the future with confidence and plan our lives. We had work and our salaries were sufficient to live on, and (when I retired) I could provide for myself and even save a little bit". But after that, "payment for all services was a bottle of Samogon (homebrew)".[12]

According to ShTAB collaborator and academic Mohira Suyarkulova, it is too simple to say that Soviet Kirghizia was

From colony to cosmos

colonial; there was a constant dialogue back and forth, with racist and condescending attitudes from Russians and from Moscow being countered from within the Communist framework. She points as an example to the way that after Stalin's death in 1953 – his rule had seen Central Asia largely as an extractive economy, for raw materials and cotton – Central Asian Communists had pushed, usually successfully, for investment in modernisation projects that would favour internal development. She points to Frunze's Special Design Bureau for the Institute of Space Research of the Academy of Sciences of the USSR, where much of the equipment for the Soviet space programme was designed; it was in "a modest building on Toktugul Street, which is now home to textile sweatshops".[13]

At the same time, Soviet Central Asia was used as a showcase for decolonisation globally; revolutionaries from Africa, India and South-East Asia would visit Frunze, just as they did Almaty and (especially) Tashkent, to see modern cities with no Jim Crow, no "colour bar", and with the Asians apparently running the show. The decline from this was sharp – from a city that designed equipment for space exploration to Third World levels of poverty in a decade, without even Kazakhstan's consolations of raw materials or Georgia's tourism income. Suyarkulova and Mamedov are keen not to just see this as a collapse, but also as a shift with its own possibilities – today's Bishkek is more relaxed, more contested, more multicultural, than was Soviet Frunze.

Frunze Today

Frunze then, the real Frunze, was a showcase, and no matter how battered it is now – and it is very battered indeed – the show is impressive, as much as Almaty, and in many ways similar. Like Almaty, it is a breathtakingly green city, with streets absolutely suffused with greenery, with concrete irrigation channels running alongside each street to water the giant acacias that shelter it from the ruthless climate; unlike in polluted and overdeveloped Almaty, neglect has left this green network fundamentally complete, so walking is a pleasure – if you keep your wits about you, because most of the pavements haven't been renovated since the 1980s, and the rushed nature of Soviet engineering is revealed everywhere. Every stretch of lush tree-lined pedestrian path has potholes, loose manholes, protruding pipes and bulges where trees have taken root through the tarmac. The city's layout is intuitive – a grid, with the Tian Shan just beyond, with the green streets all leading to a network of gorgeous parks.

Leaves and panels

A walk could start at the relatively bare Victory Square, built in 1985, to the designs of V. Lyzenko, Urmat Alymkulov and V. Bukhayev, whose lack of tree cover is conspicuous. Its expanse is paved in granite, with statues of Red Army fighters, framing a central monument of red granite arches, in the shape of what was the main form of housing here until the twentieth century, the yurt, stitched at the top by black bronze laurel leaves; when you look at it from a distance, you realise that the square isn't just bare so that the parades could be held here – although of course they were – but show that a clear view could be opened up of the Tian Shan. It's startlingly beautiful.

The parks run east-west, alongside Frunze Street, Silk Road Street and Chuy Avenue, with Yusup Abrahamanov Street – originally Soviet Street, and renamed after an early Soviet leader here who was killed in the Great Purge – and the grandiosely planted, Garden City Boulevard of Manas Avenue the main north-south routes; in places,

Victory yurt

A discourse with the founders

it's hard to know what's park and what's street, although unlike the British Garden Cities that were the influence, they're always packed full of people. The largest is Oak Park, whose axial routes pass all manner of sculptural embellishment – expressionistic sculptures of the 1980s, a Neoclassical statue of Marx and Engels, a relaxed pair sat, legs crossed, clearly engaged in the dialectic, a woman (modelled on a murdered local Communist) waving the flag of revolution aloft. Then there are Pavilions, little cafes – the 1960s Seashell Pavilion is a sculptural "Duck" in the shape of an organic yurt, and the Stalinist-Orientalist Mineral Water Pavilion is a florid rotunda designed in 1952 and decorated in Neo-Timurid plaster, looking like it had been teleported here from Moscow's Exhibition of Economic Achievements. Panfilov Park, named after the mainly Central Asian Panfilov Regiment of the Great Patriotic War, is dominated by a very carny funfair, and red obelisks abound. One monument celebrates an

Frunze Orientalism

Colonialism and/or friendship

anniversary of the "friendship" of the Russian and Kirghiz peoples, something of a comedown from the early USSR's celebration of violent anti-colonial revolt.

A subtle route between these parks leads to Ala-Too Square, one of the very largest in the Soviet Union, a plaza of staggering size, built over the first half of the 1980s, and showing some hints of Postmodernism. Going north to south, you first come to a Lenin statue where he appears to be giving the thumbs up; in front is what is now the National Museum (but was originally the Lenin Museum, in a country he never visited), an imposing, faintly Islamicised glass and marble cube, with raised walkways as circulation around it; trace these walkways around, and you see the square, an asphalt steppe furnished with fountains and neon lights, with two colonnaded domed buildings on either side, and an interesting Brutalist government complex where projecting volumes and another gold dome are raised on very tall pilotis, offering a pedestrian route through.

This is "official" Frunze, a world away from Utopian Communes, imaginary or otherwise, but it is also exemplary public space, free-flowing and intuitive to walk through, however vast it is. Adjacent is what was the Central Committee of the Communist Party of the Kirghiz Republic, which became the Parliament after independence. It is a typical Brezhnev-era government building, built in the early Eighties to the designs of Urmat Alymkulov, A. Zusik, O. Lazarev, R. Mukhamadiyev and S. Sultanov; like many, it is transparently modelled on Boston City Hall (two decades after that was built), but it is monumental and in good condition. It is surrounded with new revolutionary monuments, to the insurrections that have happened whenever Kyrgyzstan has threatened to come close to the open dictatorship that dominates its neighbours, in 2005 and again in 2010; the latter uprising also managed to close the air base that had been granted to the US as a convenient place to pursue the "War on Terror" in nearby Afghanistan and Pakistan and do some "extraordinary rendition". These revolts could equally be seen as revolts against the

Palace of Lenin turned National Museum

The Square

country's dire poverty, and in that, they were not successful. Certainly the spiked fence around it is taking no chances.

If looked at in terms of GDP or more usefully, the Human Development Index, Kyrgyzstan is indisputably part of the "Third World". Its population is slightly poorer than that of Bolivia, slightly richer than that of war-ridden Iraq. The only country poorer in the former USSR is Tajikistan, which endured a ferocious Civil War in the 1990s. But this is in no way the Third World city lately celebrated by the liberal guilt of Western planners and architects, where all outside space is a giant, unplanned informal market; it's a carefully planned city of elegant public spaces, and people do not shun this but use it, strolling through the parks and lazing on the benches.

The architecture you can see through the trees is, as in Almaty, frequently superb. The dominant housing is typical late-Soviet national style prefab, with decorative brises-soleils over the windows

The Headquarters

Posing and Overturning

and balconies, in better condition than in Georgia and even Armenia, with relatively little in the way of self-building on top – there are real shanty towns instead, on the outskirts. Bishkek has all the panoply of Soviet public buildings, from a bombastic Neoclassical Opera House of the Stalin era, described by Mamedov as being from the period of "proletarian ressentiment", all giant columns and gilding to show that we have grandeur too, and with the heroic proletarian statues recently lacquered, so that they look like Chinese statuettes. There are spectacular examples of Brutalism, such as the Sports Palace, a concrete volume designed by V. Kostin and V. Marukov and built in 1974, roaring forward on melodramatic thrusting pillars, there is another flying-saucer Circus, and so forth; but two buildings stand out. These

Bishkek Brutalism

are the Lenin Library and the Palace of Weddings, which stand opposite each other on one of the north-south streets. The Library, finished in 1983 to the designs of S. Nurgaziyev, I. Ibrayev and R. Asylbekov, is a long, marble-clad building, its reading rooms reached via a multi-level atrium criss-crossed by flamboyantly cantilevered stairways; tiled ceilings are in abstract patterns most likely "inspired by the national form" but enjoyable as pure inventions. It's a masterfully realised space. Outside it, trees shelter a drained pool, one of many in contemporary Bishkek.

This is modern architecture as it was practiced globally, but the Palace of Weddings, designed by A. Logunov and A. Klishevich and built in 1987, could only be imagined in the USSR. In terms

The Lenin Library

of its function, it is what happened instead of Queer Communism – marriage outside of religion rather than the end of marriage altogether, and the affirmation of the nuclear family overseen by the eyes of the state instead of in the eyes of God. Even so, it is an exciting building, jagged glass and marble prisms, with spiky turrets, and an astonishing interior, where a grand staircase with rooms for bride and groom on either side lead to a deeply suggestive opening in the middle, where the marriages took place; it is strafed by polychromatic shafts of light from abstract stained glass panels. If the old ceremonies could have been reimagined in such a thrilling way, think what could have been done with a new invention.

There are also two public buildings which make clearer where you are in the world. The Bathhouse, designed by A. Sogonov, S. Nasypkulov and S. Belyanchikov in the early Eighties, and the Bishkek Central Mosque, planned under Perestroika and finished in the early

Winged Eros, or Not

Mammarial

A Perestroika mosque

1990s. These are close to each other, and are more obviously "Asian" in typology. The Baths are not monumental and luxurious like in Almaty, but consist of two faintly cosmic, mammarial marble-clad domes. The decorative treatment of the bath-house's pipes and ducts is echoed in the nearby Central Mosque, where tubular, brick detailing is used to create a sense of swelling mass, somewhere between the Persian architecture still visible in some Kyrgyz cities like Uzgen, and the impure modernism of the late Soviet Modernist period, that heady and particular mix of "national tradition" and international modernism. Aside from these, and the golden domes on Ala-Too Square, there's far less than in Almaty of the "made in Moscow national style" critiqued by Boris Chukhovich. There are minarets, but no "minarets".

At the edges of the parkland city there's another, earlier set of squares and parkland spaces, around the Philharmonic, built in 1980 to the designs of A. Pechonkin, a flamboyant Brutalist-Baroque composition, sculpturally embellished with an obelisk ridden by Manas, the protagonist of a much celebrated Kyrgyz epic poem. Around this are two spiky Stalinist towers on an axis, and a lot of classical public buildings, dotted around parkland – these could be in Minsk. This classical ensemble aside, Bishkek is a modernist garden city of the absolute highest quality, a Brasilia where the pedestrian rather than the car is the dominant. A huge amount could be learned from that city, but it's not "sexy" in the required manner. Planned and designed in very large degree by Central Asians themselves, it represents instead a yearning for communal life that is ordered and logical, rather than chaotic and unpredictable, – a more than understandable desire.

There are two museums that seem to speak most about what it was to be Communist and Kyrgyz, and how seriously or not that aspiration was taken – both confidently modernist, cubic, concrete, internationalist and Brutalist. These two are the Gapar Aitiev Fine Art Museum, designed by Shailo Djekshenbayev in 1974, and the Mikhail Frunze Museum, designed by Gennady Kutateladze and Yury

Karikh in 1967. The earlier building could be absolutely anywhere in the world at the time, but for its sculptural embellishment. It is a plain concrete and glass grid, with supergraphics and two relief sculptures of revolutionary scenes integrated into its structure. Inside, a story is told which, again, seems to be much the same as that which would be told anywhere in the USSR in the Brezhnev years, a staid display at odds with the elegance of its building.

Mikhail Frunze is born to Moldovan parents in Pishpek, his father the only doctor in the town that would treat Kyrgyz patients. He becomes a Bolshevik, becomes a General in the Civil War, and leads the Red Army to victory over the both the Russian nationalist White Armies and Muslim Basmachi insurgents in what was then "Russian Turkestan". Then he dies, and we are left with this collection of maps, guns, booklets, proclamations, posters, and at the end, his divan, pianola and bookcase. Below is his house, an obviously faked

The Frunze Museum

bungalow containing a pleasant rustic interior, an example of the peculiar fact that the Soviets had lots of standard Museums of How People Lived in Olden Times and justified them by tying them to revolutionary hagiography. There are a few real nineteenth-century bungalows like it scattered around Bishkek now, all those I saw in a terrible state of disrepair; only the fake is well looked after. Other rooms sketch out the history of Pishpek, Frunze and Bishkek as cities, and have a special section on the Panfilov Regiment, who marched "from Frunze to the Elbe". The yellow peril that so terrified Central European liberals. "The Universal City will be realised when a son of the Kirghiz steppes waters his horses in the Loire, and a Sicilian peasant plants cotton in Turkmen valleys."[14]

That aside, the place seems most of all to have been for tourists from the rest of the USSR, part of a long-forgotten itinerary of revolutionary relics. By contrast, the Gapar Aitiev Fine Art Museum's abstract architecture hides a much more clearly national and anti-

The Art Museum

colonial story. The building is ingenious and original. Inclined concrete volumes on pilotis contain the galleries, with the entrance reached through a shaded courtyard; an abstract mosaic runs up the height of the interior atrium. The actual gallery spaces manage rather remarkably to recreate the creaky, stuffy ambience of a Victorian museum, which belies the radicalism of the paintings and sculptures. Most of the early rooms consist of works made at the turn of the Thirties, to depict change in Soviet Kyrgyzstan. Youths examine a globe. Miners discuss in open air as if they are intellectuals. Teenage girls, unveiled, carry books. Many of these are by Semen Chuikov, who was from a local settler family – he helped organise a commemorative exhibition in 1936 celebrating the twentieth anniversary of the 1916 uprising (attendance was massive – 20,000, a quarter of the city's population at the time), an example of what Mamedov approvingly calls "revolutionary betrayal" of his Russian roots.[15] The interest in the paintings rises and falls with the politics – the 1930s work of Gapar Aitiev himself, the first Kyrgyz painter, is fresh and vivid, and there is, after a nadir in the Forties and Fifties of Soviet jingoism, much intriguing 1960s work, but by the end of the Seventies, we're well into a form of lucrative Sunday painting, frequently sentimentally treating local themes. "Maybe that's what art will really be like in Communism", Mamedov muses. People will be concentrating on enjoying their lives, and art will be whimsical and slightly naff, no longer a place to channel sublimated energies. Soviet Kyrgyzness begins as a celebration of a new, revolutionary subject, and ends as ornamental images of yurts, pretty girls and mountains. It was probably a good time to be an artist, if you were satisfied with that.

The cityscape has become more "Asian", in a banal sense, in that there are many new Mosques, instantly identifiable by whoever has funded them – the largest being an impressive Ottoman Megamosque near Victory Square and a naff Saudi-style outgrowth of marble kitsch off Frunze Street – and these aside, there's a few gross Neoclassical/Postmodernist high-rises inserted at random into the Soviet grid.

There are also a lot of useful if shoddy shops on ground floors of the green boulevards, and most positively, a lot of cafes and restaurants spilling out onto those broad and lush streets. Lenin is still everywhere, and the hammer and sickle ubiquitous. In how unadulteratedly Soviet its imagery is, Bishkek is rivalled only by Minsk among post-Soviet capitals. Mamedov points out that the local Communist Party even threatened to sue the government when it moved Lenin to the huge square at the back of the National Museum, as opposed to the even huger square in front of it. This is most probably because of the fact it is the only democratic country in Central Asia – those revolts have ensured that – and hence, the popular Communist nostalgia is able to resist attempts to "de-Communise". It is also the most neoliberal country in Central Asia, with the Soviet welfare state dismantled even more thoroughly than everywhere else. Appearances, as ever, can be deceptive.

New Language for a New World

If that was official Bishkek, one of the Utopian Bishkeks can be found right on the city's outskirts, a "ruin porn" world of enormous derelict factories, car washes, dusty railway sidings, concrete silos, and old offices squatted by migrants from the countryside. Just beyond this, where the trolleybuses end (Bishkek's transport system is that of the Soviet city of 600,000 it was in 1991, not the nearly 1 million-strong one it is now), is a large, slightly wild park, some dilapidated houses, and a Workers Club, on a grid of dusty streets. This is the territory of Interhelpo. The name is in Esperanto.

Interhelpo was founded in the 1920s by Communists from Czechoslovakia, as an industrial co-operative, which ran at various times a power station, a textile factory, a furniture factory, and so forth; most of its thousand or so members were Slovaks, from what was then an impoverished post-Hapsburg hinterland, where it may have made some sense to move from Central Europe to Central Asia in order to build a new society. The park is named after Julius Fucik, a Czech journalist (later murdered by the Nazis) who visited and apparently "saw the birth of a new, socialist life in the nomad tent, to say nothing of the Kirghiz capital, and realised the epoch-making significance... he discerned the future in what he saw in Kirghizia". In a letter "to the builders of socialist Kirghizia", Fucik relates that "we had set out for a country which the bourgeois story-tellers described as savage and exotic", but "what we have received from you we shall take to the proletariat of the whole of Western Europe".[16] This was in a book with the title A Land Where Our Tomorrow is Already Yesterday. As was common with foreign Communists, many Communards were targeted during the Purges, and the co-operative was wound up during the war. Even so, it is remembered here still.

The Communards' enthusiasm for Esperanto wasn't unusual in the early USSR – why not speak in an invented international language, here in an area where you could find Turkic, Persian and Slavic languages constantly mixing already? In this contempt for the "natural" and belief that conditions can be changed through will, science and collective action, it's pretty close to ShTAB's Ethics of Queer Communism, a practical precursor that evidently interests Mamedov more than images of awesome ruined monuments. Interhelpo now offers little to those who would be looking for Soviet Utopias to be aesthetic and architecturally inventive – these are simple houses, the club and school is rudimentary – the Communards of Interhelpo built these themselves, after all, with no division of labour. You can go to the Workers' Club and use the privy the Communards built, walk the dusty, unlit, streets they laid out, potholed even by Bishkek standards. An early participant, as a child, was the later leader of the Prague Spring, Alexander Dubcek. There is a little tribute to him in the Workers' Club, headed "The Human Face of Politics", which was not his slogan. The area is almost shanty-town like in its state of worn, lived-in, uncared-for decay. A fence outside the Interhelpo School has, with arrogant fanfare, a plaque telling you it has been funded by the government of the Czech Republic. How good of them.

Co-operative convenience

Near to Interhelpo was a large factory complex, which built its own stadium and park for the use of its workers. It seems to have been untouched since 1991, but for the decay. In the park, Lenin gestures. A bright poster still stands over the archway to the stadium, showing young Communists gazing, grinning, into the future. Below them, are boards with the insignia of Soviet Kirghizia, and even untouched old scoreboards. Go through the grand Roman arch into the stadium itself, and sit on the concrete steps, half eaten away by spalling, and you're often just sat on steel bars. But teenagers are playing football on the green, with the trees and disused chimneys behind them. Mamedov looks rather content. "I don't feel melancholy here. It happened, and it can happen again"; not that extravagant a claim to make in a place where people travelled by train from Slovakia to build a new world and speak a new language on the borders of China.

Streets of Interhelpo

For Mamedov and Suyarkulova, the means to build their new world in the present is through Queer activism, with both of them working for Labrys, the major LGBT campaign group in Kyrgyzstan (the name comes from the double-sided axe used by the Amazons). This sort of straightforward civic activism – safe spaces, advice, public advocacy, encouragement of 'visibility' – might seem a comedown from visions of Cosmic Queer Communism, but then if Kyrgyzstan is ever mentioned in the news in the West over the last few years, it has been over its attempt to emulate the law forbidding "homosexual propaganda", implemented in St Petersburg and then across Russia. From being by far the freest country in the region for sexual difference, meetings – including those of Labrys – started being violently broken up by homophobic gangs, as the government voted to institutionalise bigotry.

Arch of Triumph

Still here

Traces

Except, and here's the twist, the government in question fell and the relevant bill was shelved. At least for the moment, Labrys won. The Neanderthal obscurantism introduced in Russia's "Window on the West" foundered when attempted in a mountainous, impoverished Republic in Central Asia. Who is "backward" now? From such sparks, all manner of things can grow. Commenting on his decision to opt for activism over art, Mamedov tells me "this doesn't mean that Queer Communism is over. But there won't be so much of the Soviet stuff". They've proved their point, that the Soviet legacy is more than the Gulag, more than Russian colonialism, and more than sentimental nostalgia: now, something else.

Before I left Bishkek, I mentioned to Mohira Suyarkulova that I was planning on taking an actual holiday elsewhere, in a place in Western Europe, that I wouldn't write about. "Why not exoticise the familiar instead?", she asked, casually but sharply. I felt embarrassed, as well I might. I hope I haven't exoticised the exotic in this book. What I wanted to do here was something else: to challenge the notion that the former Soviet Union is just an albatross, an embarrassment for the global left, where the Great Idea was tried and failed by people just too backward, too Eastern, to understand its message, and now just a wasteland of commercialised Stalinist boulevards, crumbling factory-made flats, flag-waving Babushkas and stomping skinheads. In Bishkek, I found the best confirmation that the place that generated the first real attempt at Communism can still develop it anew, and still push at the limits of the possible. After all, here, more than anywhere else, they know not only what not to do, but also what can be done. You can fly from the "periphery" into outer space. дорогу космическому эросу.

ENDNOTES

1 Lydia Ginzburg, Notes from the Blockade (Vintage, 2016, originally published in 1989), pp. 24-25

A Short Introduction

1 Dissatisfaction with these limited national narratives is the reason why alternative names of each city are given as titles, after their current official names, as a reminder of the non-"national" people that made – and in some places still make – these places home.

2 I have tried to avoid any repetition of locations from the more personal and taxonomic account of "socialist architecture" in *Landscapes of Communism* (Allen Lane, 2015). Only some of the capital cities – Moscow, Kyiv, Petersburg, Tbilisi – and one industrial city, Nizhny Novgorod, appear in both, and here I've deliberately left out places covered in the earlier book. I've tried to indicate where a relevant place is covered there in footnotes, rather than reprising them, so as not to bore anyone who has read the earlier volume, but to indicate said information to those who have not.

Microcosmos: Slavutych

1 Terry Martin, *The Affirmative Action Empire, Nations and Nationalism in the Soviet Union*, 1921-1939 (Cornell, 2001)

2 Svetlana Alexievich, *Voices from Chernobyl – the Oral History of a Nuclear Disaster* (Picador, 2006), p. 51

3 Ibid, p. 199

4 Ibid, p. 163

5 Ievgeniia Gubkina, *Slavutych Architectural Guide* (Dom, 2016), p. 26

6 Much of the fun of the event was programming speakers into unexpected parts of the town, as a means of exploring it. I delivered a lecture about British new towns in the drained municipal swimming pool.

7 Gubkina, *Slavutych Architectural Guide*, p. 19
8 Alexievich, *Voices from Chernobyl*, p. 42

Part One: The Western Periphery

Forgotten Capital: Kaunas, Kowno, Kovno

1 On the fascist aspects of the Smetona regime in the 1930s, see Anatol Lieven, *The Baltic Revolutions – Estonia, Latvia and Lithuania and the Path to Independence* (Yale, 1997), pp. 66-69
2 Note the account of these two buildings in the excellent Kaunas Architectural Guide, edited by Julija Reklaite (Lapas, 2016), pp. 60-61
3 Raul Hilberg, *Perpetrators, Victims, Bystanders – The Jewish Catastrophe* 1933–45 (Harper Perennial, 1993), pp. 98-99

A Guidebook of Revolutionary Relics: Kuldīga, Goldingen

1 Joachim Becker, "Europe's Other Periphery", in *New Left Review*, Vol. 2, 99, May/June 2016, p. 55
2 Paul Krugman, "Response", in Olivier J. Blanchard et al, *Boom, Bust, Recovery – Forensics of the Latvian Crisis*, (IMF, 2013)
3 Becker, "Europe's Other Periphery", p. 45
4 Will Mawhood describes it "Latvia's most Latvian town" in a 2015 article for *UpNorth*, http://upnorth.eu/Kuldīga-jewel-of-ancient-latvia/
5 Anatol Lieven, *The Baltic Revolutions* (Yale, 1994), p. 51
6 Andrew Ezergailis, *The* 1917 *Revolution in Latvia* (East European Quarterly, 1971), p. 5
7 Ibid, p. 79
8 For a grim account of this exile milieu, with its traumatised revolutionaries, generally unable to speak English, and many of them left scarred physically and psychologically by torture from the Tsarist authorities (including Peeters, whose fingernails were ripped out), see Donald Rumbelow, *The Houndsditch Murders and the Siege of Sidney Street* (Macmillan, 1988)

9 A useful example here is Mara Kalnins's recent *Latvia – A Short History* (Hurst, 2015); or the account in the exhibition catalogue *The Motherland Calls!* (Maksla. Mits. Dokuments, 2011), which explains away both the Latvian Riflemen and the Latvian SS legion as misguided "fighters for their country"; curious given that neither the Bolsheviks in 1917, nor, by even the wildest stretch of the imagination, the Third Reich in 1944, promised any kind of independence to Latvia. The latter didn't even promise the sort of deeply circumscribed autonomy Latvia had under the USSR. It's evidently too disturbing to imagine that at any point large groups of people could have believed in socialism, or for that matter believed in Nazism.

10 Liliana Riga's recent *The Bolsheviks and the Russian Empire* (Cambridge, 2014) finds Latvians disproportionately represented in the Bolshevik leadership, the Latvian Social Democrats disproportionately large as a Party – larger, at one point than the Russian Bolsheviks and Mensheviks put together – and also, most interestingly for Kuldīga, argues that Latvia was the only place in the Russian Empire where there was significant rural support for the Bolsheviks.

11 Ezergailis, *The* 1917 *Revolution in Latvia*, p. 21

12 Ibid, p. 103

13 Ibid, p. 52

14 Ibid, p. 138

15 Ibid, p. 139

16 Quoted in Otto Lacis, "Farewell to the Communist Party of Latvia", *New Left Review*, 182, July-August 1990

17 David Mitchell, 1919 – *Red Mirage* (Jonathan Cape, 1970), p. 88

18 Ibid, p. 89

19 The incident, deriving from an account by a Freikorps officer, is cited in Jean-Paul Kauffmann, *A Journey to Nowhere* (Quercus, 2013), p. 14

20 See Lieven, *The Baltic Revolutions*, p. 390

21 *The Latvian Soviet Socialist Republic* (Novosti, 1972), pp. 30-1

22 *In The Holocaust in Latvia* (United States Holocaust Memorial Museum, 1996), Andrew Ezergailis points out that actual spontaneity was anathema to Vyshinsky, and the "welcoming" of the Red Army was tightly controlled and organised.

23 According to Ezergailis, there is no evidence Jews were either prominent in the 1940-1 Latvian Soviet Republic, in the NKVD or otherwise, or that they were disproportionately represented in the occupying regime in general.

24 Unpaginated English text appended to A. Volanska, *Livijas Rezevskas: Darbu Katalogs Izstazu Zale* (Darbnica a Projekti, 2004)

25 This is the argument of Ivan Szelenyi, *Urban Inequalities Under State Socialism* (Oxford, 1983)

26 On the puzzling nature of Soviet concrete construction in areas with a lot of high-quality wood that could be used more easily and cheaply, see Adrian Forty's notes on Estonia in *Concrete and Culture* (Reaktion, 2012)

27 See Dimitrij Zadorin and Philipp Meuser, *Towards a Typology of Mass Housing in the* USSR (Dom, 2015)

28 Quoted from "Grand-land's Museum" leaflet, given out at the Kuldīga Art House.

A Tour with the City Architect: Ventspils, Windau, Vindava

1 *Ventspils* 700+25 (Ventspili Turismsa, 2015), p. 10

2 Ibid, p. 25

3 See Part Three of this book.

4 For example: http://www.archilovers.com/projects/141880/parventa-library.html

5 *Ventspils* 700+25, p. 5

6 Ibid, p. 100

Nuclear Model Village:
Sillamäe, Sillamäggi, Narva 2, Leningrad 5

1 Maros Krivy, "From Mining to Data-Mining" in Karlis Berzins, Jurga Daubaraite, Petras Isora, Ona Lozuraityte, Niklavs Paegle, Dagnija Smilga, Johan Tali, Laila Zarina, Jonas Zakauskas (eds), *The Baltic Atlas* (Sternberg Press, 2016), p. 193

2 These interviews were originally in my "Baltic Interplay", *TANK*, Autumn 2016

3 Aleksandra Zavjalova, "Small Voices, Big Narratives – Problems of Remembering and Identifying the Post-Soviet Space: The Case of the Stalinist Architectural Ensemble in Sillamäe, Estonia", (Kingston University, 2013)

4 Ibid, p. 8

5 Ibid, p. 15

6 Ibid, p. 21

The Cradle of Three Revolutions:
St Petersburg, Petrograd, Leningrad

1 The book to read is Alexander Rabinowitch, *The Bolsheviks Come to Power* (Pluto, 2017)

2 All the information here come from Ilya Orlov's 2014 article "On The Field of Mars", translated by Thomas Campbell at his blog The Russian Reader, at https://therussianreader.com/2014/11/13/ilya-orlov-field-of-mars/

3 A big question in Petersburg, as this city, perhaps closest in its population and scale to Berlin, has 69 Metro stations. Berlin has 173, and another 166 on the S-Bahn.

4 For a straightforward description of what got built and why, see Andreas Trier Morch and Juri Nikitin, *The Unknown St Petersburg – Architecture from 1917 to 1956* (Royal Danish Academy of Arts, 2003), pp. 64-87

5 B.M. Kirilikov, M.S Stieglitz, *Leningrad Avant-Garde Architecture* (Kolo, 2009), p. 101

6 See the Chto Delat "drift" of the district, at https://chtodelat.org/category/b7-art-projects/commisioned-works/b_4/
7 Philipp Meuser and Dmitrij Zadorin, *Towards a Typology of Mass Housing – Prefabrication in the* USSR, 1955-1991 (Dom, 2015), p. 297
8 See Richard Pare, *The Lost Vanguard – Russian Modernist Architecture,* 1922-1932 (Monacelli Press, 2007), pp. 308-315; for my "take", ill-advisedly written two years before I'd actually visited Russia, see *Militant Modernism* (Zero, 2009), p. 49
9 From the recent catalogue *Sergei Kirov Museum* (SMHStP, undated), p. 4
10 The great literary depiction of this is Victor Serge's *Conquered City* (NYRB, 2011)

Part Two: Debatable Lands

Art and Revolution: Kyiv, Kiev, Kijów, קיִעוו

1 She describes the event in the first part of Agata Pyzik, *Poor but Sexy – Culture Clashes in Europe East and West* (Zero, 2014)
2 On Viatrovych and his Institute of National Memory, a useful critical account from a by no means leftist source is Josh Cohen, "The Historian Whitewashing Ukraine's Past", *Foreign Policy*, May 2016
3 A pocket catalogue of the "art" side of the events is available as *The School of Kyiv Guidebook* (Huss, 2015); but the guide to the venues themselves is essential – *The Book of Kyiv* (Medusa, 2015)
4 There is a chapter on Lybidska Square in my *Across the Plaza* (Strelka, 2012)
5 From the booklet *Monuments of Kiev* (Mistestvo, 1963), unpaginated
6 At https://sovietmosaicsinukraine.org/
7 Boris Groys, "Communist Globalisation", in Lukasz Ronduda, Alex Farquharson, Barbara Piwowarska (eds.), *Star City – the Future under Communism* (Mammal, 2013), p. 183

8 Yevgen Nikiforov, *Decommunised – Ukrainian Soviet Mosaics* (Dom, 2017), p. 8

Oligarchy in Rocket City:
Dnipro, Dnepropetrovsk, Ekaterinoslav

1 R.W. Davies and Stephen Wheatcroft, *The Years of Hunger – Soviet Agriculture,* 1931-1933 (Palgrave, 2009), p. 113. Davies and Wheatcroft note that Peterovsky, along with other Ukrainian Party leaders, publicly took a hard line, while privately begging the Politburo for famine relief.
2 There is a good analysis of this process and the limitations of "clan" analysis in Yuliya Yurchenko, *Ukraine and the Empire of Capital* (Pluto, 2018)
3 On this, see Oliver Carroll's remarkably candid interview with the man, "Star Wars in Ukraine", *Politico*, December 2015

Streets of Crocodiles: Chișinău, Kishinev, קעשענעוו

1 A useful analysis can be found in Alexander Moldovan's "Social Unrest in Moldova: Expropriate the Mafia!", *LeftEast*, February 2016, http://www.criticatac.ro/lefteast/social-unrest-in-moldova-expropiate-the-mafia/
2 Ivan Szelenyi, *Urban Inequalities Under State Socialism* (Oxford University Press, 1983), p. 109

Part Three: The Centre

Where the Gauges Change:
Brest, Brest-Litovsk, Brześć-nad-Bugiem, בריסק

1 One of many: "Edge of Europe, End of Europe", *New York Review of Books*, July 2015
2 At the time of writing, you can enter Belarus visa-free if you get in at Minsk Airport, otherwise it's a visit to the consulate and some intricate form-filling. As, of course, it is for Belarusians going the other way, harsher still.

3 Broadly, Andrew Wilson's *Belarus – the Last Dictatorship in Europe* (Yale, 2011) is convincing on the means by which any meaningful democracy in the country was strangled at birth, though unreflective as to why.

4 There is an English language guide of the 1980s, which gives a flavour of the propaganda and the scale: Nikolai Kudryashov, *The Brest Fortress: A Guide* (Raduga, 1987)

Time, Backward!: Minsk, Miensk, מינסק

1 Again, Timothy Snyder is textbook here: "In Darkest Belarus", *New York Review of Books*, October 2010

2 For an informed and dryly witty account of the city's twentieth-century architecture, see Dmitrij Zadorin, "Architecture of the BSSR – Texture of the Standardised", in Katharina Ritter, et al (eds), *Socialist Modernism – Unknown History* (Park Books, 2012)

3 Barbara Epstein, *The Minsk Ghetto – Jewish Resistance and Soviet Internationalism* (University of California Press, 2008), esp. pp. 40-76

4 Whether the renamings of the sister organisations in Russia and Ukraine, the FSB and SBU, has resulted in them being significantly nicer or nastier, or about the same, institutions is worth considering.

5 Artur Klinau, "Minsk: the Sun City of Dreams", *Herito Quarterly*, 22–23, 2016

6 See Part Four of this book.

7 Nelly Bekus, "Ideological Recycling of the Socialist Legacy: Reading Townscapes of Minsk and Astana", *Europe-Asia Studies*, Vol. 69, 2017

8 "We see here a model social state like the one we are trying to create", said the great man. "Chávez Forges Ties with Belarus", http://news.bbc.co.uk/1/hi/world/europe/5209868.stm. For an outlandish account of Belarusian "socialism", see Stewart

Parker, *The Last Soviet Republic – Alexander Lukashenko's Belarus* (Trafford, 2007), though perhaps not more absurd than the "darkest Belarus" trope.

9 The imprisonment and violence at worst and surveillance at best that dissidents have to face is of course real, just as the near-full employment and readily available mass housing are real. But for an example of unintentionally hilarious credulity, see the *Guardian*'s Lyn Gardener repeating as gospel the Belarus Free Theatre's (tongue-in-cheek) claim that there is a set legal time limit in which people can look at each other in Minsk's public spaces. "Minsk 2011 – Review", *Guardian*, 24 October 2011

Life in the Twenty-First Century: Moscow, Moskwa

1 For an account of this melancholy period in the VDNKh's history and what it said of the society that made it and that it existed in, see Svetlana Stephenson and Elena Danilova, "Down to Earth", *Radical Philosophy*, Issue 159, January/February 2010. For a "schizoanalysis" of the place, see Andrey Monastyrsky's 1986, "VDNKh, Capital of the World", in Elena Zaytseva and Alex Anikina (eds), *Cosmic Shift – Russian Contemporary Art Writing* (Zed, 2017)

2 I discuss the replanning of Moscow as an imperial capital in my *Landscapes of Communism*, but the best introduction is Karl Schlogel's *Moscow* (Reaktion, 2005)

3 Invited to lecture at the Strelka Institute of Architecture in 2011, I asked if there was a route from the airport to the school I could take. They insisted on booking me a taxi. It took two hours. On my way back, I took the Metro and the Airport Express, and got there in 25 minutes.

4 The last chapter of Richard Anderson's *Russia – Modern Architectures in History* (Reaktion, 2015), is useful on the post-Soviet career of the likes of Mosproekt-2 and Mikhail Posokhin.

5 This building and others like it are given a rather more forgiving assessment in Bart Goldhoorn and Philipp Meuser, *Capitalist Realism – New Architecture in Russia* (Dom, 2009)

6 Full disclosure: I published a book with Strelka's press, *Across the Plaza*, on public space, in 2012.

7 For an excellent short critique of how the project has revealed the city's Stalinist face, see Clementine Cecil, "The New Moscow: Clean n Mean", October 2016, at her blog Onion Domes on Golden Lane http://clementinececil.blogspot.co.uk/2016/10/the-new-moscow-clean-n-mean.html

8 "Russians Rebel Against Plans to Tear Down Their Homes", *Economist*, May 2017 https://www.economist.com/news/europe/21721642-even-apolitical-muscovites-are-up-arms-russians-rebel-against-plans-tear-down-their-homes

9 M. Vassilev and S. Gouchev, *Life in the Twenty-First Century* (Penguin, 1961), pp. 162-3

10 Bee Flowers, "What's Wrong With This Approach, Comrades?", *Architectural Design*, No. 179, Vol. 76, No. 1, 2006

11 Philipp Meuser and Dimitrij Zadorin, *Towards a Typology of Mass Housing in the* USSR (Dom, 2016)

12 Kuba Snopek, *Belyayevo Forever* (Strelka, 2013), p. 13

13 Ibid, p. 77

14 Alexei Gutnov, et al, *The Ideal Communist City* (Braziller, 1968), p. 153

15 Ibid, p. 156

16 Ibid, p. 145

17 Ibid, p. 34

18 Ibid, p. 87

19 Ibid, p. 158

20 Lynne Attwood, *Gender and Housing in Soviet Russia* (Manchester, 2010), p. 170

21 Ibid, p. 155

22 Ibid, p. 157

23 Ibid, p. 207; and see Abel Aganbegyan, *Challenge – The Economics of Perestroika* (IB Tauris, 1988)
24 See Anna Bronovitskaya and Olga Kazakova, *Leonid Pavlov* (Electa, 2015), p. 198
25 Snopek, *Belyayevo Forever*, pp. 48-9
26 On this building, see Richard Anderson, *Russia – Modern Architectures in History* (Reaktion 2015), pp. 226-8
27 Meuser and Zadorin, *Towards a Typology of Mass Housing in the* USSR, pp. 434
28 Ibid, p. 345
29 For a comprehensive and rightly heavily critical analysis of this construction boom, largely reliant on the sweated labour of Central Asian migrants rather than automation (people are cheaper), see The Russian Reader, "A Home For Every Russian", https://therussianreader.wordpress.com/2015/05/03/a-home-for-every-russian/
30 Flowers, "What's Wrong With This Approach, Comrades?"

A Week in the Kremlin: Nizhny Novgorod, Gorky

1 I discuss Avtozavod at some length in my *Landscapes of Communism* (Allen Lane, 2015)

The Architecture of Sovereignty:Kazan, Qazan

1 On this and much else, Helen M Faller's *National, Language, Islam – Tatarstan's Sovereignty Movement* (Central European University, 2011) which makes fascinating reading.

Constructivist Capital: Yekaterinburg, Sverdlovsk

1 It was finally demolished in 2018 in "preparation for the World Cup", to much protest.
2 For an English-language piece on this, see Dmitry Lebedev, "Our City, Our Space", *openDemocracy*, 26 April 2017, at https://www.

opendemocracy.net/od-russia/our-city-our-space-ekaterinburg-residents-come-out-against-plans-to-construct-new-church

3 For a study with particular attention to public space, see Mikhail Ilchenko, "Green Utopia of the Uralmash – Institutional Effects and Symbolic Meaning", *Critical Housing Analysis*, Vol. 3, Issue 2, 2016

Part Four: The Eastern Periphery

Brand Georgia: Kutaisi, Kutais

1 Eric Lee, *The Experiment – Georgia's Forgotten Revolution, 1918-1921* (Zed, 2017). A more hostile, and in many ways more convincing, account of the Menshevik republic can be found in Alex Marshall, *The Caucasus Under Soviet Rule* (Routledge, 2010)

2 Quoted repeatedly in Leon Trotsky's often questionable justification for the Georgian invasion, *Social Democracy and the Wars of Intervention* (New Park, 1975)

3 I owe this fact to a paper given by Nano Zazanashvili in Yerevan in October 2017.

4 Branko Milanović, "For Whom the Wall Fell?", *Globalist*, 7 November 2014, https://www.theglobalist.com/for-whom-the-wall-fell-a-balance-sheet-of-the-transition-to-capitalism/

An Exhibition of Achievements: Tbilisi, Tiflis

1 Joanna Warsza, *Ministry of Highways – The Performative Architecture of Tbilisi* (Sternberg Press, 2014), pp. 27-8

2 The romantic version: Joanna Warsza (ed.), *Kamikaze Loggia – the Georgian Pavilion at the 55th Venice Biennale* (Ministry of Culture and Monument Protection of Georgia, 2013); the factual reasons behind it: Rusudan Mirzikashvili, "Everybody's Favourite", in Ritter, et al, *Soviet Modernism* (Park Books, 2012). Both are worth reading.

3 Among the many virtues of Georgi Derlugian's wonderful *Bourdieu's Secret Admirer in the Caucasus* (University of

Chicago, 2005) is its analysis of these under-investigated sides of the USSR and its collapse.

From the Purges to Paradise:
Sevan Writers' Resort, Sevanavank

1 Osip Mandelstam, *Journey to Armenia* (Notting Hill Editions, 2011), pp. 45-47
2 Nadezhda Mandelstam, *Hope Abandoned* (Penguin, 1976), p. 610
3 Vasily Grossman, *An Armenian Sketchbook* (Maclehose Press, 2013), p. 8
4 I owe this reference to "The Mountains are Still Very Wild", at the Chichikir blog, 22 April 2014, at https://chichikir.wordpress.com/2014/04/22/the-mountains-are-still-very-wild/
5 I owe these details to the exhibition, but an English language article touching on this: Ruben Arevshatyan, "An Architecture of Paradoxical Shifts", in Ritter, et al, *Soviet Modernism* (Park Books, 2012).

Mysterious Cities of Pink and Gold:
Yerevan, Erevan, Erebuni

1 On the genocide, see Ronald Grigor Suny, *They Can Live in the Desert but Nowhere Else* (Princeton 2015); on the Soviet takeover, Marshall, *The Caucasus Under Soviet Rule* (Routledge, 2010).
2 A good English source here: Karen Balian, "The City Overlooking Ararat", *Fabrikzeitung*, 1 May 2017, at http://www.fabrikzeitung.ch/the-city-overlooking-ararat/
3 Zhanna Andreasyan and Georgi Derlugian, "Fuel Protests in Armenia", *New Left Review*, September-October 2015
4 A terrific piece on this project: Ruben Arevshatyan, "Blank Zones in the Collective Memory, or the Transformation of Yerevan's Urban Space in the 60s", *Red Thread*, Issue 2, 2010, and at http://www.red-thread.org/en/article.asp?a=33

5 At the time of writing, this has just been followed by a vastly more impressive victory of the same civil movements – mass demonstrations have forced the resignation of Serzh Sargsyan, who was widely considered a potential Putin, Nazabayev or Lukashenka. It is too early to say what the upshot of this will be, but the protesters' avoidance of geopolitics or invocations of 'Europe' suggests they learned some wise lessons from the aftermath of the overthrow of Yanukovych in Ukraine.

1 See the "Moscow" chapter above.

2 Caroline Erin Elkin, "The Image of the Gorod-Sad: Searching for Howard's Garden City in Almaty", *Tom*, No. 3, 2016

3 Quoted in N. Berkova, "Vanishing Landscape – Soviet Alma-Ata from the Viewpoint of Documentary Film-Makers", *Tom*, No. 3, 2016, p. 3

4 Yuliya Sorokina, "Ghost of a Garden City", in Ritter, et al, *Soviet Modernism* (Park Books, 2012), p. 179

5 Yuri Dombrovsky, *The Keeper of Antiquities* (Longmans, 1969), p. 3

6 Ibid, p. 18

7 Ibid, p. 226

8 Alexander Wat, *My Century* (NYRB, 2003), p. 313

A City of the Future:
Astana, Akmolinsk, Tselinograd, Aqmola

1 R.W. Davies and Stephen G. Wheatcroft, *The Years of Hunger: Soviet Agriculture,* 1931-1933 (Palgrave, 2004)

2 For an informative journalistic account of immediately post-Soviet Kazakhstan that concentrates overwhelmingly on the Russian demographic "threat", see Dilip Hiro, *Between Marx and Muhammad – the Changing Face of Central Asia* (HarperCollins, 1995)

3 Philipp Meuser, *Astana Architectural Guide* (Dom, 2016), p. 158

4 *Astana Architecture Guide*, p. 107

5 Explore this, and much else, on Albo's site, https://www.astanamyth.com/
6 Nari Shelekpayev, "A French Welcome to the Kazakh Capital", *Radio Free Europe-Radio Liberty*, 22 January 2016, at https://www.rferl.org/a/a-french-welcome-to-astana/27505708.html
7 *Astana Expo-2017 Future Energy* (Bureau International de l'Expositions, 2017), p. 4
8 Goran Therborn, *Cities of Power – The Urban, the National, the Popular, the Global* (Verso 2017), p. 353
9 Ibid, p.354

"Where Our Tomorrow is Already Yesterday": Bishkek, Frunze, Pishpek

1 This work was recently translated – Selim Khan-Magomedov, *Georgy Krutikov, The Flying City and Beyond* (Tenov, 2015)
2 This is available in English at *The Kids Want Communism*, https://tkwc.tumblr.com/post/147186458225/queer-in-space-kollontai-commune-archive-%D1%81
3 ShTAB, "Manifesto of Queer Communism", at http://www.art-initiatives.org/ru/content/manifest-kvir-kommunizma-2013
4 "Manifesto of Queer Communism". This is an analysis close to that of recent historians on how the ambitious Kollontai's ideas about free sexual choice foundered on a banal "materialism" seeing the body as a mere reproductive machine – see for instance Gregory Bateson, *Sexual Revolution in Bolshevik Russia* (Pittsburgh, 2010) or Dan Healey, Bolshevik Sexual Forensics (Northern Illinois University Press 2009)
5 Georgy Mamedov and Oksana Shatalova, "Against Simple Answers" (2017) at http://artseverywhere.ca/2017/08/17/against-simple-answers/
6 Georgy Mamedov and Oksana Shatalova, 'Queer Communism is an Ethics' in Ingo Niermann and Joshua Simon, *Communists Anonymous* (Sternberg Press, 2017), p. 90

7 An English version of one, Ursula Le Guin-like, heavily homoerotic story: Synat Sultanalieva, "Element 174", at *The Calvert Journal* (2018), at https://www.calvertjournal.com/features/show/9831

8 Ben Lewis and Lars T. Lih, *Zinoviev and Martov Head to Head in Halle* (November Publications, 2011); they're referring to the Soviet attempts to bring anti-colonial movements into the Communist International. See the minutes of the 1920 *Baku Congress of the Peoples of the East* (New Park, 1977)

9 V. Vitkovich, *Kirghizia Today* (Foreign Languages Publishing House, 1961), p. 18

10 Sam Tranum (ed.) *Life at the Edge of the Empire – Oral Histories of Soviet Kyrgyzstan* (American University of Central Asia, 2012), p. 91

11 Ibid., p. 66. Recent revisionist histories against the simple 'colonial' paradigm include Adeeb Khalid, *Making Uzbekistan* (Cornell, 2015) and Ali Igmen, *Speaking Soviet with an Accent* (Pittsburgh, 2012)

12 The speaker is a dancer, Galina Timoshenko; Ibid., p. 51

13 Mohira Suyarkulova, "Soviet Frunze – a Centre for Space Research?", 1st Feb 17, available at http://cesmi.info/wp/?p=1460

14 This delightful bit of racism comes from Czeslaw Milosz's 1951 *The Captive Mind* (Vintage, 1981), p. 19

15 Samuel Goff, "Empire State of Mind", *The Calvert Journal*, October 2017, at https://www.calvertjournal.com/features/show/8287/revisiting-revolution-empire-state-of-mind-legacy-central-asia

16 Vitkovich, *Kirghizia Today*, p. 243

ACKNOWLEDGEMENTS

The following is a very probably incomplete list of the many people that have helped with this book by inviting me to places, walking round them with me, discussing them, having ideas on them I've found useful or interesting, or by arguing with me on social networks, and in at least two cases by giving me a thought-provokingly bad review: Greg Afinogenov, Ruben Arevshatyan, Karen Balyan, Mari Bastashevski, Nelly Bekus, Vytautas Biekša, Kostya Budarin, Oleksandr Burlaka, Thomas Campbell, Clementine Cecil, Jonathan Charley, Maria Chekhonadskih, Boris Chukhovich, Keti Chukhrov, Julian Duane, Ilona Elyashevich, Nikolay Erofeev, Kateryna Filyuk, Tom Gann, Mikhail Ilchenko, Iryna of Citydog.by, Olga Kazakova, Dennis Keen, Catriona Kelly, Yuliya Komska, Maros Krivy, Stefan Kubiczyn, Ksenia Litvinenko, Ruth Maclennan, Martynas Mankus, Will Mawhood, Arzu Mirzalizade, "Miss Pavlichenko", Anel Moldakhmetova, Gleb Napreenko, Natalia Neshevets, Elle O'Rourke, Natalia Otrishchenko, *Niklāvs* Paegle, Yuri Palmin, Sarhat Petrosyan, Nina Power, Mykola Ridnyi, *Agnė Sadauskaitė*, Nari Shelekpayev, Matas Šiupšinskas, Liudmila Slivinskaya, Kuba Snopek, Stefania Soich, Yuliya Sorokina, Gustavs Strenga, Aleksandra Sudnikovich, Ilze Supe, Mohira Suyarkulova, Dmytro Sysoiev, Johan Tali, Alberto Toscano, Elena Trubina, Nastia Tsourkouskaya, Mait Valjas, Kazys Varnelis, Joanna Warsza, George Zaborski, Dmitrij Zadorin, Aleksandra Zavjalova, Nano Zazanashvili.

Special thanks are due to the following: Valeria Costa-Kostritsky, Jenia Gubkina, Juliet Jacques, Georgy Mamedov, Michal Murawski, Douglas Murphy, Hannah Proctor, Agata Pyzik, Oleksiy Radynski, Dubravka Sekulic, Anya Shevchenko, Łukasz Stanek, Giuliano Vivaldi, Tom Wilkinson.

Many chapters in this book have been published before, albeit always in a different form. Most of these were "Letters From... " for the *Calvert Journal*, who have given me over several years levels of freedom and indulgence well beyond what most writers would hope for, and far better photography than I'm capable of. Thanks are due to Jamie Rann, Arthur House and especially Sam Goff. Will Mawhood let me write "Ventspils" for *Deep Baltic*, Maxim Edwards commissioned an early version of "Almaty" for *openDemocracy*, Kirill Kobrin commissioned "Kuldiga" for *Neprikosnovennyi Zapas*, and Daniel Trilling published the first version of "Slavutych" for *New Humanist* – many, many thanks to these people both for letting me test out ideas and for being good, disputatious listeners in their own right. Some parts have also appeared in *Dezeen*, with many thanks to Amy Frearson and Anna Winston, and in *Disegno*, with thanks to Oli Stratford and Kristina Rapacki. An early version of "Moscow" was published in the anthology *Economic Science Fictions* (Goldsmiths Press, 2018), with thanks to its editor Will Davies.

Thank you to Tariq Goddard, Alex Niven, Tamar Shlaim, Josh Turner and George MacBeth at Repeater for commissioning, editing and generally being encouraging with this book, and to Johnny Bull for risking the wrath of the Hergé estate.

Bisous to Carla Whalen.

REPEATER BOOKS

is dedicated to the creation of a new reality. The landscape of twenty-first-century arts and letters is faded and inert, riven by fashionable cynicism, egotistical self-reference and a nostalgia for the recent past. Repeater intends to add its voice to those movements that wish to enter history and assert control over its currents, gathering together scattered and isolated voices with those who have already called for an escape from Capitalist Realism. Our desire is to publish in every sphere and genre, combining vigorous dissent and a pragmatic willingness to succeed where messianic abstraction and quiescent co-option have stalled: abstention is not an option: we are alive and we don't agree.